The Gothi
in *Supe*

The Gothic Tradition in *Supernatural*

Essays on the Television Series

Edited by
MELISSA EDMUNDSON

McFarland & Company, Inc., Publishers
Jefferson, North Carolina

ISBN (print) 978-0-7864-9976-2
ISBN (ebook) 978-1-4766-2486-0

LIBRARY OF CONGRESS CATALOGUING DATA ARE AVAILABLE

British Library cataloguing data are available

Front cover images © 2016 Givaga/iStock

Printed in the United States of America

*McFarland & Company, Inc., Publishers
Box 611, Jefferson, North Carolina 28640
www.mcfarlandpub.com*

Acknowledgments

I would like to express my gratitude to Stacey Abbott for her support of this project and for her pioneering work in reading *Supernatural* through a critical lens.

My sincere thanks go to Wendy Catalano for her thorough reading of the entire manuscript and for her meticulous work creating the index. I am also grateful to Jeff Makala for his assistance during the preparation of this book.

And I especially want to thank all of the contributors whose work made this book possible. Each one was a delight to work with and made this a really fun project.

Table of Contents

Part 4. Gothic Others: Monstrous Selves

Introduction

MELISSA EDMUNDSON

> **SAM**: When I told Dad I was scared of the thing in my closet,
> he gave me a .45.
> **DEAN**: Well, what was he supposed to do?
> **SAM**: I was 9 years old! He was supposed to say, "Don't be
> afraid of the dark."
> —"Pilot"

Since its premiere in September 2005, *Supernatural* has followed the adventures of the Winchester brothers, Dean and Sam, as they pursue the "family business" of "saving people, hunting things." Along the way, the Winchesters have encountered almost every form of supernatural being while also battling their own inner demons. Series creator Eric Kripke has discussed the influences behind the show's conception, stating, "You really learn a lot about a culture based on what scares them, and I've always been interested in these legends, which are every bit as fleshed out as any world mythologies. They're the stories you tell by the campfire" ("Fact"). For Kripke, these urban myths are connected to the society that creates and recreates them. He calls these legends "cautionary tales" that "reflect what our culture was afraid of at a particular time." As an example, Kripke cites the Hook Man legend, a group of stories, which he says "were predominant in the '60s, about the lovers in lovers' lane who were killed by a lunatic with a hook for a hand, [and] were about a culture's fear of sex and promiscuity" (qtd. in Fernandez). From the beginning, Kripke wanted the series to emphasize the brothers' quest and the genuine fear that exists in a seemingly quiet suburban setting. He says, "It's the idea that horror can happen in your own backyard. How many viewers have to worry about the vampire in the gothic castle?" ("Fact"). Taking the supernatural out of the castle and into average, ordinary homes taps into a whole new set of fears, especially contemporary anxieties about

1

the average, ordinary home being invaded by unpredictable violent forces and bad things happening to seemingly good people (the first five minutes of almost every *Supernatural* episode). Kripke says:

> We have a folklore in mythology that is as rich and developed as any world culture's and as uniquely American as baseball.... I found that such an interesting and untapped source of stories. People have heard these stories, but they're all part of this great mythology of America that speaks to the unique fears we have in America. They're every bit as relevant today as when they were originally told because if there's any one cultural zeitgeist at the moment it is that we're living in the age of anxiety [qtd. in Fernandez].

Sam and Dean's journey is experienced alongside these supernatural elements. As Kripke says, "I landed on this idea to have this mythic road trip across the country, and it became the best vehicle to tell these stories because it's pure, stripped down and uniquely American.... These stories exist in these small towns all across the country, and it just makes so much sense to drive in and out of these stories" (qtd. in Fernandez).

Throughout its decade-plus of production, *Supernatural* has maintained an avid fan following. Since 2007, there have been fan conventions held in both America and Europe. *Supernatural* panels continue to draw huge crowds at the annual Comic-Con in San Diego, and the show has spawned both novel and anime series. It has its own comprehensive wiki site (supernaturalwiki. com), and the show's Facebook page currently boasts over 15 million followers. The series has won the People's Choice Award for "Favorite Sci-fi/Fantasy Show" in 2010, 2012, and 2013. The series also won two *TV Guide* Awards for "Favorite Sci-Fi Series" in 2011 and "Favorite Horror Series" in 2012. Likewise, Jensen Ackles, Jared Padalecki, and Misha Collins have all won awards based on their performances as leading actors on *Supernatural*. The show has also been recognized by other awards dedicated to fantasy/horror, including the Constellation Awards, Saturn Awards, SFX Awards, and the Rondo Hatton Classic Horror Awards. Television reviewers have also noticed the continuing relevance and success of the show. In 2009, Maureen Ryan of the *Chicago Tribune* ranked *Supernatural* as a top ten show, saying that the series "got bolder and more creative in 2009, coming up with hilarious and innovative episodes and taking risks with its storytelling." Likewise, Mike Hale of the *New York Times* listed the show on his annual top ten, calling it "among the wildest and most entertaining series in prime time." In 2012, *Supernatural* captured the attention of *Entertainment Weekly*, which placed the series at #19 in its ranking of the "25 Best Cult TV Shows from the Past 25 Years." The reviewer noted the growing complexity of the show, saying:

> *Supernatural* began with a pretty straightforward premise—hot guys kill spooky things—but it didn't stay that way for long. The characters have literally been to hell and back, and along the way, they have woven a complicated and compelling

mythology filled with friends (angel Castiel), recurring foes (demon Crowley), and inside jokes (Wincest!). *Supernatural* has also, however, dedicated episodes to mocking the sillier aspects of its own existence, like its hypercritical fandom. This self-referential approach has rewarded longtime viewers and helped build a community so passionate, it's almost scary [42].

Until recently (and somewhat surprisingly, given the show's continued success), there have been relatively few critical studies of *Supernatural*. Stacey Abbott and David Lavery's edited collection *TV Goes to Hell: An Unofficial Road Map of* Supernatural (ECW Press, 2011) offers the most complete overview of the series through Season Five, and from the amount of times Abbott and Lavery's work is referenced in the essays of this current collection, it is obvious that *TV Goes to Hell* has laid the groundwork for future scholarly examinations of the series. Other recent collections, including Galen A. Foresman's Supernatural *and Philosophy: Metaphysics and Monsters … for Idjits* (Wiley Blackwell, 2013) and Susan A. George and Regina M. Hansen's edited collection Supernatural, *Humanity, and the Soul: On the Highway to Hell and Back* (Palgrave, 2014) have focused on philosophical, theological, and gender issues. Yet, despite the usefulness of these studies in increasing the scholarly conversation about the socio-cultural concerns of the series, there has been scant attention paid to *Supernatural*'s involvement with the Gothic tradition. This collection seeks to fill this gap by examining how the series is directly tied to Gothic concerns about anxiety, the monstrous, family/generational trauma, and, of course, the supernatural itself. In addition to these overarching themes, the series provides a rich framework with which to discuss major Gothic sub-genres such as the Suburban Gothic, Postcolonial Gothic, Female Gothic, and Postmodern/Meta-Gothic.

From the first season, the series has included storylines based on popular Gothic legends and mythology, such as the Woman in White, Bloody Mary, Phantom Travelers, and the Hook Man, as well as numerous haunted/cursed objects, from the rabbit's foot in the comic "Bad Day at Black Rock" (3.3) and the celebrity wax museum of "Fallen Idols" (5.5), to the more sinister painting in "Provenance" (1.19) and the vengeful ghost of "Playthings" (2.11). Throughout the show's run, *Supernatural* has paid direct homage to the Gothic tradition, such as "Monster Movie" (4.5), in which the Winchesters face a shapeshifter who impersonates classic movie monsters such as Dracula, the Mummy, and the Wolfman. To complete the effect, the episode was shot completely in black and white. Other monster-of-the-week episodes have also been directly tied to various creatures of the Gothic, including ghosts, werewolves, vampires, witches, and demons, to name only a few. The series has also referenced well-known practitioners of the Gothic, most notably H. P. Lovecraft and his appearance in "Let It Bleed" (6.21) and the Brothers Grimm in "Bedtime Stories" (3.5). Yet, *Supernatural* is also not afraid to be experimental with its treatment of the Gothic. The Meta-Gothic appears in several episodes, namely "The Monster at the End of this Book" (4.18), in which Sam and Dean discover Chuck Shurley (a.k.a. Carver Edlund), author of a series of *Supernatural* books based on the Winchesters' lives as hunters, as well as the alternative universe of "The French Mistake" (6.15) where the brothers find that they are actors named Jensen Ackles and Jared Padalecki, who star in a show called "Supernatural." Other episodes are all the more unsettling because the supposed supernatural occurrences turn out to be natural disturbances based on hidden/repressed secrets that haunt the living, such as the backwoods human-hunting family in "The Benders" (1.15) and the feral children of an incestuous relationship in "Family Remains" (4.11).

The beginning of the series coincided with a significant reemergence of interest in the Gothic and its many cultural manifestations. In a review of the show's third season, "*Supernatural* is Midwestern Gothic for the Google Generation," Annalee Newitz calls attention to *Supernatural*'s unique form of modern American Gothic, remarking that the show "fits squarely into the gothic tradition that started with eighteenth century novels like *The Monk*, and goes right on up through ... Led Zeppelin and AC/DC." Newitz goes on to praise Eric Kripke and how he "has combined classic gothic storytelling— two drifter brothers with a tragic past fight demons—with pop culture quirks. Every show begins with a classic rock or metal song that brings us into the story. It's like the organ music of contemporary horror." She also notes that the show's inclusion of angels and demons plays a key role in its Gothic content: "The show also isn't afraid to tackle things that most horror series shy away from, namely Heaven. You've probably seen a million devils and demons in your time, but how often do you get a really meaty, interesting story about angels?... The plot seems partly ripped from the pages of Philip Pullman's *His Dark Materials* trilogy, and partly from *Paradise Lost*." Just as Eric Kripke describes the ability of the show to tell American Gothic stories, Newitz also points out the importance of the show's locations, as the Midwestern landscape increases the Gothic potential of the storylines:

> Another standout part of *Supernatural* is its setting. While most gothic tales center on the south, with its weepy trees and creepy history, *Supernatural* is set square in the US Midwest. Dean and Sam hail from Kansas, and they never stray far from it. Though they occasionally hit a coast, most of their jobs take the boys on a winding path between insta-suburbs cut into the empty prairies, lone farmhouses, and rusting industrial towns.... These Midwestern settings are perfect for hauntings, and for the family tragedies that often lurk at the heart of gothic tales.

In *Nightmare on Main Street* (1997), Mark Edmundson has examined the socio-cultural forces at work behind the popular interest in Gothic. He notes that since the 1990s, horror has assumed "a central role in American culture" (3). This emergence is directly tied to the complexities (and anxieties) of modern life: "Unsentimental, enraged by gentility and high-mindedness, skeptical about progress in any form, the Gothic mind is antithetical to all smiling American faiths. A nation of ideals, America has also been, not surprisingly, a nation of hard disillusionment, with a fiercely reactive Gothic imagination. Ours is the culture that produced both 'Self-Reliance' and 'The Fall of the House of Usher'" (5). This pessimism is in many ways linked to American capitalist culture. As Edmundson says, "Political Gothic entails finding the dark self, the double, that lurks inside your brightly shining adversary.... Capitalists look like heroes, captains of industry: in reality they're a gang of bloodsuckers" (20). In Season Seven of *Supernatural*, the bloodsucking capitalists are Leviathans, led by Richard "Dick" Roman, billionaire and CEO of Richard Roman Enterprises. Along with the Winchesters, viewers discover that the Leviathans are using food additives to make the American population a ready food source. Dean discovers this firsthand when, on the trail of the Jersey Devil, he eats the new additive-laced turducken burger at Biggerson's. Writer and director Sera Gamble and Robert Singer have discussed the modern anxieties that influenced these monsters: "The Leviathan have been a metaphor for corporate greed, among other things, all season. When we were crafting these villains, we talked about what freaked us out in the writers' room and we came to the conclusion that big corporations are scarier than the government. A lot of our villains over the years have been monstrous, and we thought these monster corporations and their lack of morality seemed to be a perfect fit for this ultimate monster" (qtd. in Knight).

Along with this sense of modernity comes the Postmodern Gothic. The shifting, fragmented identity works well with the Gothic obsession with unpredictable, multiple identities. And *Supernatural* engages with these preoccupations as well as any show on television. While the series itself constantly blends the genres of Gothic, drama, fantasy, comedy, and horror, the identities of the individual characters are also constantly changing: Dean/Demon Dean/Michael, Sam/Demon Sam/Lucifer/Gadreel, Castiel/Jimmy Novak/ God/Emanuel, Crowley/Fergus MacLeod/King of Hell, Leviathan Dean/ Leviathan Sam, not to mention all the alternative lives imagined by the Winchester brothers. According to Lorna Jowett and Stacey Abbott in *TV Horror* (2013), this nebulous sense of reality/unreality, good/evil, and natural/supernatural works particularly well for horror TV where "fragmentation, repetition and seriality—characteristics inherent in television—immerse audiences within horror narratives while also lending themselves to the dystopian vision of modern horror, making television an ideal place for the genre" (55). Likewise in *Skin Shows* (1995), Judith Halberstam connects this fragmentation to the monstrous, saying that one of Gothic's defining juxtapositions is "the inability to categorize." She goes on to say that the Gothic "marks a peculiarly modern preoccupation with boundaries and their collapse. Gothic monsters, furthermore, differ from the monsters that come before the nineteenth century in that the monsters of modernity are characterized by their proximity to humans" (Halberstam 23). This loosening of defined boundaries equals a loss of control and the breakdown of a reassuring sense of meaning: "The monstrous body that once represented everything is now represented as potentially meaning anything—it may be the outcast, the outlaw, the parasite, the pervert, the embodiment of uncontrollable sexual and violent urges, the foreigner, the misfit. The monster is all of these but monstrosity has become a conspiracy of bodies rather than a singular form" (Halberstam 27).

What also makes *Supernatural* unique in how it relates to a larger Gothic tradition is its television format and how the show is encountered by viewers. In *Gothic Television* (2006), Helen Wheatley states that "television is the ideal medium for the Gothic" (1) because both areas are inherently linked with the domestic space. Wheatley goes on to say that Gothic television is "the meeting of two houses: the textual domestic spaces of Gothic television (haunted houses, decaying mansions, permeable family homes under threat from within and without) and the extra-textual domestic spaces of the medium (the homes in which Gothic television is viewed)" (200). She also lists several characteristics of Gothic television: stereotyped characters and plots from the Gothic literary tradition, moods of terror or dread, the use of the supernatural, the uncanny (which takes the form of repetitions, ghosts, premonitions, doppelgängers, and animated objects), and haunted families and homes (Wheatley 3). Yet, Gothic television as a specific genre has been impeded by the fact that neither television professionals nor viewers tend to label programs as specifically "Gothic." This is true of *Supernatural* itself, as it has been variously termed horror, fantasy, and science fiction. Many other current television series that also could be termed "Gothic" are usually described under the category of horror. So, like the definition of Gothic in the literary tradition, the category of Gothic television has been notoriously hard to pin down.

Both Wheatley and Lenora Ledwon have discussed the suitability of Gothic on the small screen as opposed to film. Wheatley states that the serial drama reveals "television's full potential as a medium of Gothic fiction" (17). Likewise, Ledwon asserts that "film does not have the same Gothic potential as television precisely because of the finite time period for a film. A film must end, while a television series has a seemingly infinite potential to continue telling the story and to continue multiplying messages" (267, qtd. in Wheatley 17). Gothic television has the ability to reach us exclusively in our homes, making it more intimate than film. Wheatley discusses this in terms of character, saying that "Gothic television's heavy emphasis on the translation of character subjectivity implies a sense of connection, a simultaneity, between protagonist and viewer" (20). Likewise, Mark Edmundson has commented that "one of the common functions of the Gothic is to turn anxiety, the vague but insistent fear of what will happen in the future, into suspense. The Gothic novel or film in effect gathers up the anxiety that is free-floating in the reader or viewer and binds it to a narrative" (12). Angela Ndalianis, in *The Horror Sensorium* (2012), goes even further in describing this connection between fiction and viewer, remarking that film and television media are "modes of travel that take the spectator to fictional places and embroil them in the lives of characters who travel their own life journeys onscreen." This involvement in the narrative becomes "an emotional journey that relies on cognition and perception; our understanding of the characters, their stories, the way they interact with each other and the spaces around them affects us in immediate ways in that beyond the level of narrative comprehension (and often because of it), we're drawn into emotional journeys. The spaces 'in there' impact on our space 'out here'" (4–5).

For all its mirroring of present societal fears, the Gothic is also concerned with the pull of the past, as Edmundson notes, "Gothic is the art of haunting, and in two senses. Gothic shows time and again that life, even at its most ostensibly innocent, is possessed, that the present is in thrall to the past. All are guilty. All must, in time, pay up" (5). This is particularly true of *Supernatural*, as both Sam and Dean are constantly battling both the supernatural beings of the present as well as their own demons from the past. The show presents this struggle in the narrative arc of almost every episode, most especially in later seasons as the family mythology has become deeper and more complex. Jowett and Abbott see this as a necessary element to the audience's emotional involvement with and continuing interest in the show, noting how Sam and Dean are always at the narrative center: "The episodic format means few other characters distract from them.... While certain horror elements recur across different seasons ... character provides ultimate coherence to episodic horror action, fixing it firmly within the show's evolving mythology" (50, 51).

In addition to the haunted families and individuals that the brothers encounter each week, Sam and Dean's family history is a major component of the show. Although Sam, in particular, often wishes for a normal life away from hunting, he also cannot escape from the fact that he is indeed different, a "freak." When Dean questions his hunting methods in the Season Four episode "Metamorphosis" (4.4), Sam responds by saying that his demonic blood is like a disease, a curse that he can never be rid of. In "Bugs" (1.8), when Sam hints at wanting a normal life, Dean tells his brother that being normal is overrated. Dean outwardly relishes a life on the road, free from responsibilities and routines, but, like Sam, knows that he could not fit in with the normal world any more than his brother could. When Dean expresses doubts about his purpose in life, Bobby Singer quickly reminds him that he is a hunter, not a person ("How to Win Friends," 7.9). The line between person, freak, and monster is blurred. Sam and Dean are imprisoned by their way of life, and despite short stays in the "real" world and attempts at normality, both ultimately return to being a hunter. The nomadic life led by the Winchesters makes *Supernatural* a continuous "road trip" series. Until only recently have the brothers found any sort of permanent home, in the form of the Bunker created by the Men of Letters, which is significantly located in their home state of Kansas. Even the brothers' reactions to the Bunker are laced with meaning. Dean delights in having a memory foam mattress that actually remembers him, displays an ax from Purgatory, a prized Led Zeppelin album, and a picture of himself as a child with his mother. However, Sam is unable to settle down, ultimately admitting to Dean that he has no memories of any kind of home life and therefore cannot recreate something he never had ("Slumber Party," 9.4).

Apart from the cases Sam and Dean are constantly pursuing, they are also going down the same figurative road again and again in their personal lives. The ongoing trials of the Winchesters are symbolized by recurring motifs in the structure of the show, such as its weekly recap intro titles, "Then" and "Now," as well as each season finale's use of the intro title, "The Road So Far," and the inclusion of Kansas's "Carry on Wayward Son." Sam and Dean's Gothic labyrinth of escape and return is not located in the dark forests and storm-tossed cliffs of Europe but on the back roads of America. Their method of escape is their father's '67 Impala, and their soundtrack is not eerie winds rustling through trees or owl screeches, but classic rock. The setting is different—an abandoned house in Kansas instead of a castle in Italy—but the sense of haunting remains the same; we've been down this road before.

Along the way, there is also a good deal of guilt felt by the brothers for what they have done to their family, their friends, and, most importantly, to each other. As the brothers fight against the monster-of-the-week, viewers are also transported via flashback to past family or personal struggles undergone by one or both brothers. Dean remains the less hopeful of the two, but also the more verbal when it comes to personal guilt, often commenting that he will ultimately end up in Hell in order to "pay up" for all that he has done and for the people who, in his mind, he has let down. Throughout these ups and downs, however, the brothers remain loyal to one another; family always comes first. Dean tells Sam in the Season Five finale ("Swan Song," 5.22), that protecting his younger brother defines his own identity. And in the Season Eight finale ("Sacrifice" 8.23), Sam confesses to Dean that his greatest sin is all the times he failed his brother. The brothers are linked to each other, and this is both a blessing and a curse.

Supernatural is constantly calling into question what it means to be human and the often fine line between humanity and monstrosity. The show's creators also frequently blur the line between hunter/hunted and human/ monster. Sam consorts with demons, the angel Castiel befriends the demon Meg Masters, and Dean teams up with the vampire Benny Lafitte, who he meets while trapped in Purgatory. Castiel suffers from a hangover after drinking an entire liquor store, eats too many hamburgers, and shops for pie and porn in convenience stores. The demonic Crowley cries out for love and understanding in the Season Eight finale. The archangel Gabriel has a sweet tooth, and Death has a fondness for junk food. This blurring is also symbolized in the switching of the brothers each season. Dean goes to Hell to save Sam, Sam consorts with demons and later goes to Hell to prevent the Apocalypse, Sam returns from Hell without a soul, and Dean becomes a demon. Yet the show is equally concerned with how the brothers cope with these changes and the violent and (self)destructive lengths they will go to in order to save one another from these fates. It is these difficult choices that the brothers constantly have to make and the ongoing complexities of their relationship that we, as viewers, care about.

Imagined within the framework of a show dedicated to the supernatural, these complexities make the series an important part of the Gothic tradition, and the following essays in this book represent the many ways Gothic can be interpreted within the context of *Supernatural*. Comparisons are drawn with the earliest Gothic works, beginning in the eighteenth century with Horace Walpole's seminal novel *The Castle of Otranto* (1764) and continuing through the twenty-first century with the modern Gothic works of Neil Gaiman and Markus Zusak. The essays cover a wide range of classic Gothic characters, including Frankenstein and his Creature, Dracula, Dr. Jekyll and Mr. Hyde, Melmoth the Wanderer, and Ambrosio the Monk. Along the way, the Gothic is also connected with horror studies, postmodernism, and postcolonialism.

In "Part 1: Gothic Tropes and Traditions," contributors discuss the ways traditional themes work their way into the series. Alexandra Lykissas, in "Gothic Anxieties—Then and Now: A Post–9/11 Examination of the Gothic," discusses how the series reflects real-world anxieties in a post–9/11 world while also examining how the show deals with gender roles and the domestic space as a microcosm of the nation-state. In "The Automobile as Moving Castle," Thomas Knowles reads the Winchesters' beloved 1967 Impala as a Gothic character within the series. Knowles suggests that the interior of the car, which functions as a surrogate home for Sam and Dean, mirrors the subversive and deathly interiors that make up the more traditional Gothic castle. These early Gothic tropes also feature in Dana Fore's "Shadows of Hope: Gothic Motifs and Nihilism." Fore discusses *Supernatural*'s debt to Matthew Lewis's 1796 Gothic novel *The Monk* and argues that the moral inversion of good and evil characters on the show is part of a Gothic cynicism that foregrounds suffering in a world that is seemingly out of control.

"Part 2: Gothic Storytelling" centers on how the series uses plot, repetition, and mythology in self-aware episodes that are at once both familiar and unfamiliar. Jamil Mustafa focuses on *Supernatural*'s 200th episode in "'You can't spell subtext without S-E-X': Gothic Intertextuality and the (Queer) Uncanny." Mustafa examines "Fan Fiction" and other meta-episodes in terms of the Gothic tradition of the uncanny and also the slash fiction created by fans of the show. The discussion of the show's self-awareness is continued by Michael Fuchs in "'I know everything that's going to happen': The Self-Reflexive Compulsion to Repeat (with a Difference)." Fuchs considers how the show's creative use of repetitions signifies the close relationship between narrative and audience. The theme of the familiar/unfamiliar is then taken up by Daniel P. Compora, who, in "Gothic Imaginings: Folkloric Roots" provides a survey of the many monsters and other creatures that find their way into the series. Compora sees these ghosts, vampires, and zombies as part of a larger folklore that is then taken by the show's writers and changed into a unique mythology that resurfaces throughout numerous seasons.

Gender concerns resurface in the third part, "Gothic Women: Heroes and Victims." In "Coloniality and the Chicana Gothic: Travelling Myths in the Pilot," Leow Hui Min Annabeth continues the discussion of nation and gender. Leow reads the first episode of the series through a postcolonial lens that highlights the ways in which white patriarchal colonialism is upheld through the destruction of creatures who symbolize indigenous peoples, particularly the female ghost who represents a reimagining of the Llorona folkloric narrative. E. J. Nielsen, in "Wearing the Woman in White: The Doomed Lives and Afterlives of Women," examines the show's frequent use of women as "vessels" for demonic and angelic entities and how this bodily invasion raises issues of consent and the larger problem of female victimization within the series and other Gothic narratives. The tendency of *Supernatural* to portray women as victims or monsters is then complicated in Ashley Walton's "'What's up, bitches?' Charlie Bradbury as Gothic Heroine." Walton interprets Charlie's character through the Female Gothic tradition and suggests ways in which the character breaks with previous female stereotypes within the series.

The final section, "Gothic Others: Monstrous Selves," looks at the recurring focus on forms of monstrosity in *Supernatural*, both in how it manifests within Sam and Dean Winchester, but also how it functions in the changing portrayals of supporting characters. In "'We've all been demons': Postmodern Gothic and the Fragmented Self," Jessica Seymour uses Robert Louis Stevenson's *Strange Case of Dr. Jekyll and Mr. Hyde* (1886) as the touchstone text for her discussion of Castiel, Balthazar, Gabriel, Meg Masters, and Crowley. These characters become more divided and face greater identity issues as their characters are forced to choose between good and evil. Samantha J. Vertosick, in "'Sympathy for the Devil': The Neutralization of Traditionally Evil Figures," extends Seymour's discussion. Vertosick connects themes ranging from John Milton's *Paradise Lost* (1667) to the modern Gothic works of Neil Gaiman and Markus Zusak as she looks at how characters such as Lucifer, Crowley, Cain, and Death are "neutralized" as they progress into tragic figures in the series, which, in turn, creates conflicted feelings for viewers. Earlier discussions of sexuality and the queer uncanny within the series are taken up again by Megan Fowler in "'Psychotically, irrationally, erotically codependent': Incest and the Gothic Other." Fowler focuses on the Gothic uncanny as it relates specifically to what she sees as the subtextual queer desire between Sam and Dean. Fowler examines how the show's repeated emphasis on otherness serves to call into question the brothers' ability to live "normal" lives without one another in a traditional domestic setting. The book concludes with Lisa Schmidt's "We All Have a Little Monster in Us: Dean Winchester, the Mark of Cain and the New Monster Paradigm." Schmidt discusses how monstrosity has been a concern in *Supernatural* from the beginning of the series and how ideas of being good or evil have been developed and complicated over the course of the show's run. This new type of monster, one that defies previous stereotypes, points to how the series remains on the cutting edge of the Gothic and horror genres.

In its now 200-plus episodes, *Supernatural* has shown its audience one of the best varieties of supernatural beings ever to be seen on television. But these otherworldly creatures are not what keeps viewers returning week after week and does not account entirely for the massive fan base that the series still enjoys. The heart of the series, like many of the best Gothic novels and stories, is the ongoing question of what it means to be human and how we live and have purpose, to the best of our abilities, in an imperfect world full of unpredictable violence and seemingly pointless evil. In addition to its ghosts and vampires, *Supernatural* keeps showing us that the most dangerous monster can be within ourselves and that love and the bonds of family can be our greatest strength but also our greatest weakness. And because it is a serial drama, coming into our homes each week for over ten years, we are reminded of and affected by this struggle more so than any finite horror film. We are on the journey with the Winchesters, and as with the best of Gothic literature, we enjoy the ride.

WORKS CITED

Edmundson, Mark. *Nightmare on Main Street: Angels, Sadomasochism, and the Culture of Gothic*. Cambridge: Harvard University Press, 1997. Print.

"Fact Scarier than Fiction." *The Daily Telegraph* (8 March 2007). Web.

Fernandez, Maria Elena. "On the Road Trip from Hell." *The Age* (5 January 2006). Web.

Franick, Darren, et al. "25 Best Cult TV Shows from the Past 25 Years." *Entertainment Weekly* (3 August 2012): 36–43. Print.

Halberstam, Judith. *Skin Shows: Gothic Horror and the Technology of Monsters.* Durham: Duke University Press, 1995. Print.

Hale, Mike. "A Top Ten List That Needs an Addendum." *New York Times* (18 December 2009). Web.

Jowett, Lorna, and Stacey Abbott. *TV Horror: Investigating the Dark Side of the Small Screen.* London: I.B. Tauris, 2013. Print.

Knight, Nicholas. *Supernatural: The Official Companion Season 7.* London: Titan Books, 2012. Print.

Ledwon, Lenora. "*Twin Peaks* and the Television Gothic." *Literature/Film Quarterly* 21.4 (1993): 260–70. Print.

Ndalianis, Angela. *The Horror Sensorium: Media and the Senses.* Jefferson, NC: McFarland, 2012. Print.

Newitz, Annalee. "*Supernatural* Is Midwestern Gothic for the Google Generation." 30 April 2009. io9.com. Web.

Ryan, Maureen. "Watch This: The Top TV Shows of 2009." *Chicago Tribune* (14 December 2009). Web.

Wheatley, Helen. *Gothic Television.* Manchester: Manchester University Press, 2006. Print.

PART 1

Gothic Tropes and Traditions

Gothic Anxieties—Then and Now
A Post-9/11 Examination of the Gothic

Alexandra Lykissas

When examining how the Gothic has migrated over the centuries, an area of great import is the migration to other media, like television. Most of the traditional Gothic texts were published as novels, poetry, and drama, but the genre has maintained its influence over the last two centuries through its adaptability. As Julie Sanders and Linda Hutcheon have argued, in order for "origin" stories to be adaptable, they must be able to speak to each era's specific cultural and societal concerns. Gothic has become a genre that is seen in many different places because of the use of traditional and non-traditional tropes and themes that are relatable to different cultures and different historical moments. Gothic texts can examine those things within a society that may want to remain hidden—the unknown becomes known. This essay will argue that the TV series *Supernatural* has adapted the Gothic as a way to examine the effects of a post–9/11 world by critiquing traditional gender norming that proliferated American culture after 9/11, while also highlighting the concept of the evil or terror within. I will also briefly examine the domesticated space as it relates to the eighteenth-century concepts of the inner world of the domestic versus the outside male-dominated sphere, and how the violation of the domestic is a symbolic violation of the homeland.

Traditionally the beginnings of the Gothic have been dated to the second half of the eighteenth century, with English and German texts that combined romance, terror, and ancestral curses in a literary subset of the Romantic tradition. While few contemporary authors or critics actually termed what was happening as specifically "Gothic" in the sense that we know it today, these works helped establish the genre that has persisted for the last 250 years. One of the many reasons that the Gothic has persisted where other genres, like the novel of sentiment or morality tales, have not is because it is easily adaptable to different eras and cultures as a way to speak about the terrors that we may not want to acknowledge. This terror is typically established through the traditional—some might call cliché—settings of the dark night, creepy house, and shadowy figures. However, while these aesthetic elements may be cliché to some, they are traditional stylistic features that help to establish mood and help to firmly place these texts within the Gothic mode. In the Gothic, we are meant to fear the dark night, the shadow in the forest, or the creepy run-down castle. More than just a laundry list of spooky descriptions and supernatural events and elements, however, the authors of the Gothic are able to use the supernatural as a way to comment on the cultural and social conditions of their historical moments. E. J. Clery cites the Marquis de Sade in her book *The Rise of Supernatural Fiction, 1762–1800* (1995), as saying that "this genre [Gothic] was the inevitable product of the revolutionary shocks with which the whole of Europe resounded" (156), meaning that the rise of the Gothic was an effect of the French Revolution. Clery says, "The Marquis de Sade described a situation in which the writers of fiction were compelled to turn to effects of the supernatural in order to outdo the secular terrors that had become a commonplace reality" (170). I will argue that Clery's point about using "the supernatural in order to outdo the secular terrors" relates to our modern reaction to 9/11,[1] which also answers the questions raised by Ann McGuire and David Buchbinder in their article "The Forensic Gothic: Knowledge, the Supernatural, and the Psychic Detective" about "why *these?* And why *now?*" (290). McGuire and Buchbinder are trying to find answers to the increase in supernatural fiction in books, movies, and on television over the last twenty years. If we connect their questions with Sade's reasoning for why the Gothic made such a mark on literature after the French Revolution, we can clearly draw a line to another historically significant moment, especially in American history—9/11. While there are a number of post–9/11 narratives, I will focus on how Eric Kripke's *Supernatural* examines the return to traditional gender norms, the fear of the evil within, or the homegrown terrorist as we are constantly told of in the media, in addition to the destruction of the domestic space as symbolic of the violation of the homeland.[2]

Before I offer the post–9/11 examination, let me provide an overview of the series, for those unfamiliar with "The Road So Far…."

Supernatural began on the WB network in 2005, before the network changed to the CW. The show traces the adventures of two brothers, Sam and Dean Winchester, who are hunters. They hunt all that goes bump in the night—everything from ghosts to vampires to demons to witches. Kripke, the creator, says in the Season One DVD special feature commentary, "*Supernatural*: Tales from the Edge of Darkness," that he wanted the show to be a supernatural *Star Wars* (1977) meets *Route 66* (1960–1964) with Dean as Hans Solo and Sam as Luke Skywalker. The story began as an American road trip where the boys venture from town to town to vanquish their Monster of the Week. In the first four seasons, each monster was based mostly on traditional, particularly American, urban legends and folktales. Since then, the mythos has transitioned to more traditional good versus evil storylines, including Judeo-Christian elements such as the insertion of angels and the Devil; there are also Leviathans, and in the tenth season, the Mark of Cain (of Cain and Abel fame).

No matter the arc of each season, an element that is crucial to the *Supernatural* mythos is the hyper-masculinization of the main characters, Sam and Dean. In a recent doctoral dissertation that examines post–9/11 masculinity, "Upon Life and All Its Random Injustice: The Post-Traumatic Masculinity of Superheroes, Villains, and Vigilantes in Graphic Novels, Television, and Cinema," Shana Kraynak says that

> to reaffirm traditional gender roles, images of a remasculinized culture pervaded news media, television, and film in the months and years following 9/11. When faced with trauma and tragedy, people desperately cling to perceptions of normality. Following a world changing event like 9/11, any illusion of normality became a part of our nation's healing process. The problem with this is that "getting back to normal" ostensibly means getting back to what society deems acceptable behavior, but where does the concept of "normal" or "acceptable" come from? Who decides what is or is not normal, especially when it comes to gender roles? [1].

The reemphasis on what is "normal" and acceptable behavior is interesting because what are considered to be norms are the same as what were just being solidified in European society with the rise of the middle class and domestication in the mid-eighteenth century and into the early nineteenth century. This was when the concept of the "angel in the house" (though not fully articulated until 1854 when the poem of the same name by Coventry Patmore was published) first started as the concepts of the inner worlds and outer worlds were being articulated. The first was a space for women and the other for men. So, while we return to a concept of normality when healing from tragedy, as what happened after 9/11, it seems poignant that these norms, especially the interior versus exterior binaries, were established when Gothic was first coming into being.

In *Supernatural*, Dean represents those stereotypes of hyper-masculinity—he wears a leather jacket and heavy boots, drives a black 1967 Chevy Impala, listens to classic rock, carries an engraved .44 (and later a heavy-duty knife), has every type of weapon in the trunk of his car, gets drunk more nights than not, sleeps with almost every waitress the brothers come across, and has no problem cutting off some supernatural being's head or shooting it between the eyes. He is the stereotypical American alpha-male. It could be argued that Sam is not as masculine, but he does have many of the same traits as his brother—the difference is that Sam questions these traits. First, on a purely physical level, Dean always has his hair short and trimmed, much like a soldier would have; on the other hand, Sam's hair gets longer and longer with each season, which could be just a simple fact that he is younger than Dean, but it also could be seen as less masculine. Additionally, Sam tends to eat much healthier than Dean, which Dean constantly mocks, since it's pretty apparent that eating burgers and fries is the manly American way. More importantly, Sam is less likely to engage in sexual activities with the women they meet, especially during the first few seasons. During this time, his brother constantly questions his sexuality, by calling him gay, bitch, or other pejorative and emasculating terms. However, once he meets Ruby in Season Three and begins to trust her in Season Four, Sam's more masculine traits begin to surface, which could be linked to his penchant for demon blood as a way to increase his psychic powers and make him significantly stronger. This is further emphasized in Season Six, when Sam returns from Hell. In "The Third Man" (6.3), Sam is shown working out, shirtless, performing the masculine workout moves of pushups and pullups, after a night of meaningless sex. We find out later in the season that Sam does not have a soul, which explains his non–Sam like behavior, which is much more akin to Dean's hypermasculinity. So, for Sam to become more masculine, he needs to become more demon-like or lose his soul, not more human, which calls into question the traditional ideas of masculinity that we see in Dean's character. If one has to "turn to the dark side" in order to fit the hyper-masculine mold, does that not defeat the entire purpose of masculine hero on a white horse?

As Kraynak says, "Popular culture in the post–9/11 era reaffirmed and reconstructed the historical ideologies of masculinity, as shown in film, television, and graphic novels. These texts show how easy it can be for our culture to fall back into hegemonic representations of gender, relying on stereotypical masculine ideals of heroism in the face of apocalyptic trauma" (2). This was seen in those representations of male heroism after 9/11 that have persisted today—there was a return to these hegemonic ideals of masculinity as a way to reclaim our national identity and reclaim the homeland. Kraynak's dissertation offers an extensive discussion of the ways this was shown in the media both immediately after 9/11 and into more current discussions. These historical ideologies of masculinity are made very apparent in *Supernatural* when Dean says in "Wendigo" (1.2) that what they do is "saving people, hunting things … the family business." This statement resonates throughout the entire series and is repeated over and over again. Here Dean is explaining that the man's purpose is very traditional—hunt/kill things and save people. What he doesn't mention is that many of the people they save are the stereotypical damsels in distress who are being hunted by the stereotypical "other" or symbolic evil from within.

In addition to the hyper-masculinization of men, there is also a return to the weak female who needs rescuing from the big, strong men. If men become the epitome of masculinity after 9/11 as shown in the representation of the heroes and saviors, then women are shown to be either the grieving widows (those who lost their heroes) or the ones in need of rescue. In *Supernatural*, nearly every woman is there to be saved by men from the evil monster and to satiate their sexual appetites (usually Dean's). Even those female characters who seem to break the mold, like the angels and Lisa Braeden, eventually succumb to the traditional female roles established in the series. The fallen angel Anna Milton must be rescued by both Dean and Sam, but also eventually sleeps with Dean in the back of the Impala. Lisa, who Dean runs into initially in Season Three, serves a much more important role at the end of Season Five and the beginning of Season Six when Sam must battle Lucifer and Michael in the Cage in Hell. Despite her role as an independent single mother, she also fits the mold of the beautiful, sexualized damsel in distress who Dean rescues. Both traditional roles for women, as damsel in distress and sexual conquest, serve to reaffirm the man's masculine identity and to increase his virile nature and persona, therefore strengthening the traditional gender norming present after 9/11. This counters previous supernatural shows on the WB/CW network, like *Buffy the Vampire Slayer* (1997–2003) and *Charmed* (1998–2006), which contained strong female protagonists who didn't need men to rescue them and in fact, were doing most of the rescuing themselves. However, both of these shows premiered prior to 9/11, so I would argue that the shift in female representations can be seen in a simple comparison. Prior to 9/11, women could be powerful and strong, and even save men. After, however, men needed to save the weak woman as a way to reaffirm their masculinity and in a way that can be likened to men protecting the symbolic representation of the domestic, which in turn represents protecting the homeland and nation-state. This is discussed more in McGuire and Buchbinder's article, as well as Julia M. Wright's article "Latchkey Hero: Masculinity, Class, and the Gothic in Eric Kripke's *Supernatural*." Wright ties these concepts of masculinity with class, and concludes her article by saying that "'overcompensating' through masculine performance for a childhood trauma tied to downward class mobility, a gun-toting hero who is chastised by powerful male figures for his pathologically low self-esteem, Dean Winchester functions as the site at which popular depictions of class and masculinity unravel, including those embodied, though occasionally complicated, by his more conventional brother" (29). I would argue that this unraveling of masculinity, as Wright argues, happens because the traditional gender roles as established in the show cannot last in a modern world, even after 9/11. It could be argued that this return to normalcy, as Kraynak argues, is important to reestablish society after such a tragic event, or maybe it just reaffirms the societal terrors that we've all become accustomed to, as the Marquis de Sade suggests.

Susan Faludi adds to this by saying that after 9/11 "we were also enlisted in a symbolic war at home, a war to repair and restore a national myth" (13, qtd. in McGuire and Buchbiner 301). It seems clear that this myth was the myth of the all-powerful American man to overcome the big-bad invading other. Faludi adds to my argument as well as Kraynak's about the hypermasculinization of men and the weakening of women in media when she says,

> Taken individually, the various impulses that surfaced after 9/11—the denigration of capable women, the magnification of manly men, the heightened call for domesticity, the search for and sanctification of helpless girls—might seem random expressions of some profound cultural derangement. But taken together, they form a coherent, and inexorable whole, the cumulative elements of a national fantasy in which we are deeply invested, our elaborately constructed myth of invincibility [14, qtd. in McGuire and Buchbinder 302].

This myth of invincibility as evidenced through the weakened woman and hyper-strengthened man is clearly seen in the characters of *Supernatural*. The Winchesters are seen to be invincible as they fight every type of monster, demon, folklore legend, and even Lucifer himself, yet they always seem to return from the brink of death and even Death himself, Purgatory, Hell, and Heaven, to come back to Earth to fight the big fight. They are the representatives of the man who pulls up his bootstraps, returns to normalcy, and continues to fight our enemies, which seemed to be the resounding rhetoric after 9/11.

In addition to the gendered representations of the characters in *Supernatural*, the domestic also becomes an important space for both a Gothic and post–9/11 discussion. As Kate Ferguson Ellis thoroughly examines in her book *The Contested Castle* (1989), within the Gothic there was an emphasis not on the external terrors, but on the internal terrors, especially those found within the walls of the home. According to Ferguson Ellis, the only way for women to deal with the internal terrors was to do what seemed counterintertuitive—don't lock yourself in to guard against the evil; open up the gates so the terrors can be let out.

Ferguson Ellis argues less about the nationalistic sentiments of the terrors within and more about the cultural commentary that the Gothic makes about the domestic sphere. We see these types of examinations in Ann Radcliffe's novels and in Charlotte Dacre's *Zofloya* (1806), among many others, where the female characters resist domesticity because of the fear of what is within the home. These types of terrors are also seen in earlier sentimental and coquette novels, such as Eliza Haywood's *The History of Miss Betsy Thoughtless* (1751), where the coquette finally marries, but her husband becomes a tyrant and then, after he dies, she ends up with her beloved, Trustworthy; however, the reader is left wondering if she is just going to experience the same treatment at the end of the novel, when her voice and story are taken away, and it is only about him.

In *Supernatural*, there is an obvious conflict between the domestic and class, as Julia Wright examines, but I would argue that the domestic, as the symbol of the nation-state and the homeland, is violated in the show as representative of the violation that occurred on 9/11. Samira Kawash argues that "throughout the postwar period, the house has held a signal place in the American cultural imaginary, providing an affective and symbolic locus for the virtues and desires through which the national subject is interpellated and normalized" (185, qtd. in Wright 17). On 9/11, those virtues were destroyed when the planes hit the Twin Towers. Similarly, the Winchesters' mother was violated in their home when Sam was a baby. She was put on the ceiling, with a large gash in her stomach—which could be seen as similar to the gash left by the planes on the Twin Towers on 9/11—with blood dripping down on her son's head. She then erupts into flames, resulting in the destruction of the domestic space, e.g., the symbol of the nation-state. Again, this could be seen as being similar to how the Twin Towers erupted into flames and turned into ash, a smoldering remain of what had once been. While this analysis may seem heavy-handed, the visual symbols of this act are extremely significant, especially as it repeated a second time when Sam's girlfriend is killed in the exact same manner, much like how the second tower was hit and destroyed on 9/11. The show repeatedly returns to moments of the women/representations of the domestic being violated in flashbacks at the beginning of each show, much like the way in which the images of the Twin Towers were shown again and again for years after 9/11, and are still shown in anniversary memorial specials each year. The space of the home that once was (both the Twin Towers and the Winchesters' home) becomes a "history-haunted space" (101) as Anne Williams describes, that is now the symbolic shell of the idyllic American myth of what once was.[3]

I would also argue that the two main characters are constantly battling the internal versus external worlds, as traditionally represented in the domestic. Wright offers a thorough explanation of how Sam is constantly seeking upward mobility, as represented in the domestic space, but I would add that there is also a constant male voyeur looking in on the domestic, even from the pilot episode. The masculine is looking in at the domestic space—a space he is only able to enter temporarily, if at all. At the beginning of this episode, we see John Winchester outside his burning house with his two sons, all of whom are looking in on the domestic that they can no longer have, as John's wife, Mary, has been murdered and burned by a demon, leading to the house burning. Both domestic ideals, mother/wife and home, are reduced to ash. This exact scene is replicated at the end of the episode, when Jessica, Sam's girlfriend, is similarly killed. Dean rescues Sam and both look in on the ideals of the domestic as males who are not allowed inside, as they did with their father at the beginning of the episode.

There is a similar scene of the male voyeur gazing into the domestic space from outside at the end of the Season Five finale. By the end of the episode, Sam is sent to Hell to battle Lucifer and Michael in the Cage, but the episode does not end there—pan to an outside shot of Dean in a two-story house in what looks like a suburban neighborhood with a beautiful woman (Lisa) and her son (Ben). The viewer is now the voyeur—but, the shot then pans to a streetlamp, heavily shadowed except for the light under the lamp, where Sam stands. Dean is no longer on the outside looking in; Sam is alone on the outside while Dean has been allowed into the domestic, albeit temporarily as we discover in Season Six. A final example of the male voyeur gazing on the domestic is at the beginning of Season Eight—when Dean escapes from Purgatory after a year of battling monsters—only to find that Sam was in domestic bliss with Amelia Richardson. However, Dean forces him out of domesticity to return to their life of hunting. Sam later returns to watch Amelia, as the voyeur looking in (from the street in the Impala this time) on the domestic internal security he can never have. This male voyeur looking in on the domestic sphere connects to the traditional Gothic ideas of the inner female space versus the external male world. Additionally, this relates to post–9/11 concerns about the violation of the internal world from without, as well as to the surveillance state as a voyeur of citizens' lives.

In addition to the reaffirming of gender roles as seen in many forms of media after 9/11, the show also thoroughly examines the concept of the terror within—a traditionally Gothic notion that has many connotations, from psychological to nationalistic. As Kripke says in "The Devil's Road Map," the *Supernatural* DVD commentary for Season Two, "the scariest monster is the monster you face in the mirror." He continues by saying that "all monsters are our own internal fears and anxieties made manifest." While Kripke refers specifically to monsters, these monsters can be seen as any of the supernatural figures we see in the "original" Gothic texts. I would argue that those internal fears and anxieties after 9/11 are societal fears.

As I've already mentioned, following 9/11 there were many socio-cultural changes, and in the arts, many writers were left wondering how they should respond to the event or even if they had the right to respond. Prior to 9/11, as Richard Gray explains in *After the Fall: American Literature Since 9/11* (2011), "America had been impervious.... Then everything changed. On September 11, 2001, as the media did not fail to point out over and over again, America came under attack. It was—at least, according to the national sense of things—invaded. The homeland was no longer secure and, to that extent, no longer home" (5). Americans were invaded, but as more and more information came out about the hijackers, the American public felt as if they were invaded from within since the hijackers spent significant time in the United States prior to the attacks and learned how to fly planes in the U.S. The concept of battling the evil within continues today with the presence of the "homegrown terrorist" as seen in increasing numbers of mass shootings (admittedly, many of these shooters have not had ties to any sort of terrorist organization). However, the battle of the evil from within has been a constant concept in the media since 9/11 and it doesn't seem to be letting up anytime soon.

McG, one of the original producers for *Supernatural*, says in the commentary for Season One, "*Supernatural*: Tales from the Edge of Darkness," that he got involved in the series because he was interested in "what [was] happening at movie theaters … with scary films really having a lot of resonance with today's audiences." Those scary films resonated with audiences who wanted a sort of catharsis after 9/11 and were able to speak about evils and monsters in a way that audiences could connect with. We had experienced real-life monsters and evil on 9/11 and watching the monsters get vanquished on TV and in movie theaters helped us to resolve our fear, anger, and trauma caused by the horrific nature of that day. Gray says that "what was remarkable, and arguably unique, about the response of American writers to the crisis of 9/11 was that it reignited their interest in a paradox that lies at the heart of writing at least since the time of Romanticism: the speaking of silence, the search for verbal forms that reach beyond the condition of words, *the telling of a tale that cannot yet must be told*" (14, emphasis added). If we look at Gray's words, we can understand why the Gothic has become a place for this "telling" the last fifteen years. The Gothic has always been an arena where the unspeakable can be spoken and where the audience can experience things that they cannot experience in other texts.

The pilot of *Supernatural* sets up the series as the travel story of two hyper-masculine men who search for and destroy all aspects of supernatural beings. Many of the monsters they experience in their travels are examples of the internal becoming manifest—the vampire is hidden and looks human until it needs to feed and its second row of teeth are shown; the demon possesses a body and can only be differentiated by its black eyes; the ghost was a normal human before it died, typically from a violent death, and has stayed on Earth long enough to become a vengeful spirit. These monsters used to be part of society—used to be normal—and they changed, much like the "homegrown terrorist." Now they are all extreme threats to the homogenous, acceptable society.

A show like *Supernatural* uses the Gothic as a way to examine many of the traditional tropes and themes found within the original Gothic that are still haunting and manifesting in our modern society. Fifteen years after 9/11, society is still coming to terms with the concerns about gender-norming, the domestic space as symbolic of the nation-state, and the terror/evil within. However, while *Supernatural* examines these concepts, I want to argue that the show is critiquing these societal tendencies rather than reaffirming them, but I am not sure if this is actually the case, and that is a truly disturbing conclusion.

Notes

1. I am purposely focusing on the American reaction after 9/11 since *Supernatural* is set in, though not filmed in, the United States and was set up as the quintessential American road trip. While other countries had their own post-9/11 reactions, the American reaction is unique and is deeply reflected in *Supernatural*.

2. There are many excellent examinations of the other post-9/11 concerns, including the surveillance state and protection of the homeland, but that is outside the scope of this essay.

3. For more on the male and female Gothic, see Chapter Seven, "Night*mère's* Milk: The Male and Female Formulas," in Williams's *Art of Darkness: A Poetics of Gothic* (Chicago: University of Chicago Press, 1995), pp. 99–107.

Works Cited

Clery, E. J. *The Rise of Supernatural Fiction, 1762–1800*. Cambridge: Cambridge University Press, 1995. Print.

"The Devil's Road Map." *Supernatural: The Complete Second Season*. Exec. prod. and creator Eric Kripke. DVD extra. Warner Bros., 2007.

Ferguson Ellis, Kate. *The Contested Castle: Gothic Novels and the Subversion of Domestic Ideology*. Urbana: University of Illinois Press, 1989. Print.

Gray, Richard. *After the Fall: American Literature Since 9/11*. Oxford: Wiley-Blackwell, 2011. Print.

Hutcheon, Linda, with Siobhan O'Flynn. *A Theory of Adaptation*, 2d ed. London: Routledge, 2013. Print.

Kraynak, Shana. "'Upon Life and All Its Random Injustice': The Post-Traumatic Masculinity of Superheroes, Villains, and Vigilantes in Graphic Novels, Television, and Cinema." Diss., Indiana University of Pennsylvania, 2015. ProQuest Dissertations and Theses Database. Web. 25 July 2015.

McGuire, Anne, and David Buchbinder. "The Forensic Gothic: Knowledge, the Supernatural, and the Psychic Detective." *Canadian Review of American Studies* 40.3 (2010): 289–307. Project Muse. Web. 24 July 2015.

Sanders, Julie. *Adaptation and Appropriation*. The New Critical Idiom. London: Routledge, 2006. Print.

"*Supernatural*: From the Edge of Darkness." *Supernatural: The Complete First Season*. Exec. prod. and creator Eric Kripke. Exec. prod. McG and Kim Manners. Warner Bros., 2006. Blu-Ray.

"Wendigo." *Supernatural: The Complete First Season*. Writ. Eric Kripke. Dir. David Nutter. Perf. Jensen Ackles and Jared Padalecki. Warner Bros., 2006. Blu-Ray.

Wright, Julia M. "Latchkey Hero: Masculinity, Class and the Gothic in Eric Kripke's *Supernatural*." *Genders* 47 (2008): n. pag. Web. 15 July 2015.

The Automobile as Moving Castle

Thomas Knowles

This essay explores the Gothic in *Supernatural* through the vehicle of Dean Winchester's 1967 Chevrolet Impala. *Supernatural* certainly ticks many of the boxes of a "shopping-list" approach to the Gothic, but Gothic purists might be tempted to deny *Supernatural* a generic classification as such because of its seeming lack of that central Gothic component: the castle.[1] I will attempt to read the Impala—in many respects the third central character of the show, besides the brothers Sam and Dean Winchester—as the Gothic castle of the series. In so doing, I will consider the automobile as a cultural symbol and emblem of normative North American concepts of identity and authenticity. Conversely, I see the homosocial space of the interior of the car that the brothers share, combined with the filmic fetishization of the car's paintwork, body panels, instrument binnacles, and chromium detailing, as gesturing toward a subversive literature and cinema of the car as both pornographic and deathly.[2]

The Impala, castle-like, provides a safe haven and bulwark against the threatening outside world for Sam and Dean, and it is quite literally the vehicle that delivers the brothers both from and into danger. This duality is in keeping with the castle's traditional role in Gothic fiction as the problematic seat of family and order, which nonetheless harbors secrets and dangers, which upon emerging transform an ostensible sanctuary into a prison of horrors. Dean's obvious self-identification with the Impala,[3] and Sam's status as "guest" or "other" within the car—Dean maintains the right to choose all of the music that they listen to in the car, as well as doing most of the driving and maintenance—marks the car as the fulcrum of the brothers' strained relationship. Its status as family heirloom contributes to this sense of the car having taken the place of the familial home as the arena for fraternal contestation, much as television in the twentieth and twenty-first centuries has succeeded the novel as the preeminent medium for the representation of societal taboos and anxieties.

But the Impala might also be said to reverse the traditional role of the castle. In Sam and Dean's world, drawing upon the Gothic tradition, the four-walled house is the last place the brothers would turn for safety. In becoming the mobile fortress of the duo, the Impala invokes the powerful symbolic role of the motorcar in the American psyche, recalling the glory days of American manufacturing might, and of the freedom of the open road in Jack Kerouac's *On the Road* (1957) and classic road movies, such as *Vanishing Point* (1971).[4] The gas-guzzling, pedestrian and passenger-imperiling image of the motorcar is resisted in this representation, and in the contemporary world of climate change and safety consciousness, I ask to what extent the show can be said to recapitulate the classic Gothic ambivalence of both social critique and reactionary retrenchment.

Before discussing my reading of the Impala in detail, I will give a brief outline of some of the critical assumptions about the Gothic castle upon which I will be drawing. In the final section I will draw upon the cultural theory of John Ruskin and Roland Barthes to draw out the competing modes of production and identity that I see the Impala as problematically enshrining. Firstly, though, I would like to acknowledge some extant critical responses to *Supernatural's* Impala.

Melissa N. Bruce, in "The Impala as Negotiator of Melodrama and Masculinity in *Supernatural*," has read the Impala as a structural hinge for melodrama, which enables the expression of non-normative emotion between the two central characters and in fact comes to embody their relationship. Bruce draws upon the sense of succor and support that Dean in particular draws from the Impala, and sees the space within and around the vehicle as one which enables the brothers to recognize the strength of the emotions that they feel for one another, in a heteronormatively acceptable fashion: "As the only constant physical space in their lives, the Impala offers a stability that can be provided by no other object, and Dean's ownership of the car only solidifies his role as protector. By acting as the sole space of home, therefore, the Impala is placed within a specifically feminine framework, which allows Dean the freedom to display overt emotionalism that might not otherwise be acceptable" (4.3).

The Gothic castle is often figured as a feminine space and thus as belonging to what is called the Female Gothic. This space in Gothic fictions would metamorphose into the middle-class family home over the course of the nineteenth century, but whether as traditional castle or monastery, or as bourgeois town house, its enclosed and private sphere was contrasted with what has been seen as the male Gothic principle of the wanderer in the wilderness.[5] *Supernatural's* car, then, as a machismo space of petrol-powered exploration and classic rock music, is nonetheless a domesticated and private space of emotion and family contact. Stan Beeler, in his "Two Greasers and a Muscle

Car: Music and Character Development in *Supernatural*," identifies the Impala and the classic rock that invariably accompanies its scenes as the default setting of the series: "the car and chronologically consistent music anchor the show to an anachronistic mood with the same regularity that establishing shots of identifiable location items are used in other television series. This is particularly important in a series that does not have a regular setting or location" (20).

Beeler is concerned with the overtly masculinist elements of the Impala and of the brothers—the "two greasers" of his title—but in identifying the car as the "home" of the series, alternative gendered readings are released. In this way, once again, the car can be seen to replicate the castles of classic Gothic fiction, which are both the seat of power for sublimely terrible patriarchs, symbolized by phallic towers and ramparts, and yet also the domain of female ministrations that can be seen to work against such figures and their nefarious designs. Missing from both Bruce and Beeler's accounts of the Impala are the uncanny and disquieting aspects of the car, the sense in which it is as much a prison and a curse for the brothers as it is the means of achieving the freedom of the open road, and a place of sanctuary. In discussing the struggle for primacy that is one of the drivers of Sam and Dean's relationship, Bruce actually invokes those Gothic tropes in an attempt to reinforce the positive effects of the car: "At this moment, both brothers are well aware of the roles they occupy, regardless of Sam's hopes of changing them.... As this new struggle for the place of protector begins, therefore, the Impala is foregrounded as a means of both physical and emotional support for the boys" (4.4).

I would argue that an appreciation of the Gothic in *Supernatural*, and particularly of the Impala seen as the Gothic castle of the series, helps to demonstrate the car's implication in the inescapable nature of Sam and Dean's roles; the car will, vampire-like, return from the dead again and again throughout the seasons, so that the boys can never escape its seductive enticement to the open road, and its whisperings of legacy and family debt. In addition, the safe haven of the car is frequently penetrated by Dean and Sam's enemies, and it suffers violent wreckage on more than one occasion. It may represent the only home that the brothers can lay claim to, but it is as terrifying and contingent as it is comforting and familiar.

Catherine Tosenberger, in "The Epic Love Story of Sam and Dean," explores the incestuous tension between the brothers in the TV show, as well as the explicit "Wincest" fan fiction in which the boys very often acknowledge and act upon their repressed desires. Again, the centrality of the Impala as the paradoxically unfixed location of the series is assumed in a reading that sees echoes of the incestuous Gothic of Virginia Andrews's classic modern Gothic novel *Flowers in the Attic* (1979): *Supernatural* fan writers have jokingly christened the series "Flowers in the Impala," a reference to Andrews's novel.[6] Drawing upon Andrew Richardson's theorizing of incestuous siblings in the poetry of Romanticism, Tosenberger sees the childhood bonds of Sam and Dean intensified and made almost transcendent in the fan fiction realizations of their forbidden love: "The bond forged between Sam and Dean when they were children on the road, with an unreliable, often-absent father, is the deepest and most profound relationship that they will ever have with anyone … the most intense Sam/Dean moments—and the moments when they are mistaken for gay—often take place in episodes that concern family relationships, especially when those family relationships involve children" (4.2). The threat of incest is never far from the castle or home in Gothic fiction, and as a cultural taboo it still holds much of its power today. But if the Gothic is a means of exploring the specific "hang-ups" of a given society in a "safe" fashion, what are we to make of this paradoxical intermingling of masculine pride and power with anxiety around homosexuality and incest? In the age of mass-media and production-line manufacturing, I will argue, the core anxiety of the show is that of the impossibility of, and yet the persistent desire for, authenticity.[7] The incestuous tension between Dean and Sam, which the fan fictions fully realize, can be seen as a further destabilizing element in the identities of both Dean and his avatar, the Impala.

The Castle

I will now outline some of the classic features of the Gothic castle, and begin to draw some parallels with the Impala. Eino Railo, in his seminal study *The Haunted Castle* (1927), defines the structure of the castle in what he calls "horror-romanticism": "The reader quickly observes that this 'haunted castle' plays an exceedingly important part in these romances; so important, indeed, that were it eliminated the whole fabric of romance would be bereft of its foundation and would lose its predominant atmosphere" (7). Describing the secret tunnels and passageways that lie beneath the titular castle in Horace Walpole's *The Castle of Otranto* (1764), Railo tells us that "an awesome silence reigns in these subterranean vaults, a silence only broken by the creak of rusty hinges as a breath of air somewhere sets an old door moving" (7). Such obscure passages in the dark below, coupled with the lighter and airier reaches of the upper castle, where the decisions of state are made and guests are entertained, has led to the frequent mapping of models of the mind onto the structures of the castle—the subterranean vaults becoming a projection of the unconscious, the upper courts the domain of consciousness and presumed rationality. Carol Margaret Davison has said of the Gothic's central symbol: "If we conceive of Gothic literature as a type of castle—its most preeminent symbol—it is fair to say that it has long been besieged" (2). Indeed, its foundations have continued to be undermined by its transplantation and/or dissemination into other mediums, such as television and film. There have been readings of the castle as architectural incarnation of the body, too, with all of the obvious phallic connotations attached to tall towers and turrets; the private chambers and secret subterranean passages suggestive of the protected orifices of virgin heroines under siege; and the queering of such design features as back passages and portholes.

A less overtly sexualized reading might see the castle as a symbol of the mind or soul trapped in the prison of the body, but this too is open to a gendered interpretation in which the frustrated heroines of Ann Radcliffe's fictions, for instance, find their taste for the sublime and for picaresque curtailed by their gender. It may be pushing the analogy too far to say that we can hear an echo of Railo's rusty hinges in the Impala's creaking doors, or that the cubby holes, vents, and other secret compartments of the car are miniaturized equivalents of subterranean passages and sealed vaults of the Gothic castle, but as a repository for memories and incommunicable emotions, they do have structural similarities, and there are strong sexual overtones to the marketing and consuming of automobiles, which the camera-work of *Supernatural* and the repartee of the boys certainly plays up to.

The Impala

Commonly referred to by fans as "the Metallicar," in reference to the classic rock that provides the soundtrack to the brothers' epic road trips, and as "Baby" by Dean, the Impala is as central to *Supernatural* as the castle was to the Gothic novels of the eighteenth century. As an icon, the American muscle car could easily have been represented by a Mustang, a Dodge, or a Pontiac, but there is something menacing about the brooding architecture of the Impala that suits its Gothic employment very well. Any discussion of the Impala's role in *Supernatural* must surely hinge upon the climax to the original five-season story arc. In "Swan Song" (5.22), Chuck Shurley—the hack author/ prophet who is writing the fan fiction/gospel based on the exploits of Sam and Dean Winchester—narrates a passage of his scripture that details the origins of the Impala. Having described the celebrations around the hundred-millionth car rolling off the line at the General Motors plant in Janesville, Wisconsin, Chuck tells us of the "birth" of Dean's beloved car: "Three days later another car rolled off that same line. No one gave two craps about her, but they should've. Because this 1967 Chevrolet Impala would turn out to be the most important car … no, the most important object in pretty much the whole universe."

Later in the same episode the author treats us to some sentimental background story about the boys taking time out between hunting, living the dream of the open road, providing the narration for a montage of cheap motels, pool-hustling, and the Impala travelling through wilderness at speed: "They could go anywhere and do anything … and when it was clear, park her in the middle of nowhere, sit on the hood and watch the stars … sure, they never had a roof and four walls, but they were never in fact homeless."

At the climax of this episode, the half-brothers Sam and Adam,[8] possessed by the brother archangels Lucifer and Michael respectively, face off in a graveyard setting. The "God made evil" argument is rehearsed by Sam/Lucifer and, just before they join in (im)mortal combat, the growl of the Impala's engine is heard. Dean has arrived and, playing Def Leppard's "Rock of Ages" on the car's cassette player, he pulls up in front of the warring brothers to the strains of "it's better to burn out than fade away." God, who on one understanding of evil is responsible for the battle about to commence, is missing. The human bodies that heavenly and diabolic forces have possessed in order to wage their war are also the product, on one Gothic reading of the unconscious forces that influence our actions, of their absent father. In this scenario, then, the car (which Dean inherited from his hunter father, John, and whose legacy he and Sam must act out) is the symbol of both the biological father and God the father. All of this heavy symbolism is relieved the second that Castiel, the falling but not-yet-fallen angel, arrives to temporarily dispatch Adam/Michael with a Molotov cocktail of "holy fire," but not before calling him an "assbutt." It gets pretty brutal again soon after that moment of light relief, and Sam/Lucifer, having already exploded Castiel and snapped Bobby's neck, looks to be about to kill Dean. However, the sun glinting on the chromium trim of the door panel of the Impala miraculously awakens Sam from his possession by Lucifer, causing him to pause long enough for his gaze to fall upon the toy soldier that he had crammed into one of the ashtrays. Cue a montage of the boys' shared time in the car from childhood to present—a cocktail of nostalgia strong enough to give Sam supremacy in his own mind, and to hurl himself and Adam into the maw opened up by the rings of the Four Horsemen of the Apocalypse. The Impala has prevented the Apocalypse through a combination of its polished chromium detailing and Sam's personalization or territorial marking of its interior.

Beneath the symbolism of family, devilment, and divine entanglement, I read a moral that is an attempt to alleviate concerns about mass-produced culture and individuality. Dean and Sam's personalization of the mass-produced Impala is what renders it unique, although as the beginning of "Swan Song" makes clear, when it rolls off the production line it is merely the latest of over a hundred million cars already produced by General Motors. When it is destroyed by a collision with a possessed truck in "Devil's Trap" (1.22), Dean remakes it from the ground up including all of the imperfections, such as the soldier mentioned above, and the Lego bricks that Dean pushed into its air vents as a child. This raises intransigent questions about representation and reality, and about the mass-produced product and individuality. Is the remade Impala the same car that was wrecked by the truck?

Modes of Production and Authenticity

In an attempt to answer this question, I will now consider two antithetical but often paradoxically combined notions of the car, drawing on John Ruskin's writings about craftsmanship in Gothic architecture, and on Roland Barthes's consideration of the motorcar as the twentieth century's equivalent of the Gothic cathedral. I wish to consider the Impala, as both phenomenal and narrative object, in the light of two contrasting theories of production—that which is outlined by Ruskin in his "The Nature of the Gothic" (1852), and that which Barthes proposes in his "The New Citroën" (1957). This will prove to be a discussion of mass-produced identity crisis as against hand-crafted authenticity, and the Impala is seen to fulfill the criteria for both of these models such that it can be said to be an uncanny icon built to contain a homely/unhomely space, and to reflect the unresolvable dialectic of the desire and impossibility of authenticity. Finally, I consider the Beats and their celebration of itinerant life on the road as a possible product of this creative tension, and which *Supernatural* draws upon to make sense of its irreconcilabilities.

There is an idea of the large, square American car that pertains in Europe and that American literature, film, and television perpetuates. It is of a frontier-spirit realized in the ruggedly put-together and simplistic machines that privilege size, power, and comfort above all else. It is something of an historical irony—given that the United States is the birth place of the mass-produced vehicle, thanks to Henry Ford's Model T—but the image of American cars with large panel gaps; monstrous, unsophisticated engines; supremely soft suspension and brute power, over and above maneuverability and handling, persists. This is not to say that the manufacture of American vehicles is in any sense inferior, but that the priorities are different; the manual transmissions and precision handling of a European hatchback are an irrelevance to the vast distances of the American highway. Jean Baudrillard, in his travelogue/anthropological study *America* (1986), describes his experience of driving on Los Angeles's freeways thus: "The way American cars have of leaping into action, of taking off so smoothly, by virtue of their automatic transmission and power steering. Pulling away effortlessly, noiselessly eating up the road, gliding along without the slightest bump ... riding along as if you were on a cushion of air" (56–57). This comes close to an experience of flight, and as a symbol of freedom and the wandering spirit the American car has about it the resonances of Romantic transcendence that were heralded by images of birds, wind, and preternatural travel through the air. The apparent tension between simplistic design and construction and mass-production is key to the maintenance of this myth of the automobile, and it is this tension that is at work in the episode of *Supernatural* that I have been discussing. For Dean to be able to rebuild the Impala from scratch in Bobby's scrap yard, it cannot require factory precision, yet at the same time what he produces is an exact replica of the car that was destroyed in "Devil's Trap."

In a letter to his father dated 22 February 1852, concerning his planning of the chapter of *The Stones of Venice II*, which would become "The Nature of the Gothic," John Ruskin stated his intention to "show that the greatest distinctive character of Gothic is in the workman's heart and mind" (180n.1). For Ruskin, it was the imperfections of a hand-crafted architecture that revealed to him the heart and mind of the craftsman, as opposed to the lowly perfection of the factory-produced modernity that he sought to resist through his approbation of the Gothic: "It is not, truly speaking, the labour that is divided; but the men:—Divided into mere segments of men—broken into small fragments and crumbs of life; so that all the little piece of intelligence that is left in a man is not enough to make a pin, or a nail, but exhausts itself in making the point of a pin or the head of a nail" (196).

Ruskin's assertion here speaks to the inefficiency of a mode of production that the manufactories of his day were already endangering. Ruskin lists the properties of the Gothic artifact, but also and of equal importance are the character traits of its builders or craftsmen and the passion that they bring to their creative endeavors. Ostensibly the Impala—constructed in a General Motors plant that had already built over a hundred million cars—is very far from the Gothic ideal of a hand-crafted, imperfect machine. But when we factor in its squeaking doors, and the modifications, vandalism, and ad-hoc maintenance of the Winchesters over the years, Dean's car can be seen to have transcended its production-line similitude to its fellow 1967 Chevrolet Impalas. To return to Chuck Shurley's narration in "Swan Song," these are the Gothic elements of the Winchester Impala. Sam's army man and Dean's Legos "are the things that make the car theirs—really theirs. Even when Dean rebuilt her from the ground up, he made sure all these little things stayed, 'cause it's the blemishes that make her beautiful." There is more at stake here than the personal touches and imperfections that accrue to a long-owned possession; Chuck's narration seems to be reiterating a Romantic conception of the self—one that celebrates the individual quiddity of each and every person, no matter that they are one amongst a hundred million, or even amongst billions—and it is the childhood experiences and memories of that individual that makes them what they are. For Ruskin, the acknowledged imperfections of the Northern Gothic architecture combine as fragments to make a "stately unaccusable whole" (190).

Roland Barthes, in his short essay "The New Citroën" (1957), identifies the modern motor car as a truly transcendent object—"a transformation of life into matter" (101). For Barthes, the motorcar is as a mass-produced symbol, consumed "in image ... by a whole population which appropriates them as a purely magical object" (101). But in comparing the car to a Gothic cathedral, by which he means "conceived in passion by unknown artists," Barthes seems to be conflating two quite contradictory aesthetics: the perfection of the smooth and frictionless surface, which seems to effortlessly support itself—the classical—and the rough, human assemblages of the Gothic, which make a feature of their structural necessities. In Barthes's formula, the act of possessing a car, of touching and besmirching the factory-fresh sublimity of the new Citroën in the showroom, is a parable for "petit-bourgeois advancement" (103). It is the layering of the human over the transcendent object that seems to disgust Barthes here in what is a rejection of the passion that Ruskin had sought in imperfection as mere consumerist desire. However, in Dean's refusal to "consume" the Impala as object, even when it is itself consumed by road accidents or supernatural misadventure, can be seen an appeal to that American mythology of the self-sufficient frontier, as opposed to middle-class consumption. As emblem of the family, Dean protects the car perhaps above all else, like the classic Gothic villains of Horace Walpole and Ann Radcliffe, and he will stop at nothing to maintain not just the family but, over and above that, that which represents the family. By imbuing the rebuilt Impala with the memories and individualities that he and Sam accrued in a lifetime on the road, Dean becomes the type of Ruskin's Gothic craftsman, but in making an identical replica of the destroyed Impala he also uncannily resurrects that which was dead in a Victor Frankenstein fashion. The two modes of production become inseparable: the painstakingly imperfect recreation perpetuates the infinite reproduction of the mass-produced product even as it resists it. We can link this back to the unrealized incestuous tensions between the brothers discussed above, which are most powerfully felt in the homosocial space of the car. For Dean, the best of all possible worlds is one that maintains the creative and unresolved tensions embodied by the Impala. This is why Dean refuses to accept any "endings"—either for the Impala, for Sam, or for himself. For the brothers' feelings to end in the climax of incestuous fulfilment would be incompatible with Dean's hetero-normative, machismo self-image, and so he prefers the perpetuation of unrealizable possibility that is manifest in the moving car. For Dean it really is about the journey and not the destination.

Conclusion

Supernatural's Impala might be said to flicker disconcertingly between the conceptual realms of mass-produced consumable (Barthes) and spiritually-invested object (Ruskin). As noted in the discussion of "Swan Song," the Impala is one of hundreds of millions of cars produced by General Motors, and its destruction and resurrection further troubles its presumed status as unique object. Is the repeatedly reborn Impala really Dean's car, or is it a mere facsimile, a Gothic imposter? And if that is so for the car, this raises the further doubt that the multiply-resurrected Winchesters themselves might be mere copies or shadows of their former selves.[9] Here the car can be seen to take on the form of the Creature in Mary Shelley's *Frankenstein* (1818)—rebuilt from salvaged and scavenged parts the problematic imperfections, which are also perfect recreations of a former incarnation, serve to remind the brothers of their own serially dismembered and recapitulated bodies and souls. As much as the car can be said to be a source of continuity and permanence in the boys' itinerant existence, it is also the uncanny reminder of the Gothic horror of their own bodies. Each time that Sam and Dean come back from the dead, from heavenly or hellish imprisonment, or from demonic possession of one form or another, they appear outwardly to be the same Sam and Dean, but they can never be certain as to whether they have been irrevocably changed by their experiences, or if they are merely the latest product of the Winchester production line.

This problematic of troubled identity and authenticity taps into one of the core anxieties of American Gothic, which Charles L. Crow, in his *American Gothic* (2009), has formulated as "we are not who we believed ourselves to be. We are something else" (24). This rendering of the familiar unfamiliar, the homely unhomely, speaks to the pervasive current of the uncanny running through the Gothic, and it is central to the castle's status as both safe haven and prison. The serial wrecking of the Impala, if we consider the symbolic status of the muscle car in this extended road movie of a series, is then an act of almost compulsive iconoclasm—an attempt to break open the symbol and understand its contents. Thus through its seeming goal of perpetual speed, which can only result in the stasis of the crash, Sam and Dean's vehicle of deliverance also appears in the guise of a hearse, delivering the boys to their graves, or worse, and this is made the more unsettling because it masquerades as home and the nexus of familial feeling.

If the paradoxical goal of speed is the permanent stasis of the crash, leaving behind the Gothic ruins of smashed cars and disfigured bodies, this gives a particularly dark resonance to the end of "Swan Song," when the resurrected Castiel tells Dean that he would not be happy in either Heaven or Hell, and that what he really wants is freedom and not happiness: the freedom of the mythology of the car is the freedom to crash, to self-destruct, or perhaps it is the period between embarkation and inevitable crash realized in the speed and motion. We can see this in Ruskin's assertion that the craftsman released from the directions of lowly manufacturing perfectionism will continually err, misstep and even reveal a disturbed imagination, but will be free (192). It seems likely that the Christian Ruskin was applying a theological justification for moral freedom and evil to his aesthetic argument, and this might be said to be echoed in this episode of *Supernatural*. That Dean ends the story arc in the retirement of bourgeois family life would almost seem to refute Castiel's words, were it not for the sizeable tumbler of bourbon he sips at the dinner table, and the Gothic return of Sam (or is it Lucifer?) who looks in on his brother's "domestic bliss" with an enigmatic expression. Dean's retirement will, of course, be short-lived, and he will be on the road again, chasing the only kind of ending capable of satisfying him: the endless pursuit of an unrealizable one. On this reading the Impala is a metaphor for the ever-quest for identity in a multiply-mediated world; the only safe place by virtue of its continual passage through space and time. But just as in the Gothic castles of old, that safety proves to be illusory. When the forces of darkness emerge into the light from the secret passages and hidden chambers of the Gothic castle, it can be seen as the forces of the repressed unconscious resurfacing to exert uncanny control over the rational, conscious mind. This very easily maps onto the idea of the driver losing control of his or her vehicle in some way. The Impala's identification with safety and freedom is in fact undermined right from the very beginning of *Supernatural*: possessed by a vengeful spirit in the pilot episode, it careers after the boys over a bridge in an attempt to run them down. Moreover, just as the retreat from the dangers of the outside world into the vaults of ancestral power is seen to raise the specter of the past, no matter how fast Dean guns the Impala's engine, he is encased in the repository of his past. What is perhaps most Gothic about this circumstance, as the possession of the car by malignant forces and its repeated resurrections (read: mass-productions) demonstrate, is that this is an entirely unremarkable state of affairs; there might be a hundred Deans on a hundred highways across the United States.

Notes

1. See, for instance, Carol Margaret Davison, *Gothic Literature, 1764–1824* (Cardiff: University of Wales Press, 2009), pp. 2–4.

2. I am thinking here of J. G. Ballard's controversial novel *Crash* (1973), David Cronenburg's 1996 film adaptation of the same, and of Quentin Tarrantino's *Death Proof* (2007), but there are many more examples, such as Don DeLillo's *Cosmopolis* (2003), which was also adapted for the cinema by Cronenberg in 2011.

3. When the Impala is stolen by a shapeshifting doppelgänger in Season One, Dean says to Sam: "The thought of him driving my car....It's killing me" ("Skin," 1.6).

4. Show creator Eric Kripke has stated that *On the Road*'s Sal and Dean were the inspiration for the names Sam and Dean ("Fact Scarier than Fiction," *The Daily Telegraph* [8 March 2007]).

5. For overviews of male and female Gothic, see Davison, *History of the Gothic*, pp. 83–111.

6. V. C. Andrews's novel concerns the plight of siblings trapped in an attic for most of their childhood by wicked and uncaring relatives. Routinely whipped and starved, and deprived of daylight and company, they turn to one another for comfort and support. With the onset of puberty the closeness of the two eldest children, Cathy and Chris, inevitably takes an incestuous turn. The portrayal of this great taboo is sympathetic in this novel, seen as a natural consequence of the children's isolation and emotional deprivation.

7. Authenticity is a problematic that is very much at home in the Gothic, beginning with Horace Walpole's mock-Gothic residence Strawberry Hill, and continuing into his publication of the first Gothic novel, *The Castle of Otranto* (1764), with its layers of disavowal of authorship.

8. John Winchester fathered a child by another woman, Kate Milligan, and kept his existence a secret from Sam and Dean.

9. The Winchesters die with alarming regularity in the course of the show, sojourning in Heaven, Hell, and variations of Limbo and alternate universes before being brought back to the fight.

Works Cited

Barthes, Roland. "The New Citroën." 1957. *Mythologies*. Trans. Annette Lavers. London: Vintage, 2009. Print.

Baudrillard, Jean. *America*. 1986. London: Verso, 2010. Print.

Beeler, Stan. "Two Greasers and a Muscle Car: Music and Character Development in *Supernatural*." Ed. Stacey Abbott and David Lavery. *TV Goes to Hell: An Unofficial Road Map of* Supernatural. Toronto: ECW Press, 2011. Print.

Bruce, Melissa N. "The Impala as Negotiator of Melodrama and Masculinity in *Supernatural*." *Transformative Works and Cultures* 4 (2010). Web.

Crow, Charles L. *American Gothic*. Cardiff: University of Wales Press, 2009. Print.

Davison, Carol Margaret. *Gothic Literature, 1764–1824*. Cardiff: University of Wales Press, 2009. Print.

Railo, Eino. *The Haunted Castle: A Study of the Elements of English Romanticism*. London: Routledge, 1927. Print.

Ruskin, John. Letter. 22 February 1852. *The Works of John Ruskin, Volume 10: The Stones of Venice II*. Ed. Edward Tvas Cook and Alexander Wedderburn. Cambridge: Cambridge University Press, 2010. Print.

"Swan Song." *Supernatural: The Complete Fifth Season*. Writ. Eric Kripke. Dir. Steve Boyum. Perf. Jensen Ackles and Jared Padalecki. Warner Bros., 2010. DVD.

Tosenberger, Catherine. "'The Epic Love Story of Sam and Dean': *Supernatural*, Queer Readings, and the Romance of Incestuous Fan Fiction." *Transformative Works and Cultures* 1 (2008). Web.

Shadows of Hope
Gothic Motifs and Nihilism

Dana Fore

Given the matter-of-fact way the Winchester brothers declare themselves monster "hunters" and face new apocalyptic threats every season, there can be little doubt that they come from a long line of paranormal warriors that extends through Buffy the Vampire Slayer and back to the stalwart crew created by Bram Stoker in 1897. But an equally compelling case can be made that the Winchesters owe as much—if not more—to Matthew Lewis's 1796 novel *The Monk* as to Stoker's *Dracula*.

Lewis scholar Emma McEvoy could just as easily have been talking about the style and content of a typical episode of *Supernatural* when she remarked that *The Monk* "seems constantly to recur to certain literary styles and allude to other genres only to transgress their limits. It veers dangerously between the Gothic and the grotesque, the moralizing and the burlesque.... [The] reader is assailed not only by Gothic horror, but also by the tones of mocking rationality, and, most elusively, of comedy" (xxvii). The heady mix of grotesque visuals and high melodrama in both *The Monk* and *Supernatural* make it easy to dismiss both works as simply successful "low" cultural artifacts that endure because they pander to the need for new sensations in the jaded and the young. This view echoes the Marquis de Sade's assessment of Lewis in 1800. In his *Reflections on the Novel*, Sade praised Lewis for "call[ing] upon hell for aid" and thereby re-energizing the flagging Gothic genre, even while he faulted Lewis for failing to re-ground his work in the real world in order to make it relevant as literature. According to Sade, Lewis "never rais[ed] the curtain," and thus stranded his readers "in the most horrible unreality" (qtd. in McDonald 111).

But such sweeping assessments seem too reductive: closer examination of thematic links between *Supernatural* and *The Monk* suggests that the dramatic sensibilities of the older novel help to make *Supernatural* a form of escapist entertainment that paradoxically creates a theater for grim critiques of the modern world even while it invites viewers to indulge in broadest fantasy. Using the philosophy of Southern Gothic writer Flannery O'Connor to help further define the allure of *Supernatural*, one finds that the series drives viewers toward a point of horror that O'Connor defined as demonic "nihilism"—the idea that God does not exist, simply because horrible things happen in the world. Paradoxically, for O'Connor this state of despair is the point one must reach in order to truly feel "grace," the presence of the divine, because for O'Connor, there is no true salvation unless people struggle and suffer as they move toward it (Edmondson 3–4).

An examination of what Fred Botting calls the "negative aesthetics" of the Gothic genre helps to clarify how Lewis's novel redefines conventions that later energize the *Supernatural* series. In *Gothic* (1996), Botting explains that elements of paradox are integral to Gothic plots, since the genre draws energy from the struggle to not only entertain but also to educate through the presentation of potentially disturbing scenes and ideas (42–43). Discussing Gothic literature of the eighteenth century, Botting explains that the age of "Enlightenment and reason"

> [required] carefully constructed antitheses, the obscurity of figures of feudal darkness and barbarism providing the negative against which it [could] assume positive value. The interplay of light and dark, positive and negative, is evident in the conventions, settings, characters, devices and effects specific to gothic texts. Historical settings allow a movement from and back to a rational present … the movement does not long for terrifying and arbitrary aristocratic power, religious superstition or supernatural events but juxtaposes terrors of the negative with an order authorized by reason and morality [3].

Peter Brooks has characterized the sort of vacillation outlined here—in this case, between order and chaos, reason and superstition—as integral to the pleasure of narratives as a whole, because movement of this sort works best to heighten the anticipation or "forepleasure" that reaches its climax at the end of the story ("The Idea" 29–30). This sense of final mastery over conflict was most pronounced in the seminal works of Gothic novelist Ann Radcliffe, whose narratives won critical praise for their ability to promote "virtue" in ways that were exciting, yet suitably decorous (Botting 61). In novels like *The Mysteries of Udolpho* (1794) and *A Sicilian Romance* (1790), the existence of supernatural forces was often suggested as a possibility, only to be dismissed in favor of a more rational worldview by the end of the narrative. Radcliffe relied on this basic plot structure to create what she defined as "terror"—the power to "[expand] the soul and [awaken] the faculties to a high degree of life" (qtd. in Botting 68). Opposed to this positive quality of Gothic melodrama was "horror," which "contract[ed], [froze] and nearly annihilate[ed]" the soul and finer feelings through the presentation of graphic violence, gore, or perversion (Botting 68–70).

Lewis did not share Radcliffe's squeamishness about "horror" and recognized that the bait-and-switch quality of her Gothic tales diluted the power of her plots, in contrast to narratives that embraced the otherworldly without reservations. Jettisoning an unambiguously happy ending was another innovation that Lewis added to Radcliffe's basic structure, as he presented plots that did not necessarily confirm a sense of inevitable justice and order in the end. The success of his supernatural thriller *The Monk* among the general public proved his intuition correct, even if mainstream critics accused him of trying to "[defile] ... the public mind" (qtd. in McDonald 74), and readers like Sade (himself no stranger to horrific novels) implied that Lewis's terrors were too artificial to accurately suggest "all the ills that are brought upon men by the wicked" (qtd. in McDonald 111).

At least one recent critic counters Sade's assertion that *The Monk* has no grounding in the real world. In *Monk Lewis: A Critical Biography* (2000), D. L. McDonald aligns himself with readers who see Lewis as a closeted gay man, and he argues that key scenes of mob violence in *The Monk* bear an uncomfortable resemblance to newspaper reports of vigilantism against British men convicted of homosexual acts (75–76). McDonald concludes that *The Monk* is a "virtuoso exercise in subversion. Its two plots add up to a *reductio ad absurdum* of the logic of sexual repression in Lewis's culture" (79–80). As persuasive as McDonald's view is, there is room to move beyond the idea that homophobia is the primary target of *The Monk's* social critique—that the book is, in McDonald's words, "the revenge fantasy of a man whose sexuality put him at lifelong risk" (80). There is also a strong anti-utopian cynicism driving Lewis's novel, and it is this anti-utopian impulse that is resurrected through the equally monstrous adventures of the Winchester brothers.

In his groundbreaking work, Lewis tells the story of the Spanish monk Ambrosio, a man taken in by Capuchin monks as a foundling and raised in a monastery in Madrid. As an adult, Ambrosio achieves renown as a great orator and pious ascetic; acute awareness of his social status breeds pride and hypocrisy within the monk, who secretly relishes the adulation of the masses. At the height of his power, Ambrosio is set on a path to destruction: he discovers that Agnes, a nun from the affiliated Convent of St. Clare, is plotting to break her vows and flee the order because she is pregnant. Fearing the vengeance of the implacable Prioress who runs the convent, Agnes begs Ambrosio for mercy, but he is resolute. As she is dragged away to punishment, Agnes curses the monk:

> Hear me, Proud, Stern and Cruel! You could have saved me; you could have restored me to happiness and virtue, but would not! You are the destroyer of my Soul; you are my Murderer, and on you fall the curse of my death and my

unborn Infant's! Insolent in your yet-unshaken virtue, you disdained the prayers of a Penitent.... And where is the merit of your boasted virtue? What temptations have you vanquished? Coward! you have fled from it, not opposed seduction. But the day of Trial will arrive! Oh! then when you yield to impetuous passions! when you feel that man is weak and born to err.... Oh! In that fearful moment.... Think upon Agnes, and despair of pardon! [48–49].

Agnes's curse creates a thematic affinity with the television show by introducing a primal scene—analogous to the murder of Sam's fiancée Jessica—which will drive Ambrosio into the arms of a demonic lover and put him on a course to meet the Devil himself. This scene also establishes that the fragility of *virtue* will generate many of the conflicts that follow, in much the same way that the adventures of the Winchesters underscore the ambivalent nature of *heroism*. Like the murder of Jessica in *Supernatural*, Ambrosio's betrayal of Agnes is also a sin that casts a very long shadow—one that darkens the lives of people only tangentially connected to the original crime. Like Sam Winchester on his quest for vengeance, Ambrosio becomes a man driven by a dark destiny. The unfolding of this destiny exposes "impetuous passions" in both men as their virtue is tested, and in the course of their trials, questions are raised about the possibility of justice in the world as others begin to suffer simply because of their proximity to these cursed figures.

The fragility or absence of justice in the larger world is suggested primarily through Lewis's sustained use of irony: characters frequently incur disaster while trying to uphold what initially seem to be morally correct standards of behavior. Consider the back-story of Agnes and her lover, the nobleman Raymond de las Cisternas. During his travels abroad, Raymond meets Agnes's guardians, the Baron and Baroness Lindenberg. When he learns that Agnes is being coerced into becoming a nun, he ingratiates himself with the Baroness, hoping to change her mind. The Baroness, however, misinterprets Raymond's attention as the flirtations of a lover; she subsequently declares her love for Raymond as well as her willingness to desert her husband. When Raymond rebuffs her advances, she vows revenge. When she discovers that Agnes is Raymond's true love, she determines to expedite the girl's transfer to the Convent of St. Clare.

Forced to take extreme measures to gain Agnes's freedom, the couple hatch a plot worthy of an Ann Radcliffe novel: To escape without interference by her guardians or the servants, Agnes will exploit their superstitious natures and impersonate the Bleeding Nun, a ghost said to haunt Lindenberg Castle. After waiting for the day and time the specter traditionally appears, Agnes will don a disguise and make her way through the castle and out the gates to where Raymond and a carriage will be waiting.

On the night of the escape, a sinister figure in a white, bloodstained habit runs through the castle gates to freedom. Raymond embraces her and pledges his love. She faints. During the couple's escape, the horses are terrified by a raging storm; they run wild, and the carriage is smashed to bits in a crash. While recovering from his injuries, Raymond learns that he is the sole survivor of the accident—there was no woman among the dead. He realizes his mistake when the true Bleeding Nun appears at his sickbed, returning his pledge of love and eternal fidelity.

This encounter with the Bleeding Nun prefigures not only the unabashedly gory narratives found in *Supernatural*, but also the use of iconic, "urban legend"-type monsters in the series, and the show's frequent use of morbid humor. Agnes and Raymond initially discuss the Nun in terms of condescending mockery: with "burlesqued gravity" (Lewis 139) Agnes describes the Nun as a capricious nobody who simply decides to make noise after death; with that aim in mind, the specter takes up the "best room" in the castle and proceeds to howl, and shriek, and make "many other agreeable noises of the same kind" (Lewis 139). When Raymond not only meets this legendary figure, but also blunders into binding himself to her for eternity, the target of the humor shifts—he becomes the object of a grim jest, a sort of inside joke between Lewis and readers who appreciate a darkly humorous parody of the wild coincidences in Radcliffe-type Gothic novels. This same mockery of genre conventions—wherein sensible people from the "normal" world receive a spectacular (and morbidly comical) come-uppance from famous monsters and paranormal forces—reappears, for instance, in episodes like "The Real Ghostbusters" (5.9), "I Believe the Children Are Our Future" (5.6), and "Monster Movie" (4.5). But the morbid humor in both Lewis's text and Kripke's series often goes beyond mere comic relief by creating a nagging sense of imbalance—oftentimes victims suffer inordinately for having the trivial flaw of being non-believers in supernatural powers, or simply because they are in the wrong place at the wrong time.

In *The Monk,* this disturbing sense of collateral damage moves the novel into the realm of horror just as much as the presence of overtly supernatural occurrences. Granted, Ambrosio dies in spectacular fashion: after being caught for his crimes, he sells his soul to the Devil in order to escape the tortures of the Inquisition; he escapes not to safety, but to a mountain peak, where Lucifer bears him aloft and then drops him to the rocks below. As he dies, insects drink his blood and sting his wounds, and eagles "[dig] out his eye-balls with their crooked beaks" (Lewis 441–42). Yet even this gruesome death is too quick to feel like satisfying punishment, given the victories the monk has already achieved: He has successfully captured, raped, and murdered Antonia, the object of his sexual obsession; he has murdered Antonia's mother; his betrayal of Agnes leads to the lingering death of her newborn child in the dungeons of the Convent of St. Clare, and her imprisonment causes a riot that kills innocent bystanders when she is finally rescued.

Supernatural recreates this world under siege by supernatural forces, where the forces of evil may be equally as strong (or stronger) than the forces of good, and where first impressions can be deceptive, often disastrously so. This idea drives Seasons Three and Four, by introducing characters on both sides of the divide between good and evil who share contempt for mankind and a willingness to kill or torture anyone who interferes with their scorched-earth policies. Fighting for Lucifer's army is the demon Ruby, a sister in spirit to Matilda, Ambrosio's lover and a witch who uses magic to help the monk fulfill his nefarious desires. Ruby offers her services to the Winchester brothers as an additional hunter and seems to prove her good intentions by murdering a score of her own "people." Yet in the end she is unmasked as a double agent for Lucifer, whose main purpose was to seduce Sam Winchester into relying on his demonic powers, thus hastening his damnation and triggering the Apocalypse. Ruby's counterparts among the angels are Uriel and Zachariah, who behave more like Nazi bureaucrats than divine messengers in their blind obedience to "orders," and who think nothing of murdering innocents on a genocidal scale if it will accomplish their goals.

This moral inversion of stereotypically good and evil characters seems to express bluntly for a modern audience the kind of irreligious cynicism that Lewis could only present ironically for his contemporaries. Upon discovering that Antonia, the target of his lust, has been reading the Bible, the hypocritical Ambrosio feels a pang of righteous indignation, since he believes that the Bible is too graphic a text for young minds to read without guidance. It has the power to corrupt untutored minds because in it, "every thing is called plainly and roundly by its name ... the annals of a Brothel would scarcely furnish a greater choice of indecent expressions," and the frequent violence and sex in the stories all "too frequently [inculcate] the first rudiments of vice, and [give] the first alarm to the still sleeping passions" (Lewis 259).

This debased Christian cosmos is even darker in Kripke's version. Universal disorder is conveyed through explicit references to God's absence by the angels Zachariah and Castiel; and in "Dark Side of the Moon" (5.16), the character Joshua raises the specter of God as an indifferent or sadistic deity. Joshua is introduced as the only person who still talks to God face-to-face; when the Winchesters meet him and ask for God's aid, Joshua simply says that God does not consider the Apocalypse "His problem" anymore, provoking Dean to retort that God is simply another "deadbeat dad."

The suffering within this chaotic universe achieves an intense, excruciating quality when it confronts viewers with the horror of what Holocaust scholar Lawrence Langer has described as the "choiceless choice"—situations where people are forced to choose between equally horrible actions that rob the participants (and by extension, audience members) of the sense that "moral effort" promotes any higher purpose (46). The harbingers of this cosmic despair are sometimes Ambrosio-type figures who are typically false prophets or con men. The pattern for their particular style of depredation is established in episodes like "Faith" (1.12) and "99 Problems" (5.17). In these episodes, there is an additional tinge of sadism to the crimes of the supernatural creatures because they are abetted by the weaknesses of human cohorts who are driven to extremes of desperation.

In "Faith," for example, Dean is electrocuted and later diagnosed with heart damage that will eventually kill him. Sam takes him to the faith healer Roy LeGrange, who affects a miraculous cure in front of a crowd of awestruck witnesses. Later the brothers learn that LeGrange does not have true healing power: Behind the scenes, LeGrange's wife Anna has used witchcraft to bind a soul-collecting Reaper to her service, and for every person her husband heals, the Reaper must take another life to restore a compensatory balance to the universe. Similar exploitation of human despair takes place in "99 Problems," where a community of demon hunters falls under the sway of the young sybil Leah Gideon, who claims to receive messages from angels. The Winchesters learn that the real Leah Gideon is dead, and her body has been possessed by the demonic Whore of Babylon. The creature is eventually destroyed, but not before it has led a grieving mother to the brink of a Jonestown-style massacre of "non-believers" in the hopes of achieving the resurrection of her murdered teenaged son.

But even in the absence of such demonic catalysts, the Winchesters are often faced with choiceless choices simply because they are committed to a job that requires them to make life-and-death decisions while stepping outside the boundaries of ordinary law. For example, in "Heart" (2.17), Sam is forced to kill a woman he loves when it is clear she cannot be freed from the curse of lycanthropy, and in "The Girl Next Door" (7.3), Dean kills the equally sympathetic Amy Pond, a monster who must murder to keep her ailing son alive. This last murder is complicated further because Pond's son witnesses the killing of his mother and vows revenge against Dean, becoming yet another traumatized child in the Winchester saga whose life is blighted by a vendetta.

As if these hellish events were not enough to convince viewers that we live in the worst of all possible worlds, Season Seven introduces the idea that the real catalyst for the destruction of humanity lies closer to home, within the hearts and minds of our trusted heroes. In "Meet the New Boss" (7.1), "Hello, Cruel World" (7.2), and "Repo Man" (7.15), we see the profound breakdown of the social network that functions as the Winchesters' psychological support system, and we are confronted with the idea that the relentless violence to which these heroes have been exposed can create post-traumatic stress that threatens to turn our favorite crusaders into shell-shocked wrecks or malefic spree-killers.

Elisabeth Bronfen's work on Gothic creatures explains how the fantasy horrors in episodes like these can create unsettling associations with real-world trauma. In "Cinema of the Gothic Extreme," Bronfen analyzes the psychological impact behind conventional monsters like ghosts, doubles, zombies, aliens, and cyborgs. She suggests that such creatures are doubly "haunting" because the mythic, supernatural plots in which they appear facilitate a "return of the repressed" in viewers (111). These creatures exert their most uncanny effects when they appear in narratives that "[blur] ... the distinction between bodies and belief systems," because these stories, in turn "[continue] to *reflect* and *reflect on* cultural anxieties which remain unfinished business in Western culture" (112, italics in original).

This uncanny distortion of bodies and belief systems is an integral part of Season Seven because the Winchesters' primary nemeses are the man-eating Leviathan: these voracious shapeshifters serve easily as symbols of predatory capitalism, given that their leader Dick Roman prefers to assume the mantle of a charismatic politician. Rather than retaining his true form and simply launching a war on humanity with his physically superior legions, he attempts to lure the masses to their doom through the proliferation of utopian promises and tainted junk food.

But the most disturbing distortion of beliefs and bodies occurs in "Meet the New Boss," after the angel Castiel fights to free Sam from imprisonment with Lucifer. The battle warps his personality, and he returns to Earth successful, but with a towering sense of megalomania. After declaring himself God, he embarks on a mission to destroy anyone he does not consider sufficiently pious or obedient, including scores of his fellow angels and hundreds of religious leaders. Castiel's metamorphosis introduces Season Seven's motif of heroic figures breaking down and becoming monstrous or ineffectual. Discovering that the strength of an angel is no protection against madness makes the Winchesters' predicament even more disturbing, since we see Sam apparently losing his own battle with encroaching insanity.

"Hello, Cruel World" introduces the threat of Sam's collapse. We learn that the post-traumatic stress of having been imprisoned with Lucifer has created terrifying hallucinations of the Devil's return, visions that make Sam question the nature of reality: Has he really escaped? Or is the "free" world around him—as Lucifer suggests—merely a grand illusion that the Devil has created to torment Sam with false hope while he remains trapped in Hell? This problem seems to be resolved once Sam learns a coping strategy: The self-infliction of pain on his recently wounded hand makes the visions of Lucifer disappear. Dean seems to provide further proof that Sam's visions are imaginary. The hallucinations seem most real to Sam—and to the audience—when he is alone, and there is no outside source to confirm that his torments are false. When Dean is there to help Sam work through these psychotic breaks, the camera includes reaction shots from Dean's point of view—for example, he sees an empty corner of Bobby Singer's library, where Sam sees Lucifer casually chatting away. This strategy primes the audience to "trust" the camera as the final arbiter of reality. But the audience is robbed of even this small degree of certainty and comfort in subsequent episodes.

In "Repo Man," Sam's visions of Lucifer return full force after his self-help strategies fail. The nature of reality becomes an issue again when the brothers arrive at a crime scene, and it is the specter of Lucifer—and not Sam or Dean—who remembers the name of the lead detective first. The situation becomes dire after Dean is held hostage by a serial killer, and Sam is forced to rely on Lucifer as a "partner" in his absence. In a key scene, Sam and Lucifer are arguing in a library while tracking the killer. The Devil says that Dean is probably dead. Sam tells Lucifer to "Shut up," and he stalks out of the room. Rather than providing the reassurance of a "normal" POV shot that shows Sam leaving an empty table, the camera remains behind, for a shot of the Devil sitting by himself. Sulking, Lucifer says, "He said 'Shut up' to me."

The implications of this bit of throwaway humor are more sinister: On one hand, the scene implies that Lucifer has some kind of independent existence outside of his prison after all, which revives questions about the power of good against evil in Sam and Dean's world. Furthermore, by showing that viewers can no longer "trust" the camera to help them distinguish between what is real and what is not, the scene creates uncomfortable questions about human vulnerability and the power of evil in our own world, since the camera is used to guide the viewers rather than the characters themselves, and we—like Sam and Dean—rely heavily on what we see to determine what (and who) is good and bad, true or false.

Season Seven's insistence that heroism in the modern world is a grand—and potentially destructive—illusion seems to validate critic Joseph Maddrey's view that modern American horror stories have become essentially "postmodern" through highly self-reflexive plots that promote cynicism as a survival strategy (68–83). There is much to recommend this view when it is applied to individual horror films; but before one can conclude unequivocally that the belief system being mocked in *Supernatural* is a religious one, it is helpful to consider the philosophies of Southern Gothic writer Flannery O'Connor: Her worldview provides a complementary explanation for the communal appeal of such horror stories, beyond the idea that they serve chiefly as a safety vent for the despair or sadism of American viewers in a post–9/11 world.

Flannery O'Connor (1925–1964) was dubbed a "Southern Gothic" writer because she favored grim stories set in the American South, where her typically arrogant, eccentric, or grotesque protagonists struggle for existence in a capriciously violent world of serial killers, sexual predators, con men, and sociopathic children. Like Lewis and Poe before her, O'Connor did not shy away from the use of shocking violence, and her critiques of human nature were laced with mordant wit. Like the early Gothic novelists, O'Connor believed that Gothic conventions were powerful tools for inculcating a sense of virtue in her audiences. According to biographer Henry Edmondson, O'Connor felt that modern Americans devalued the importance of Christian redemption, thanks to misplaced faith in materialism and the Nietzschean ideal of life "beyond good and evil." These false ideals created, in turn, a society that disdained "firm moral judgment," where evil was merely an abstraction and being "good" simply meant being "tolerant" to the point of being "indiscriminate" (Edmondson 2). O'Connor declared that for an audience of this sort, Christian writers would "have to make [their] vision apparent by shock—to the hard of hearing you shout, and for the almost-blind you draw large and startling figures" (*Mystery* 34).

What links O'Connor's works to the ethos of *Supernatural* is the use of paradox and shocking violence to gesture toward a grim kind of religious faith, culminating in the idea that the struggle for God's assistance or "grace" is worth continuing, even if the world seems to provide proof on all fronts that God is dead and human existence is futile. Even though the extremity of her plots tacitly acknowledged that atheists might have good reasons to believe in the futility of religion (Bacon 108), she refused to embrace such "nihilism," declaring that a "massacre of the innocents" was still not enough reason to reject Christ's divinity (qtd. in Bacon 108).

In spite of its lack of an explicitly Christian agenda, *Supernatural*'s cavalcade of monsters incarnates O'Connor's idea that in order to revive humanity's faith in a divine "mystery," we need "a sense of evil which sees the devil as a real spirit who must be made to name himself … with his specific personality for every occasion" (*Mystery* 117). And to establish this paradoxically redemptive sense of evil effectively, characters must suffer intensely and reach the point of darkest hopelessness because "it is the extreme situation that best reveals what we are essentially" (*Mystery* 113).

O'Connor explains that this degree of despair is necessary in stories because modern readers have only a superficial sense of the nature of evil and have forgotten that redemption often requires a supreme effort on the part of individuals: "There is something in us, as storytellers and as listeners to stories, that demands the redemptive act, that demands that what falls at least be offered the chance to be restored. The reader of today looks for this motion … but what he has forgotten is the cost of it. His sense of evil is diluted or lacking altogether, and so he has forgotten the price of restoration" (*Mystery* 48).

Considering the way in which *Supernatural* yokes together elements as disparate as grindhouse gore, comedy, atheistic humanism, and revivalist piety, perhaps the most pressing question that remains after examining the show's Gothic roots is "To whom is all this energy directed? What sorts of ideal viewers keep the show alive?" Are they cynical inheritors of post–9/11 paranoia who embrace the show's casual blasphemy and gore to work through fears of terrorist-inspired guerrilla war abroad and "lone wolf" attacks at home? Or are they a generation disenchanted with the false promises of the past who (in the words of Peter Brooks) still "thirst for the Sacred?" (*Melodramatic* 16). I believe the answer is "All of the above." *Supernatural* speaks to viewers who have discovered, like Goethe's Faust, two souls within their breasts: one that strives to accept, without collapsing, the darkest monstrosities of a world without God; and another—one that hopes beyond hope that on the day we fall to the bottom of the Abyss, there will finally be a benevolent hand to pull us out.

WORKS CITED

Bacon, Jon Lance. "Gory Stories: O'Connor and American Horror." *Flannery O'Connor in the Age of Terrorism.* Ed. Avis Hewitt and Robert Donahoo. Knoxville: University of Tennessee Press, 2010. 89–112. Print.

Botting, Fred. *Gothic,* 2d ed. New York: Routledge, 2014. Print.

Bronfen, Elisabeth. "Cinema of the Gothic Extreme." *The Cambridge Companion to the Modern Gothic.* Ed. Jerrold E. Hogle. Cambridge: Cambridge University Press, 2014. 107–122. Print.

Brooks, Peter. "The Idea of a Psychoanalytic Criticism." *Psychoanalysis and Storytelling.* Oxford: Blackwell, 1994. 20–45. Print.

_____. *The Melodramatic Imagination.* New Haven. Yale University Press, 1976. Print.

"Dark Side of the Moon." *Supernatural.* Writ. Andrew Dabb and Daniel Loflin. Dir. Jeff Woolnough. Perf. Jensen Ackles and Jared Padalecki. CW Network, 1 April 2010. Television.

Edmondson, Henry. *Return to Good and Evil: Flannery O'Connor's Response to Nihilism.* New York: Lexington Books, 2002. Print.

Langer, Lawrence. *Admitting the Holocaust: Collected Essays.* New York: Oxford University Press, 1995. Print.

Lewis, Matthew. *The Monk.* 1796. Ed. Howard Anderson. Oxford: Oxford University Press, 2008. Print.

Maddrey, Joseph. *Nightmares in Red, White and Blue.* Jefferson, NC: McFarland, 2004. Print.

McDonald, D. L. *Monk Lewis: A Critical Biography.* Toronto: University of Toronto Press, 2000. Print.

McEvoy, Emma. "Introduction." *The Monk.* Ed. Howard Anderson. Oxford: Oxford University Press, 2008. vii–xxx. Print.

O'Connor, Flannery. *Mystery and Manners.* Ed. Sally and Robert Fitzgerald. New York: Farrar, Straus and Giroux, 1969. Print.

"Repo Man." *Supernatural.* Writ. Ben Edlund. Dir. Thomas J. Wright. Perf. Jensen Ackles and Jared Padalecki. CW Network, 17 February 2012. Television.

PART 2

Gothic Storytelling

"You can't spell subtext without S-E-X"

Gothic Intertextuality and the (Queer) Uncanny

Jamil Mustafa

Although "Fan Fiction" (10.5) appears anomalous, the two hundredth episode of *Supernatural* is in fact a synecdoche for the entire series and thus both marks and elucidates its longevity. The most striking aspect of "Fan Fiction," and among the most salient features of the series as a whole, is intricate self-referentiality. More subtle are the ways in which "Fan Fiction" and other meta episodes exemplify the Gothic features at the core of *Supernatural*, together with the relationships among these features and the program's characteristic allusions to and inclusions of other texts. This intertextuality is itself a hallmark of the Gothic, whose earliest incarnations feature elaborately framed stories, and whose most recent iterations are thoroughly postmodern in their complex narrative structures and concern with the nature and mechanics of storytelling. The Gothic intertextuality of the meta episodes in particular and *Supernatural* in general is linked to other Gothic features—most notably the uncanny, which involves phenomena that are at once familiar and unfamiliar and which often reveals itself in narrative doubling and in confrontations between doppelgängers. The uncanny also informs fan fiction inspired by *Supernatural*, in which characters and their relationships are both familiar and, most notably in slash fiction, queerly unfamiliar. In "Fan Fiction" and other meta episodes, *Supernatural* continues and complicates the Gothic narrative tradition through intertextuality and the uncanny.

Since "intertextuality" may be construed in ways that are more or less useful in understanding *Supernatural*, I define it broadly to describe how one text incorporates another and use the term "intertext" for a text that "the reader

51

[or viewer] must know in order to understand a work of literature [or TV] in terms of its overall significance" (Riffaterre 56). While the Gothic is typically intertextual, the intertextual need not be Gothic. The original Gothic novel, Horace Walpole's *The Castle of Otranto* (1764) is certainly intertextual: the first edition is framed by a Preface in which Walpole (falsely) claims to have discovered a 1529 manuscript based on a story from the time of the Crusades (59). Other, realistic novels of the era are also framed, however. Gothic works are distinctively intertextual insofar as they use frames to link unconventional works to canonical ones, to vouch for strange narratives, and to insulate readers from the immediate impact of these extraordinary stories. Mary Shelley's *Frankenstein; or, The Modern Prometheus* (1818) exemplifies all three forms of Gothic intertextuality. Its alternate title links it to classical mythology and its title-page epigraph, to John Milton's *Paradise Lost* (1667). The novel is constructed as a nested series of increasingly improbable tales told by progressively stranger narrators: the Arctic explorer Robert Walton's letters to his sister Margaret frame the autobiography of Victor Frankenstein, which frames that of the Creature. Reading Robert's letters as if we were Margaret, we suspend our disbelief in stages, until at last we inhabit the consciousness of a being stitched together from corpses.

The uncanny is related to the intertextual, since both are forms of haunting. The uncanny is linked to "spirits and ghosts" (Freud 241), and "intertextuality is a ghost effect" in which "each text is haunted by the others" (Clayton 54). For Freud, "the uncanny proceeds from something familiar which has been repressed" (247) and which has reemerged into consciousness. Although these (un)familiar objects and ideas range from life-like mechanisms to a sense of déjà vu, all relate to reproduction and repetition. Not surprisingly, the doppelgänger is among the most uncanny of manifestations. Again we may look to *Frankenstein*, in which Victor and his creation mirror each other, pursue and are pursued by each other, and exchange roles as protagonist and antagonist. Their doubling, argues Eve Kosofsky Sedgwick, is bound up with anxieties about homosexuality.[1] It is therefore one example of Nicholas Royle's observation that "the uncanny *is* queer. And the queer is uncanny" (43).[2] If queerness is repressed by an individual, a society, or a text, then the queer uncanny signifies the return of the repressed.

"Fan Fiction" epitomizes the many ways in which *Supernatural* draws upon Gothic intertextuality and the (queer) uncanny. Although intertextuality marks every episode, only in the meta episodes is narrative itself investigated and problematized. This approach is truly Gothic intertextuality, since it leaves characters and audiences alike uncertain and anxious about how storytelling and reality interrelate. No wonder that when Marie declares, "I kinda hate the meta stories," the Winchesters—and, perhaps, viewers—concur. From (before) the start we are disoriented, when the usual opening frame,

"THEN," begins with a blank computer screen on which the title page of a script appears: "SUPERNATURAL 'Pilot' Created by Eric Kripke." As this computer screen is conflated with the viewer's screen, so too is the viewer/fan fused with the creator of the show. These conflations foreshadow Marie's creation of the musical *Supernatural*, echo the fan fiction of "The Monster at the End of This Book" (4.18), and—thanks to the uncanny sound of typing that inexplicably accompanies the appearance of digitized letters—hark back to an opening frame from the previous season, in which Metatron is typing "Meta Fiction" on a manual typewriter, with copies of Carver Edlund's works nearby, in a *Masterpiece Theatre*-style setting haunted by the one in the opening scene of "Ghostfacers" (3.13). Doubles proliferate, echoes re-echo—and, to paraphrase Dean in "The Monster at the End of This Book," our heads hurt.

That the episode is "Created By" rather than "Written By" or simply "By" is significant. In the punningly titled "Meta Fiction" (9.18), Metatron addressees the viewer, asking, "What makes a story work? Is it the plot, the characters, the text? The subtext?" Metatron's reference to the subtext and the episode title's to the metatext mirror his own uncanny double name, which not only denotes the Judaic archangel but also conflates opposites: the prefix *meta* (above, beyond) and the suffix *tron* (associated with the sub-atomic). Scribe and would-be replacement for a Creator whose Word brings all existence into being, Metatron writes at every level. He and Chuck—who declares, "Obviously, I'm a god" because he "write[s] things and then they come to life"—are linked not only by their creative writing but also by the typing sound in "Fan Fiction," which involves both Metatron's manual typewriter and Chuck's word processor in Eric Kripke's writing process. The means by which Kripke himself writes is left ambiguous. In "The French Mistake" (6.15), he is "off in some cabin somewhere writing his next pilot." On a typewriter, a computer, or a hybrid of the two? In any event, his writing a "pilot," thereby beginning "in the beginning" (Gen. 1:1 KJV), underscores his God-like status, for "in the beginning was the Word, and the Word was with God, and the Word was God" (John 1:1). But the fusion of creators and fans means that Kripke, Metatron, and Chuck share divine creative control with viewers. Metatron suggests as much when he asks fans, "Who gives a story meaning? Is it the writer? Or you?" A reader-oriented critic would respond that meaning is created by the interaction of writer, text, and reader. Our knowledge and experiences, including our reading, inform and shape our apprehension of texts—and intertexts. When Metatron, whose vast knowledge comprehends everything from divine tablets to popular culture, becomes frustrated with Castiel's relatively limited mental depository, he transforms him into an "ideal reader"—that is, one who can "understand perfectly" a writer's words and intentions, one "capable of interpreting the infinity of texts that … can be found in one specific text" (Prince 9); or, in Metatron's own (quoted) words, one who appreciates that "the universe is made up of stories, not atoms." In such a universe, reading is fundamental—as are writing and viewing.

By linking *Supernatural* to divine creation and thus to works—most obviously, the Bible—associated with it, the first image of "Fan Fiction" functions as an authenticating Gothic frame.[3] This function is duplicated in the innermost (and most outré) story, wherein Calliope declares that *Supernatural* is "epic." Given her status as the muse of epic poetry, her authority on this topic is unimpeachable. Indeed, authorship, authenticity, and authority are closely related and very much at issue throughout the episode, as they have been since Calliope's day.[4] They are also associated with intertextuality. The action begins with a dispute between Marie and Siobhan about the Samulet in which Marie invokes the authority of Carver Edlund's latest book. Shortly thereafter, Dean and Maeve argue over whether there is singing in *Supernatural*. The moment is highly ironic. Dean ought to be the authority on things *Supernatural*, but—as we discover when Marie and Maeve laugh at his and his brother's claim to be the real Winchesters—in this situation his expertise is compromised. Ironically, Sam and Dean are granted authenticity and authority only when they act as fans, as they do for the man working in the comic-book store and for Edlund's publisher in "The Monster at the End of This Book," and for Barnes and Demian in "The Real Ghostbusters" (5.9). When Maeve explains to Dean that the musical *Supernatural* is "Marie's interpretation," he relaxes, acknowledging that if there were singing in *Supernatural*, it would have to be "classic rock"—which, as Marie points out, the show does include. The irony is that there *is* singing in *Supernatural*, both within the scenes (diegetic) and in the soundtrack (extradiegetic): diegetic songs play from the Impala's cassette deck, while extradiegetic ones punctuate the episodes, often playing when the camera is positioned not within but outside the car. That these songs are *classic* rock emphasizes their originality—a quality reinforced when they are contrasted with inferior, contemporary, and presumably derivative music. Dean's classic rock, like his classic car, signifies authenticity, authority, and canonicity.

The correspondence among originality and these other features is complicated, however, by questions of precedence. In "Fan Fiction," as "THEN" is replaced by "NOW," the shot dissolves from the word in the title card to its projection on a stage curtain. The dissolve draws parallels among card, curtain, and screen, suggesting that both *Supernatural* and its musical double appear not simply *after* but also *behind* or *beyond* these objects—a concept explored more fully in "Changing Channels" (5.8) and underscored when the curtain parts to reveal the musical *Supernatural*. The curtain and its parting mystify us; but, having seen "Changing Channels" and its like, we understand that "Fan Fiction" is among the meta episodes. Since *meta* means *beyond*, we suspect that we will again be going behind/beyond the curtain to see the show's wizards at work, and our suspicion is confirmed long before a scare-crow appears and a member of the musical's cast admits, "I was hoping we'd do *Wicked*." There are literally explosions of intertextuality in the sequence of title cards that follows Marie's critical appraisal of her own show's marquee. These thirteen cards comprise those from previous seasons, including mod-ified cards from "Monster Movie" (4.5), "Meta Fiction," "Season Seven, Time for a Wedding!" (7.8), and "A Very *Supernatural* Christmas" (3.8), together with nods to *The X-Files* and *Bonanza*. Clearly, this episode is going to be *very* meta. But what is the foundation for this meta approach? Which comes first: the musical, the Carver Edlund books, or *Supernatural*? The musical appears to follow the books, which follow the show. But their relationships are uncanny. The books appear well into the series, in Season Four; thus, the show would seem to be the urtext. Once the books are introduced, however, they take precedence: they cover not only "THEN" but also "NOW"—and they even foretell future events and episodes. The books, then, frame the show, which frames the musical—which, in turn, frames the show.

The outermost frame of a Gothic text not only establishes authenticity but also buffers readers from the more bizarre inner narratives. This structure is retained in "Fan Fiction," which positions attacks by the scarecrow and Calliope within the benign frame of a school musical—complicated though that frame might be by its uncanny links to the *Supernatural* books and show. The episode acknowledges its debt to classical Gothic framing by having Ms. Chandler wish, right before she is supernaturally assaulted, that the students had staged *Godspell* instead of an "unbelievable horror story." This intertext is appropriate, since *Godspell* features plays within the play, and among these is the story of Jesus—whom (the musical) *Supernatural* aligns with Sam, the son of Mary. The scene is framed visually as well as textually, and again in classical Gothic style: the camera is positioned within some trees, providing a menacing subjective shot from what we later learn is the scarecrow's point of view, while ominous extradiegetic musical cues signal the attack. Vines shoot from the trees to snatch the drama teacher, evoking the testy, anthro-pomorphic trees of *The Wizard of Oz* and reminding us of that story's own framing, in which the extraordinary is enclosed by the mundane. Another fantastic framed narrative is evoked by the poster of *Alice in Wonderland* in Marie's dressing room, and Maeve's declaring that the show has gone "through the looking glass."

Marie resembles Alice and Dorothy insofar as all three girls envision comprehensive imaginary worlds. But her vision, unlike theirs, is Gothic—not only because it features ghosts, demons, and monsters, but because its mimetic relationship with reality is far more uncanny. Whereas Wonderland and Oz are dreams that may be interpreted as allegories for the real world, the musical *Supernatural* is, ostensibly, a reflection of this world. Sam and

Dean's experience while watching their doubles perform onstage is uncanny precisely because, in the *Supernatural* universe, the Winchesters really exist. Ms. Chandler's question, "Where is the truth in *Supernatural*?," is both easy and difficult to answer. She sees the truth, literally and figuratively, when she sees the scarecrow. She thereby comes to accept the donnée of *Supernatural*, as telegraphed by its title: a supernatural world doubles—and, indeed, frames and governs—our natural one. When the audience for the musical sees the scarecrow, however, they accept the play's fictional frame and react to the creature's onstage fights and ultimate gooey explosion with shocked delight. The scarecrow is at once real and unreal, depending on who views it.

The same may be said of Sam and Dean, whose ontological status in the meta episodes is indeterminate. When the Winchesters out themselves, Marie draws a line. She echoes Demian, who in "The Real Ghostbusters" recognizes the reality of ghosts but reminds Dean that he and Sam are "fictional characters." In "Sympathy for the Devil" (5.1), Becky Rosen initially takes the same position, assuring Chuck, "I know that *Supernatural* is just a book." Ironically and comically, Marie and Maeve reject that Sam and Dean are who they really are, but accept their roles as FBI agents—like those in *The X-Files*. Likewise, when Chuck tells Becky that *Supernatural* is real, she cries, "I knew it!" Despite their professed grounding in reality, fans—both within and outside *Supernatural*—crave fantasy. More precisely, they want their world to be as large, mysterious, and exciting as the one in the show. This longing is articulated by Virgil in "The French Mistake." Like the Winchesters themselves, he is appalled by and anxious to leave a universe in which there is "no magic"—and no meaning to Sam and Dean's lives. Or is there? Fans who idolize, identify with, and pretend to be the Winchesters understand what Demian has to explain to Dean: that reality can disappoint, but "to be Sam and Dean" is to live with purpose. Bob Singer in "The French Mistake" likewise resists Dean's characterization of *Supernatural* as "nonsense"—though when the Winchesters declare their brotherhood and genuineness to him, he believes them to be suffering from "psychotic breaks." His argument with them about fantasy versus reality is one instance of a larger contest, both within and outside the show, over its meaning.

In *Supernatural* knowledge is power, and textual interpretation is associated with conflict. Struggles ensue over who can and will decipher the Leviathan, Angel, and Demon tablets—and, most recently, *The Book of the Damned*. The meta episodes concentrate on the clashes and negotiations among writers, texts, and viewers. By describing his relationship with fans as "tempestuous, loving, [and] conflicting" ("Eric Kripke"), Kripke evokes (unintentionally, we hope) the covenant between the God of the Old Testament and His chosen people. In "The Monster at the End of This Book," he "lovingly [makes] fun" of both fans ("Eric Kripke") and himself, given that his avatar is the disheveled Chuck. The same sense of self-deprecating humor is evident when he appears as himself in "The French Mistake" and is killed by Virgil, in a scene that apparently pleased him ("'The French Mistake'"). But this *Frankenstein*-like moment also graphically depicts the threat posed by a creation to his creator, which is underscored in "The Monster at the End of This Book" when Chuck, fearful of Sam and Dean, likens them to the crazed, author-stalking fan in Stephen King's *Misery* (1987). The perils of power-sharing among authors, characters, and audiences appear most clearly in "Fan Fiction." Among the episode's many title cards is the one from "Season Seven, Time for a Wedding!," in which Becky Rosen uses a love potion to compel Sam to marry her. Becky the fan's threat to Sam the character is essentially amusing, though she eventually realizes that the potion is offered at the price of her soul. Less comically, Marie is menaced by a scarecrow—not "the one in the books" or in "Scarecrow" (1.11)—but her own authorial conception. She is likewise threatened by Calliope, who in the *Supernatural* universe is more monster than muse, inspiring and protecting authors only in order to consume them. Or, as Marie speculates, Chuck might be Calliope's true target. This uncertainty strengthens the link between the two creators while emphasizing the risks of creation. Calliope is a fan of both the play and its source material, who would kill Marie (or Chuck) and the Winchesters, but she is instead killed by Sam. Thus, authors, characters, and fans alike are in danger.

This multifaceted hazard is quelled when Calliope is dispatched, the musical and the episode approach their conclusions, and the conflict over who will control and benefit from storytelling is resolved. Dean encourages Marie to keep writing, ending their struggle over the meaning of *Supernatural* by acknowledging that they both have their own versions. Marie appears to accept Dean as genuine, or at least to enter into his role-playing: she refers to him by his real name and gives him the Samulet. While both concessions are remarkable, his is perhaps the more significant, since it involves relinquishing his privileged position as character and sharing hers as fan. It evokes a similar moment near the conclusion of "The Real Ghostbusters," when Dean stops arguing with Barnes and Demian about role-playing and accepts that their interpretation of his experience differs from his own—and that their understanding might enable him to (re)discover meaning in his life and work. Likewise, he admits to Marie that "seeing the story from [her] perspective is educational." Sam also learns from Marie's interpretation, reaching the conclusion that he and Dean ought to hit the road again—even as his realization is acted out onstage. The musical ends in literal and figurative harmony, as the cast sings a touching choral version of "Carry on Wayward Son" while, seeing representations of their friends and family assembled onstage, the Winchesters are visibly moved. In the following scene, Dean replaces the Samulet on the rearview mirror of the Impala, the brothers exchange meaningful looks, and "A Single Man Tear" plays extradiegetically as they drive into the sunset. The music recalls the scene in which Marie and Siobhan, as Sam and Dean, sing about wearing the mask of masculinity: "A single man tear, / That's all we fear." The song's silly title and refrain, coupled with its lovely melody, render it at once ridiculous and affecting. To ensure the symmetry of its framing, "Fan Fiction" ends not with this scene but with one that recalls its opening, in which Marie mistakes Sam and Dean for associates of Carver Edlund. In the closing scene, the author himself appears and approves her interpretation of his work.

Marie's being a woman is an important reason why she can successfully interpret *Supernatural*, which is also embraced by Becky, Calliope, Carver Edlund's female publisher, and hundreds of thousands of young women in the CW's (original) target demographic ("Ratings").[5] The show recognizes, parodies, and caters to its fangirls, who relish what Marie terms the scenes of "Boy Melodrama." As the publisher explains, uncannily addressing the real Winchesters, "If only real men were so open and in touch with their feelings." As "A Single Man Tear" and the Boy Melodrama scenes demonstrate, Marie recognizes that the *Supernatural* books and musical capitalize upon the wish-fulfillment of fangirls (and gay fanboys) seeking emotionally expressive men. Initially unable to see themselves from a feminine perspective, the Winchesters misconstrue her shorthand term, "BM scene," as "bowel-movement scene," thereby equating sentiment with excrement. Likewise, Dean is discomfited to the point of agitation by the BM scene between Siobhan/Dean and Maggie/Sam. When he asks Marie why the two are standing so close together, she responds evasively and suggestively, "Reasons." His next question, "You know they're brothers, right?," is noteworthy because it signifies that his primary source of uneasiness is (W)incest, not homosexuality. Dean's response to seeing Siobhan/Dean and Kristen/Castiel's hugging and holding hands is similarly illuminating. He is reassured—though startled and intrigued—to learn that they are "a couple in real life." Marie's casual reference to Destiel's appearance in Act Two then bewilders him, and her dismissing the relationship as "just subtext" fails to soothe—especially since, as she observes slyly, "You can't spell subtext without … S-E-X." Looking disapprovingly into the camera, Dean reproaches those fans who explore such queer subtexts. To defeat Calliope, however, he resigns himself to slash: "I want you to put as much *sub* into that *text* as you possibly can." In contrast, Sam, the younger, more sensitive, and—as "Fan Fiction" emphasizes—more artistically inclined brother, is amused rather than perturbed by these slash relationships.

Taking its cue from deconstruction, (the musical) *Supernatural* configures slash not as opposed but as collapsing binaries: TV show/musical, canon/fanon, text/subtext, male/female, straight/queer—each is fused. Women portray men; queer actors, straight characters. The *Supernatural* universe is replete with portmanteau words, most of which denote slash relationships: Destiel, Wincest, Sampala, Samifer, Samelia, Sastiel, Sazekiel, Chestervelle, Cockles, Crobby, Padackles, Crowstiel, Annaby, Robdam, fanon, adorkable, and even Carver Edlund. Uncannily, these terms remove the slash from the equation, thereby calling into question binary thinking. Slash can even transcend binaries altogether, as Marie demonstrates. After introducing herself to the Winchesters as "writer slash director," she becomes writer/director/actor, declaring her intention to "Barbra Streisand" the show. Since Streisand assumed all of these roles for *Yentl* (1983), while playing a woman playing a man, the reference is especially apropos. In yet another intertextual twist, Marie plays Sam by wearing a (woman's) wig from her "one-woman *Orphan Black* show"—an intertext based on a TV series in which one double proliferates into multiple selves. Given her own protean qualities, it makes sense that Marie writes an ending in which "Dean becomes a woman," though "just for a few scenes." In her musical, a queer woman plays a straight man who becomes a woman before transforming back into a man. Slash, which renders the familiar unfamiliar, is powerfully and queerly uncanny.

If the uncanny emerges from the repressed, then *Supernatural* represses queerness. In recent years, the show has been criticized for queer-baiting and other homophobic tendencies,[6] but these characterizations are facile. *Supernatural* is replete with queer (sub)texts, those who create and consume it recognize these, and especially the latter group appreciates and develops them—in slash fiction, explicitly and at length. Although queerness enhances the show's artistic and popular success, repression is evident in its depiction of queer characters and situations—as is the return of the repressed in the form of the queer uncanny. Particularly significant are phantoms and doubles. As Diana Fuss observes, in the relationship between heterosexuality and homosexuality "each is haunted by the other" (3). This mutual haunting, another manifestation of doubling and the collapse of binaries, is signaled from the beginning of the musical. When a prop ghost drops from the ceiling, we find ourselves in a place (un)familiar to us: the haunted house, which Freud describes as *unheimlich* or *un-homely* (220), and which is perhaps the ultimate manifestation of the uncanny. This comic haunting replicates grimmer ones—most notably, the Morton House haunting in "Ghostfacers," which is also referenced by the cast's pre-show chant: "Ghooooost-facerssss!" The only casualty in that episode is Alan J. Corbett, a gay man who serves as intern and (stereotypically) as cook for the hapless paranormal investigators. That he becomes a death echo, a ghost compelled to reenact its own demise, is quintessentially and queerly uncanny.

Corbett's "compulsion to repeat" (Freud 238) is among the features that distinguish the uncanny, and his becoming a ghost exemplifies "society's attempt to suppress homosexuality by relegating the queer subject to the role of 'phantom other'" (Palmer 7) and representing "the homosexual as specter and phantom, as spirit and revenant" (Fuss 3). Corbett's repression is elegantly signified by his being dragged into the id-like basement. In a return of the repressed, he reappears on the ground floor; and, his consciousness awakened by Ed's profession of love for him, he defeats the episode's phantasmal antagonist, Freeman Daggett. A Wisconsin homeowner and taxidermist looking for male company who doubles the mama's boy Norman Bates, the would-be transsexual Jame Gumb,[7] and the maternally fixated Ed Gein (who uncannily inspired Bates and Gumb), Daggett kills Corbett by driving a rod through his throat. Given the manner and significance of Corbett's murder and spectralization, Ed's memorializing him by observing that "gay love can pierce through the veil of death" is nearly as odd and ironic as the nomination that "Ghostfacers" received for "Outstanding Individual Episode" from the Gay & Lesbian Alliance against Defamation (GLADD).[8] Ed's observation, as Darren Elliott-Smith notes, "implies something unnatural, an inherent morbidity and a spectrality in homosexuality that is configured as transient perhaps due to an assumption of its non-procreative associations" (111–12). Yet "Corbett's position on the margins of masculinity" is precisely what enables him to move "from life to death and back again" (Elliott-Smith 112–13), and to rescue the Ghostfacers and Winchesters alike. His lethal liminality condemns him to death but saves the lives of others.

Although *Supernatural* kills both Corbett and the (late) lesbian Charlie Bradbury, other queer characters survive. Particularly significant are Barnes and Demian, the gay couple in "The Real Ghostbusters." By role-playing Sam and Dean and doubling Sam/Dean, they join queer Gothic doppelgängers including Victor/Creature, George Colwan/Gil-Martin, William Wilson/William Wilson, Jekyll/Hyde, Dorian Gray/picture—and, more recently, Willow/Vampire Willow. Typically, (queer) doppelgängers play a zero-sum game in which one partner kills the other, or both die. The lethality of both doubling and queerness is illustrated in "Slash Fiction" (7.6), whose title conflates slash-as-(horror-movie)-murder with slash-as-fan-fiction, whose plot focuses on Sam and Dean's efforts to destroy their Leviathan doppelgängers, and whose (sub)text features slash(er) references likening Sam/Dean to male-female killer couples from films. That both Sam/Dean and Barnes/Demian survive and continue to mirror one another is noteworthy and progressive, though hardly the realization of Destiel that some fans have hoped for. Dean's reaction to learning that Barnes and Demian are "partners" is typical: he understands but rejects the term's sexual significance, reframing the word within a macho, cowboy context by saluting them with "Howdy, partners."

Thus *Supernatural*, like the Gothic writ large, is at once transgressive and conservative, familiar and unfamiliar. The show draws upon and updates a long and distinguished tradition of Gothic intertextuality and (queer) uncanniness. In established Gothic fashion, while doubling artifacts from a range of cultures past and present, it proves itself time and again to be exquisitely aware of its position within an artistic and societal nexus, of its ability to challenge or reinforce the values of its era, and of its many interpreters and imitators. *Supernatural* continues to engage in complex, inventive, and sometimes contentious ways with its viewers—including academics like myself who attempt to analyze it. In "The Real Ghostbusters," for instance, the convention manager announces a panel on "The Homoerotic Subtext of *Supernatural*," whose papers would no doubt mirror mine and others like it. This playfully postmodern moment not only parodies (and knowingly conflates) fans and scholars, but also, and more significantly, demonstrates how all of us—writers, actors, fans, and critics—co-create this genuinely Gothic phenomenon.

NOTES

1. See "Toward the Gothic: Terrorism and Homosexual Panic" in *Between Men: English Literature and Male Homosocial Desire* (New York: Columbia University Press, 1985), pp. 83–96.

2. For a discussion of how queer theory and the uncanny intersect, see Paulina Palmer, *The Queer Uncanny: New Perspectives on the Gothic* (Cardiff: University of Wales Press, 2012).

3. The Bible's authenticity and authority are, however, questioned by Castiel, who observes in "I Believe the Children Are Our Future" (5.6), "Your Bible gets more wrong than it does right."

4. See Stephen Donovan, Danuta Fjellestad, and Rolf Lundén, "Introduction: Author, Authorship, Authority, and Other Matters" in *Authority Matters: Rethinking the Theory and Practice of Authorship* (Amsterdam: Rodopi, 2008), 1–19. DQR Studies in Literature 43.

5. For an in-depth discussion of female fans and fandom, see Katherine Larsen and Lynn S. Zubernis, *Fangasm: Supernatural Fangirls* (Iowa City: University of Iowa Press, 2013).

6. See Sadie Gennis, "*Supernatural* Has a Queerbaiting Problem That Needs to Stop," *TV Guide*, CBS Interactive, 17 Nov. 2014. Web. 19 May 2015. See also Eliel Cruzjuly, "Fans Take *Supernatural* to Task for 'Queer Baiting,'" *The Advocate*, Here Media, 17 July 2014. Web. 19 May 2015. Larsen and Zubernis also address this topic (pp. 111, 142–44).

7. The episode aligns Corbett, Daggett, Gumb, and Clarice Starling by echoing the film version of *The Silence of the Lambs* (1991), in which Starling reconnoiters Gumb's basement while he secretly watches her through night-vision goggles. Corbett puts on such goggles to explore the Morton House, unaware that he is being observed by Daggett.

8. See "GLAAD Awards," *Supernatural Wiki*. Also (and perhaps more understandably) nominated were "The Real Ghostbusters" and "LARP and the Real Girl."

WORKS CITED

The Bible: Authorized King James Version, with Apocrypha. Ed. Robert Carroll and Stephen Prickett. 1997. Oxford: Oxford University Press, 1998. Print. Oxford World's Classics.

Clayton, Jay. "The Alphabet of Suffering: Effie Deans, Tess Durbeyfield, Martha Ray, and Hetty Sorrel." *Influence and Intertextuality in Literary History*. Ed. Jay Clayton and Eric Rothstein. Madison: University of Wisconsin Press, 1991. 37–60. Print.

Elliott-Smith, Darren. "'Go be gay for that poor, dead intern': Conversion Fantasies and Gay Anxieties in *Supernatural*." *TV Goes to Hell: An Unofficial Road Map of Supernatural*. Ed. Stacey Abbott and David Lavery. Toronto: ECW Press, 2011. Print.

"Eric Kripke." *Supernatural Wiki*. 2006. Web. 15 May 2015.

"Fan Fiction." *Supernatural*. Writ. Robbie Thompson. Dir. Phil Sgriccia. Perf. Jensen Ackles and Jared Padalecki. CW Network, 11 November 2014. Television.

"The French Mistake." *Supernatural: The Complete Sixth Season*. Writ. Ben Edlund. Dir. Charles Beeson. Perf. Jensen Ackles and Jared Padalecki. Warner Bros., 2011. DVD.

"'The French Mistake' Pop-Up Trivia." *Supernatural Wiki*. Web. 15 May 2015.

Freud, Sigmund. "The Uncanny." 1919. *The Standard Edition of the Complete Psychological Works of Sigmund Freud*, Vol. 17. Trans. and ed. James Strachey. London: Hogarth Press and the Institute of Psycho-Analysis, 1955. 217–256. Print.

Fuss, Diana, ed. Introduction. *Inside/Out: Lesbian Theories, Gay Theories*. New York: Routledge, 1991. 1–12. Print.

"Ghostfacers." *Supernatural: The Complete Third Season*. Writ. Ben Edlund. Dir. Phil Sgriccia. Perf. Jensen Ackles and Jared Padalecki. Warner Bros., 2008. DVD.

"Meta Fiction." *Supernatural: The Complete Ninth Season*. Writ. Robbie Thompson. Dir. Thomas J. Wright. Perf. Jensen Ackles and Jared Padalecki. Warner Bros., 2014. DVD.

"The Monster at the End of This Book." *Supernatural: The Complete Fourth Season*. Writ. Julie Siege. Dir. Mike Rohl. Perf. Jensen Ackles and Jared Padalecki. Warner Bros., 2009. DVD.

Palmer, Paulina. *Lesbian Gothic: Transgressive Fictions*. New York: Cassell, 1999. Print.

Prince, Gerald. "Introduction to the Study of the Narratee." *Reader-Response Criticism: From Formalism to Post-Structuralism*. Ed. Jane P. Tompkins. Baltimore: Johns Hopkins University Press, 1980. 7–25. Print.

"Ratings." *Supernatural Wiki*. Web. 15 May 2015.

Riffaterre, Michael. "Compulsory Reader Response: The Intertextual Drive." *Intertextuality: Theories and Practices*. Ed. Michael Worton and Judith Still. Manchester: Manchester University Press, 1990. 56–78. Print.

Royle, Nicholas. *The Uncanny*. Manchester: Manchester University Press, 2003. Print.

"Sympathy for the Devil." *Supernatural: The Complete Fifth Season*. Writ. Eric Kripke. Dir. Robert Singer. Perf. Jensen Ackles and Jared Padalecki. Warner Bros., 2010. DVD.

Walpole, Horace. *The Castle of Otranto* and *The Mysterious Mother*. Ed. Frederick S. Frank. Toronto: Broadview Press, 2003. Print. Broadview Editions.

"I know everything that's going to happen"

The Self-Reflexive Compulsion to Repeat (with a Difference)

MICHAEL FUCHS

In his book *Difference and Repetition* (1968), Gilles Deleuze remarks that "repetition is in essence symbolic" (17). More importantly, however, he stresses that "difference is included in repetition by way of disguise" (17). As Deleuze elaborates in *The Logic of Sense* (1969), "only that which resembles differs," and "only differences can resemble each other" (261). In his attempt to counter Sigmund Freud's concept of compulsive repetition, Deleuze thus suggests a generative principle inherent in repetition—that of (ever so slight) difference. J. Hillis Miller spells out this argument in more detail in his book *Fiction and Repetition* (1982), in which he distinguishes between repetition-as-sameness and repetition-as-difference and—in truly poststructuralist manner—claims that "each form of repetition inevitably calls up the other as its shadow companion" (16). This "shadow companion," Miller emphasizes, "is not the negation or opposite of the first, but its 'counterpart'" that exists "in a strange relation whereby the second is the subversive ghost of the first, always already present within it as a possibility that hollows it out" (9). Echoing Roland Barthes's assertion that a "text is a tissue of quotations" (146), Miller concludes that any cultural artifact "is a complex tissue of repetitions and of repetitions within repetitions, or of repetitions linked in chain fashion to other repetitions. In each case there are repetitions making up the structure of the work within itself, as well as repetitions determining its multiple relations to what is outside it" (2–3).

Serial television thrives on the use of both repetition-as-sameness and repetition-as-difference. Indeed, as early as 1985, Robert Allen argued that soap operas are characterized by "paradigmatic complexity," for even though plots may not necessarily advance, events cause ripple effects across the storyworld due to their apparently endless repetitions (69–72). Jason Mittell has more recently emphasized that even though contemporary primetime serials have reduced repetition, television narratives still rely heavily on iteration in order to, on the one hand, offer entry points to new viewers and, on the other hand, remind longtime viewers of narrative strands that have been dormant for several episodes (81–96). In this context, Lorna Jowett and Stacey Abbott have observed that in the case of *Supernatural*, images of "the (character-based) start point of Mary's death," for example, "repeatedly return," as does "the (mythology-based) endpoint of the apocalypse," which is "glimpsed in various episodes" (51).

However, in *Supernatural* this (over)reliance on repetition not only springs from a poetics that strives for internal coherence and owes much to the serio-episodic storytelling typical of contemporary television but also self-reflexively draws on the American Gothic, repeating its conventions in the process.[1] Of course, *Supernatural* is far from the first Gothic text to consciously employ the "reservoir of recognizable and repeatable features" (Łowczanin 185) that define the American Gothic. Accordingly, Allan Lloyd-Smith concludes that "any study of genre is a study of repetitions, the patterns that constitute a tradition and the way that writers imitate, learn from, and modify the work of their predecessors" (1). Catherine Spooner has elaborated on this point, highlighting that even though any given genre "is profoundly concerned with its own past, self-referentially dependent on traces of other stories, familiar images and narrative structures, [and] intertextual allusions," the "Gothic has a greater degree of self-consciousness about its nature, cannibalistically consuming the dead body of its own tradition" (10).

Despite the apparent self-awareness that guides the employment of conventionalized plot structures, (stereo)typical characters, clichéd settings, and self-conscious intertextual references in many examples of the American Gothic, scholars have repeatedly returned (possibly even felt compelled to return) to Freud in analyses of the significance of repetition to Gothic texts, for he "identified repetition as one of the central characteristics of the uncanny" (Lloyd-Smith 2).[2] Roger B. Salomon has perhaps taken this line of argumentation to the extreme, for, in his exploration of horror texts, the reliance on repetition creates a genre that "offers" recipients "neither the consolations of meaningful causal explanations nor the promises of some temporal pattern suggesting a movement toward some significant resolution" (97).[3] In effect, Salomon suggests that the entire genre suffers from a compulsion to repeat, which "leads away from meaning rather than encouraging its generation" (98), because "horror narrative can only dramatize one paradigmatic experience or multiply meaningless events toward no other possible end than random death" (99). In the end, he argues, "the structure of horror narrative denies, obfuscates, or otherwise inverts any possible meaning that goes beyond the mere assertion of present horror" (100).

Compare Salomon's perspective on the functions (or even lack thereof) of Gothic texts' repetitive structure (and the attendant "compulsive" return to the same settings, characters, motifs, and plots) to Stacey Abbott's introduction to *TV Goes to Hell: An Unofficial Road Map of* Supernatural (2011), in which she remarks that *Supernatural* takes its viewers on a "journey through the horror tradition, building upon what has come before, but taking the genre further and making it darker" (xi). While I agree with the notion of *Supernatural* "taking the genre further," in this essay, I will argue that rather than "making it darker," the show emblematizes the playful engagement with the Gothic tradition omnipresent in our day and age. Whereas, despite their playfulness, other recent examples of meta-Gothic (e.g., Mark Z. Danielewski's book *House of Leaves* [2000] and the video game *Alan Wake* [2010]) succeed in eliciting the "staple emotional responses" typical of Gothic texts (Botting, *Gothic* 6), *Supernatural* epitomizes a type of ludic relationship with the genre's past that is less interested in producing "fear, anxiety, terror, horror, disgust and revulsion" (Botting, *Gothic* 6) than playing with conventions. Some critics may thus be spurred to consider *Supernatural* as emblematic of the "candygothic" (Botting, "Candygothic") that embodies the Gothic's loss of "its older intensity" (Botting, "Aftergothic" 287).[4] However, I maintain that far from performing the superficial intertextuality Fredric Jameson considered defining of postmodernism (12), *Supernatural*'s ludic text creates an excess of meaning and functions as an anchor for establishing an imagined community, a secret handshake of sorts, which establishes an intimate bond between the creators and the fans.

Supernatural's playful, tongue-in-cheek dialogue with the Gothic tradition was already evident in its pilot episode. Apart from highlighting the Gothic trope of intratextual repetition—which the show would (re)turn to time and again—the visually excessive and structurally iterative display of Mary and Jessica's burning bodies that (more or less) bookended the episode emphasized that the American Gothic is "firmly centred around images of the family and familial trauma" (Wheatley 123). In addition, the pilot established *Supernatural*'s creative use of folklore, urban legends, and (American) mythology through its semantically loaded monster of the week, the Woman in White—which came packed with highway horror associations, connections to the "monstrous-feminine" (Creed), and a spectral haunting—as a defining feature of the series. Finally, when Dean addressed two FBI agents as "Agent Scully, Agent Mulder" in the diegesis, this brief utterance tipped the show's proverbial hat to one of *Supernatural*'s most important ancestors, a series that "is more Gothic than numerous horror films which aim to shock" (Robson 243), and established the show's brand of excessive intertextuality. This allusiveness, as Alison Peirse has noted, is part of the series' success, which "can be partially attributed to its popular culture references, exploration of urban legends, and incorporation of horror film tropes" (264).

These allusions—these repetitions of texts created in the past, which have truly come to define the show—are sometimes made blatantly obvious and other times left more implicit. Consider, for example, the Season One episode "Asylum" (1.10), which borrows its plot from *The House on Haunted Hill* (1999) (itself a remake of the 1959 movie directed by William Castle and starring Vincent Price) and sees Sam and Dean trying to dispose of the titular asylum's former head doctor's ghost. When the two hunters first explore the building, Dean asks, "What do you think, ghosts possessing people?" Sam theorizes, "Maybe it's … like Amityville." "Yes, ghosts driving them insane. Kinda like my man Jack in *The Shining*," quips Dean. "The dialogue," as I have remarked elsewhere, "effortlessly moves from present to past and from reality to artifice" in this scene (Fuchs, "Hauntings" 66), as the genre's past evoked by *The Amityville Horror* (1979) and *The Shining* (1980) both segues into the real-life events that took place in Amityville, New York, in 1974 and the reality of the world the Winchester brothers inhabit. This creation of a hyperreal space is continued later in the episode when the brothers encounter teenagers who are looking for a little thrill ride in the local attraction, the sanatorium.[5] Dean asks one of the teenagers, "You've seen a lot of horror movies, yeah?" and then emphasizes, "Do me a favor, next time you see one, pay attention! When someone says a place is haunted, don't go in!" Dean thus advocates applying movie knowledge to the real world, thereby implying that the same rules apply to the fictional world of the movies and the diegetic world. Although, at other times, the characters distinguish between their world and fictional universes—"*The X-Files* is a TV show. This is real," Dean stresses in "Monster Movie" (4.5)—Dean's insistence on applying movie knowledge to the real world suggests that the Winchesters' reality is invaded, possibly even replaced, by artifice, which would become a staple of the show in later seasons.

This desire to build a hyperreal space in the diegetic space (or even establish the diegetic space as hyperreal) is made truly explicit in the episode "Monster Movie." This highly self-aware and intertextual episode opens with a Warner logo that is reminiscent of the company's logo used in the 1930s, which establishes the episode's aura of days gone by right from the outset, an aura that is further amplified by the fact that the episode is presented in monochrome colors. The coloration (or, rather, the lack thereof) emphasizes that the entire episode is steeped in nostalgia; a nostalgia for a time when things were easier. This applies both to the episode's meta-discourse on the Gothic's past—a time when, fittingly, one could differentiate between black and white, with no shades of gray in-between (so the episode implies, that is)—and Dean's yearning for simpler times. The older Winchester, tellingly, longs for "a straightforward, black and white case"—an utterance that is effectively repeated in "Swan Song" (5.22) when Sam wonders, "Remember when we used to just fight wendigos?"

To return to the repetition of the Gothic's past, however, Victor Sage and Allan Lloyd-Smith have pointed out that the genre's penchant for referencing "its own ... past ... tends to imply a critical relation between the present and the past" (1). From this perspective, the genre's past becomes a "site of terror, of an injustice that must be resolved, an evil that must be exorcised," as "the past chokes the present" and "prevents progress" (Spooner 18). Indeed, this notion of purging the past may be linked to the aforementioned nostalgia, which highlights the differences between the good-old, simple times and the complex present. In fact, this notion is supported intradiegetically through a monster who tries to escape the complex realities of the early twenty-first century by creating a simulacrum based on the Universal horror movies of the past.

The important point, though, is that as ridiculous as the monster's attempts to re-create fiction in the "real" world are, this re-creation of the past not only takes place within the story, but also on the discursive level of the television show. Just as the episode's monster tries to imitate, indeed even simulate Dracula, the Mummy, Victor Frankenstein, and other iconic monsters of the 1930s and 1940s, "Monster Movie" effectively does the same. After the Warner Bros. logo, the credits further highlight the episode's invocation of the Gothic horror movies of the 1930s and 1940s by providing the character names of lead actors Jensen Ackles and Jared Padalecki using an antiquated style for the credits, which leads straight into the prototypical shot of a crescent moon wrapped in foreboding fog accompanied by an ominous, violin-heavy horror theme. As is typical of *Supernatural*, the diegetic action begins on a remote road, as the black '67 Chevy Impala passes a "Welcome to Pennsylvania" sign in a Gothic-inspired font that the camera lingers on for a few seconds before the letters transform into "Welcome to Transylvania" when lightning strikes, thus hammering home the show's invocation of its Gothic forebears. The viewers are then virtually transported to Canonsburg, a small town somewhere in Pennsylvania that is celebrating Oktoberfest (complete with lederhosen and dirndls), which serves as a simulacrum of the "real" Bavaria. What the boys find in Pennsylvania is a monster-of-the-week that re-stages villainous acts from *Dracula* (1931), *The Wolf Man* (1941), and *Frankenstein* (1931). Tellingly, the witness to the second murder describes the killer as follows: "It was a werewolf.... With the furry face and the black nose and the claws and the torn-up pants and shirt—think from the old movies." The flurry of near-campy references does not end until the monster is killed by the girl he thinks he is expected to love. His reaction after being hit by silver bullets? Quoting *King Kong*'s conclusion: "It was beauty that killed the beast."

As Sam notes, "This is stupid." Indeed, even though the episode fleshes out the changes Dean has gone through after returning from Hell and thus expands on the show's serialized narrative, on another level, "Monster Movie" truly is stupid—consciously so. At one point, for example, the monster—dressed up as a Lugosian Dracula—escapes on a Vespa, while Dean is saved from electrocution when the pizza boy rings the doorbell. If "Monster Movie" had been intended to confront or even to exorcize the demons of the Gothic past in order to lead the genre into the future, it would have been a rather lame attempt, since the episode resurrects the past rather than putting a nail into the coffin of the Gothic's past (and burning it to ensure that it will return no more). Admittedly, "oppositional postmodernism only functions through the repetition of the very dialectical structure it is attempting to overcome" (Muckelbauer 8). Yet the episode's humorous tone, which emerges from the parody of both monster movies of the past and the self-deprecating humor directed at *Supernatural* itself, reveals a lack of the oppositional impetus characteristic of postmodernist cultural artifacts. In light of the episode's tongue-in-cheek approach, it is not surprising that Alberto N. García has suggested that "Monster Movie" is "a work of terror from the '30s, but without the terror" (153). While this assertion seems undeniable, eliciting horror or terror in the audience is obviously not one of the goals of this episode (nor, I would argue, of the show at large). Rather, the references to the Universal classics of the 1930s and 1940s create an in-group, a community of those who understand these allusions, these effective repetitions of past movies that thus become part of the present moment.

The episode's excessive intertextuality, however, also capitalizes on the affordances of digital media, be they DVRs, DVDs, or Blu-Rays, and it encourages and supports repeat viewings. The home video, as Laura Mulvey has noted, already made it possible that films and television shows "can be seen and re-seen and reinterpreted along lines that might change with changes in interest and knowledge but also are open to the chance insights and unexpected encounters that come with endless repetition" (230), a tendency that has increased in the digital age. In other words, the episode's repetitions invite further repetitions through repeat viewings. In this way, "technological advancement" sparks, as James Walters has stressed, "critical endeavor" (66), which results in the creation of wikis and other fan practices. At the end of the day, the various repetitions employed in the show are thus the foundation for the establishment of an intimate relationship between the text and its audience.

A similar idea drives a specific kind of the show's intradiegetic repetitions. Of course, as indicated above, intradiegetic repetitions abound in seri-alized television, from recaps to recurring motifs and much more. However, *Supernatural* has also employed diegetic mirrorings of a metatextual kind. This dimension was introduced in the Season Four episode "The Monster at the End of This Book" (4.18), the title of which refers to a *Sesame Street* book. In this highly metafictional book, Grover constantly seeks to stop the reader from turning the pages, since Grover is absolutely certain that "there will be a Monster at the end of this book." On the final page, Grover (and the reader) comes to understand, "I, lovable, furry old Grover, am the Monster at the end of this book" (Stone). In light of what happens in the final hours of *Super-natural's* fourth season, the episode's title foreshadows that the monster the two Winchesters are really after (or, rather, should be after) is not Lilith, the demon who emerges as their nemesis in Season Four, but one of them.

Yet beyond this intertextual dimension, the episode also introduces Chuck and his pulp fiction series titled *Supernatural*. The existence of these books in the storyworld is established in the episode's opening moments when a comic book store clerk mistakes Sam and Dean for LARPers imitating the characters from the books. Dean's flabbergasted response is merely, "Excuse me?" The vendor explains that they are fans, which only leads to more confusion, as Sam wonders, "Fans of what?" Dean is still befuddled by the shop assistant's previous utterance and asks what LARPing is. The assis-tant, with a self-assured grin across his face, responds, "Live-action roleplay-ing. And pretty hard-core, too." After Dean has clarified that he still doesn't understand, the salesman explains, "You're asking questions like the building's haunted, like those guys from the books.... What are their names? Steve and Dirk? Sal and Dane?" Sam, somewhat afraid of the response, inquires, "Sam and Dean?" "That's it!" replies the sales clerk and shows them the first book in the series. Dean reads the blurb: "Along a lonely California highway, a mysterious Woman in White lures men to their deaths ...," words that obvi-ously evoke the events of *Supernatural's* pilot. After leafing through a few more volumes in the series, the Winchesters conclude that the author, Chuck Shurley (a.k.a. Carver Edlund), must be able to somehow follow their actions.

However, when the action moves to Chuck's home, the audio-visual text suggests that things are not so simple. Chuck, working on his latest manu-script, reads, "Sam and Dean approach the run-down ... approach the ram-shackled house with trepidation." Once he has finished the sentence, Sam and Dean get out of the Impala and do exactly that—approach the run-down house and meet the author who might be their creator. Beyond the humor that emerges from the absurd situation of a writer meeting his creation, the paradoxical setup also taps into the postmodern fear of artifice supplanting reality. As Slavoj Žižek has maintained, "The ultimate American paranoiac fantasy is that of an individual living in a small idyllic Californian city, a consumerist paradise, who suddenly starts to suspect that the world he is living in is a fake, a spectacle staged to convince him that he is living in a real world, while all the people around him are in fact actors and extras in a gigantic show" (12–13).

When applied to *Supernatural*, the paranoiac fantasy diagnosed by Žižek suggests that rather than depicting a prime mover who is the primary cause of all events in the universe, "The Monster at the End of This Book" reflects the postmodern fear "of substituting the signs of the real for the real" (Baudrillard 2). Effectively, the episode repeats and performs a hypodiegetic reality (i.e., that of the books-within-the-show) in the diegetic world. Yet even if the characters, similar to "Monster Movie," try to stress, or possibly even to re-establish, the boundary between reality and fiction (Chuck insists that "Sam and Dean are fictional characters, I made them up; they are not real!"), the textual evidence presented to audiences indicates quite the opposite: The uncanny repetition suggests that "reality" is preceded, to conjure up Baudrillard's ghost again, and predetermined by representations(-within-the-representational-apparatus-of-the-TV-show).

While this intradiegetic repetition amplifies the theme of predestination vs. free will that is essential to the show in Seasons Four and Five, as it implies that nothing in the diegetic reality is the result of free will, the intratextual mirroring presents another instance of the show's ludic self-reflexivity. In his book on play in postmodernist fiction, Brian Edwards asserts that "the metonymic play between writing and building" (254), exemplified by the ways in which Chuck's writing apparently builds the world he and the other characters inhabit, is one of the most important kinds of textual play. Yet, more importantly, "play is always already interplay" (xii), for it "blur[s] distinctions between observation and participation, and between spectators and collaborators" (17) and thus encourages interaction. As a result, *Supernatural's* ludic textuality may be said to have sparked the overabundance of *Supernatural* fan productions.

As the examples have shown, rather than offering the meaninglessness Salomon considers characteristic of Gothic repetitions, the intertextual repetitions in "Monster Movie" and, to a lesser extent, "Asylum" and the intra-diegetic repetitions in "The Monster at the End of This Book" produce an excess of meaning. Yvonne Leffler has suggested that repetitions create a "determinist pattern … so intense that the fictional world is portrayed as containing nothing that is unique" (191). There is a paradoxical process at work here, as Matt Hills has noticed, for this "pan-determinism offers completely controlled—and thus completely and precisely meaningful—fictional repetitions" (65). The déjà vu elicited by repetition thus implies semantic annihilation caused by semiotic excess.

Rather than vacating meaning, *Supernatural's* effective compulsion to repeat conventionalized narratives, well-established tropes, and clichéd monsters opens up the series' semantic potentials. Indeed, the show's ludic dialogue with its ancestors (and its self-deprecating attitude) not only "problematises the relationship between reality and fiction" (Beville 7) in typical postmodernist Gothic fashion, but also builds upon the expectation of its fans' "familiarity with the rules of the game" (Crane 148). In this way, *Supernatural* encourages a playful engagement with the series. Tellingly, Eric Kripke said in an interview, "I wanted to create a universe where we welcome others to come and play" (qtd. in Zubernis and Larsen 214). Fans have most certainly accepted this invitation.

Finally, *Supernatural's* ludicity questions the prominent categorization of horror as one of the "body genres," an umbrella term for the genres "which sensationally display bodies on the screen and register effects in the bodies of spectators" (Williams 4). Xavier Aldana Reyes has more recently emphasized that such an "affective approach is not predominantly preoccupied with whether something *is* actually scary but rather with the conventions followed by a genre or mode *in the hope that it will be*" (16, italics in original). However, as early as 2006, Catherine Spooner diagnosed a problem that arises from such an approach, namely that "as a genre deliberately intended to provoke horror and unease," the Gothic "plays to audience expectations and therefore is rather too self-conscious to illuminate our most secret fears" (8) and, thus, also largely fails to elicit bodily responses. *Supernatural* does not simply highlight the practical impossibility of Gothic texts to generate emotional and bodily effects that "exceed reason" (Botting, *Gothic* 2) in the (post-)postmodern age, but rather employs this impossibility for its own purposes and, indeed, thrives on its viewers' cognitive responses instead. Thus, the show emerges as an exemplary text that clarifies that the Gothic may rather be considered a "mind genre" (Hills 171). As Hills explains, repetition allows the Gothic to "[become] a matter of performed cultural value ... for sections of its ... audience" (171). Janet Staiger has argued along similar lines, noting that "intertexuality obviously serves ... to give [the audience] cultural capital" (186). However, it is not only the fans who accumulate cultural capital, but also the show itself, which thereby aspires toward cultural spheres usually inaccessible to Gothic texts. In this way, *Supernatural* may, indeed, take the Gothic to uncharted territories.

NOTES

1. Both fans and scholars (not to mention aca-fans) may release cries of despair upon hearing "coherence" with reference to *Supernatural*, especially in view of reinterpretations of the show's mythology in the post-Kripke era. As the selection of examples in the following pages may indicate, for me, *Supernatural* concluded in May 2010. I am still trying to forget the roughly eighty episodes that were broadcast after this date of a show with the same title that mere scholarly thoroughness drove me to watch.

2. For (in part) Freudian-inspired analyses of repetition in *Supernatural*, see Fuchs, "Temporality," and Fuchs, "Time Loop."

3. Please excuse the slippage between "Gothic" and "horror." I do not mean to suggest that these were synonymous or that one were a hyponym and the other its attendant hypernym. However, since repetition proves key to both horror and Gothic narratives, the equation of Gothic and horror seems adequate in this case.

4. As Xavier Aldana Reyes has recently stressed, while "an affective approach" to the Gothic "allows for a model of the gothic that encompasses texts from horror film and fiction that do not 'look' but 'act' the part," this emphasis on the affective dimensions of the Gothic does not entail "a denial of the gothic qualities of other texts that are not experientially so" (20).

5. On the creation of a hyperreal space in *Supernatural*, see also Fuchs, "Trapped."

WORKS CITED

Abbott, Stacey. "Then: The Road So Far." *TV Goes to Hell: An Unofficial Road Map of* Supernatural. Ed. Stacey Abbott and David Lavery. Toronto: ECW Press, 2011. ix-xvii. Print.

Aldana Reyes, Xavier. "Gothic Affect: An Alternative Approach to Critical Models of the Contemporary Gothic." *New Directions in 21st Century Gothic: The Gothic Compass*. Ed. Lorna Piatti-Farnell and Donna Lee Brien. New York: Routledge, 2015. 11–23. Print.

Allen, Robert. *Speaking of Soap Operas*. Chapel Hill: University of North Carolina Press, 1985. Print.

"Asylum." *Supernatural: The Complete First Season*. Writ. Richard Hatem. Dir. Guy Norman Bee. Perf. Jensen Ackles and Jared Padalecki. Warner Bros., 2010. Blu-Ray.

Barthes, Roland. "The Death of the Author." 1967. Trans. Stephen Heath. *Image—Music—Text*. Ed. Stephen Heath. New York: Hill & Wang, 1978. 142–148. Print.

Baudrillard, Jean. "The Precession of Simulacra." 1978. Trans. Sheila Faria Glaser. *Simulacra and Simulation*. Ann Arbor: University of Michigan Press, 1994. 1–42. Print.

Beville, Maria. *Gothic-Postmodernism: Voicing the Terrors of Postmodernity*. Amsterdam: Rodopi, 2009. Print.

Botting, Fred. "Aftergothic: Consumption, Machines, and Black Holes." *The Cambridge Companion to Gothic Fiction*. Ed. Jerrold Hogle. Cambridge: Cambridge University Press, 2002. 277–300. Print.

_____. "Candygothic." *The Gothic*. Ed. Fred Botting. Cambridge: D. S. Brewer, 2001. 133–151. Print.

_____. *Gothic*, 2d ed. London: Routledge, 2013. Print.

Crane, Jonathan L. "'It was a dark and stormy night...': Horror Films and the Problem of Irony." *Horror Film and Psychoanalysis: Freud's Worst Nightmare*. Ed. Steven Jay Schneider. Cambridge: Cambridge University Press, 2004. 142–156. Print.

Creed, Barbara. *The Monstrous-Feminine: Film, Feminism, Psychoanalysis*. London: Routledge, 1993. Print.

Deleuze, Gilles. *Difference and Repetition*. 1968. Trans. Paul Patton. New York: Columbia University Press, 1994. Print.

_____. *The Logic of Sense*. 1969. Trans. Mark Lester and Charles Stivale. New York: Columbia University Press, 1990. Print.

Edwards, Brian. *Theories of Play and Postmodern Fiction.* New York: Garland, 1998. Print.

Fuchs, Michael. "Hauntings: Uncanny Doubling in *Alan Wake* and *Supernatural.*" *Textus: English Studies in Italy* 25.3 (2012): 63–74. Print.

_____. "'It's like *Groundhog Day*': Remediation, Trauma, and Quantum Physics in Time Loop Narratives on Recent American Television." *GRAAT On-Line: A Journal of Anglophone Studies* 15 (2014): 93–113. Web. 1 June 2015.

_____. "Play it Again, Sam … and Dean: Temporality and Meta-Textuality in *Supernatural.*" *Time in Television Narrative: Exploring Temporality in Twenty-First-Century Programming.* Ed. Melissa Ames. Jackson: University Press of Mississippi, 2012. 82–94. Print.

_____. "Trapped in TV Land: Encountering the Hyperreal in *Supernatural.*" *Simulation in Media and Culture: Believing the Hype.* Ed. Robin DeRosa. Lanham, MD: Lexington Books, 2011. 47–55. Print.

García, Alberto N. "Breaking the Mirror: Metafictional Strategies in *Supernatural.*" *TV Goes to Hell: An Unofficial Road Map of* Supernatural. Ed. Stacey Abbott and David Lavery. Toronto: ECW Press, 2011. 142–160. Print.

Hills, Matt. *The Pleasures of Horror.* London: Continuum, 2005. Print.

Jowett, Lorna, and Stacey Abbott. *TV Horror: Investigating the Dark Side of the Small Screen.* London: I. B. Tauris, 2013. Print.

Leffler, Yvonne. *Horror as Pleasure: The Aesthetics of Horror Fiction.* Trans. Sara Death. Stockholm: Almqvist & Wiksell, 2000. Print.

Lloyd-Smith, Allan. *American Gothic Fiction: An Introduction.* New York: Continuum, 2005. Print.

Łowczanin, Agnieszka. "Convention, Repetition and Abjection: The Way of the Gothic." *Text Matters* 4.4 (2014): 184–193. *De Gruyter Open.* Web. 3 May 2015.

Miller, J. Hillis. *Fiction and Repetition: Seven English Novels.* Cambridge: Harvard University Press, 1982. Print.

Mittell, Jason. "Previously On: Prime Time Serials and the Mechanics of Memory." *Intermediality and Storytelling.* Ed. Marina Grishakova and Marie-Laure Ryan. Berlin: Walter de Gruyter, 2010. 78–98. Print.

"The Monster at the End of This Book." *Supernatural: The Complete Fourth Season.* Writ. Julie Siege and Nancy Weiner. Dir. Mike Rohl. Perf. Jensen Ackles and Jared Padalecki. Warner Bros., 2009. Blu-Ray.

"Monster Movie." *Supernatural: The Complete Fourth Season.* Writ. Ben Edlund. Dir. Robert Singer. Perf. Jensen Ackles and Jared Padalecki. Warner Bros., 2009. Blu-Ray.

Muckelbauer, John. *The Future of Invention: Rhetoric, Postmodernism, and the Problem of Change.* Albany: SUNY Press, 2008. Print.

Mulvey, Laura. "Repetition and Return: Textual Analysis and Douglas Sirk in the Twenty-First Century." *Style and Meaning: Studies in the Detailed Analysis of Film.* Ed. John Gibbs and Douglas Pye. Manchester: Manchester University Press, 2005. 228–243. Print.

Peirse, Alison. "*Supernatural.*" *The Essential Cult TV Reader.* Ed. David Lavery. Lexington: University Press of Kentucky, 2010. 260–267. Print.

"Pilot." *Supernatural: The Complete First Season.* Writ. Eric Kripke. Dir. David Nutter. Perf. Jensen Ackles and Jared Padalecki. Warner Bros., 2010. Blu-Ray.

Robson, Eddie. "Gothic Television." *The Routledge Companion to the Gothic.* Ed. Catherine Spooner and Emma McEvoy. Abingdon: Routledge, 2007. 242–251. Ebook.

Sage, Victor, and Allan Lloyd Smith. "Introduction." *Modern Gothic: A Reader*. Ed. Victor Sage and Allan Lloyd Smith. Manchester: Manchester University Press, 1996. 1–5. Print.

Salomon, Roger B. *Mazes of the Serpent: An Anatomy of Horror Narrative*. Ithaca: Cornell University Press, 2002. Print.

Spooner, Catherine. *Contemporary Gothic*. London: Reaktion, 2006. Print.

Staiger, Janet. *Perverse Spectators: The Practices of Film Reception*. New York: New York University Press, 2000. Print.

Stone, Jon. *The Monster at the End of This Book*. 1971. Ill. Michael Smolin. New York: Random House, 1999. Print.

"Swan Song." *Supernatural: The Complete Fifth Season*. Writ. Eric Kripke and Eric Gerwirtz. Dir. Steve Boyum. Perf. Jensen Ackles and Jared Padalecki. Warner Bros., 2010. Blu-Ray.

Walter, James. "Repeat Viewings: Television Analysis in the DVD Age." *Film and Television After DVD*. Ed. James Bennett and Tom Brown. New York: Routledge, 2008. 63–80. Print.

Wheatley, Helen. *Gothic Television*. Manchester: Manchester University Press, 2006. Print.

Williams, Linda. "Film Bodies: Gender, Genre, and Excess." *Film Quarterly* 44.4 (1991): 2–13. *JSTOR*. Web. 7 Jan. 2010.

Žižek, Slavoj. "Passions of the Real, Passions of Semblance." 2001. *Welcome to the Desert of the Real! Five Essays on 9/11 and Related Events*. New York: Verso, 2002. 5–32. Print.

Zubernis, Lynn, and Katherine Larsen. *Fandom at the Crossroads: Celebration, Shame and Fan/Producer Relationships*. Newcastle: Cambridge Scholars, 2012. Print.

Gothic Imaginings
Folkloric Roots

DANIEL P. COMPORA

During its run of ten years (and counting), *Supernatural* has entertained and terrified its many avid viewers. Focusing on the lives, and occasional deaths, of Sam and Dean Winchester, the series deals with the struggle these paranormal hunters face while ridding the world of various evil creatures. Along the way it has consistently incorporated elements of ancient prophecy, visitations of angels, and attacks by demons and other monsters. In addition to these otherworldly beings, *Supernatural* also adapts elements from folkloric and fairy tale sources within the Gothic tradition. Elizabeth MacAndrew states that the worlds created in Gothic fiction "[use] an amalgam of materials, some torn from the author's own subconscious mind and some stuff of myth, folklore, fairy tale and romance" (3). This blending of cultural elements certainly is true of *Supernatural*, which does not restrict its focus to simply folkloric subgenres. Though a number of episodes have taken their inspiration from urban legends and fairy tales, much of the show's larger context draws on variants from popular culture. As a result, *Supernatural* moves beyond the folk and Gothic traditions and creates its own particular mythology.

The pilot episode wastes no time in establishing its Gothic and folkloric roots. The opening scene portrays the death of Sam and Dean Winchester's mother at the hands of the yellow-eyed demon Azazel. Twenty years later, the same force attacks and kills Sam's girlfriend Jessica. This death, coupled with the disappearance of their father, leads a reluctant Sam to join his brother as a *Supernatural* hunter. As the series develops, it is discovered that Sam and Dean's father, and other ancestors, come from a long line of demon and monster hunters, establishing a Gothic element to the series. MacAndrew states, "The characters who must carry the burden of this theme of inherited evil are also typically Gothic, being highly simplified figures useful for the embodiment of ideas" (12). Although Sam and Dean become much more complex as the series develops, at the stage of the pilot episode, very little is known about them; and what is shown is very stereotypical. Dean is a roguish drifter intent on following in his father's footsteps; Sam is the prodigal son who is trying to remake his identity in college. Sam and Dean inherit the family business from their father: Dean, willingly, and Sam, reluctantly. However, Sam and Dean's evolution throughout the series adds a complexity and depth not usually seen in Gothic characters. Though they may be "highly simplified" at the beginning of the pilot episode, by the end of the first season, they establish themselves as unique characters, carrying on a multi-generational fight against evil.

Ghosts and Urban Legends

The brothers' first case temporarily abandons the demon backstory to focus on a scenario in which, for nearly a decade, unmarried men have been disappearing along an empty stretch of road. The Winchesters learn that years earlier, a woman named Constance Welch jumped to her death off a nearby bridge after drowning her children. She eventually leads Sam to her home, where she is confronted by the apparitions of her children. This episode blends at least three urban legend archetypes together: a Woman in White (or White Lady), a Vanishing Hitchhiker, and a weeping woman, known in Mexican folklore as "La Llorona." Constance is clearly a variation of the White Lady, who "dislikes men and seeks vengeance" (Schlosser). Variations of this tale date back to the 1800s and often tell of a mother who searches day and night for the body of her daughter, who she believes has been raped and murdered. Unable to deal with her loss, the mother jumps off a cliff into a lake. Her spirit then continues to wander in search of her daughter. *Supernatural* departs from this storyline considerably, although it retains its defining element: the Woman in White.

In the pilot, this White Lady is also a hitchhiker, borrowing heavily from the imagery from the Vanishing Hitchhiker lore collected by noted folklorist Jan Brunvand. Such tales have been identified all over the world and have been reported for centuries, and they are classified in Ernest Baughman's folklore motif classification system as motif E332.3.3.1 (148). In the most common versions of this legend, a male driver and his companion pick up a young hitchhiker, usually female, who mysteriously vanishes during the journey. It is usually discovered that the hitchhiker haunts a particular stretch of road, continuously attempting to complete her journey home. Again, the episode departs considerably from the most common variations of this legend. Revenge and malice are not typically elements of the Vanishing Hitchhiker tales—instead, it is usually a simple desire to return home that motivates the apparition. In the *Supernatural* universe, though, ghosts are often driven by the desire to atone for something they did wrong while living, or to right wrongs that were done to them.

Understanding the character's life is essential to understanding the motivations of the ghostly apparition. In this series, ghosts are often fearsome entities of tortured souls, which raise obvious fears of death and the afterlife. It is fitting that the tale would be adjusted in this fashion in the pilot episode, as the simple desire to go home does not provide many opportunities for a moralist argument or high drama. Constance is clearly a tortured soul, and Sam and Dean, at this early stage of their hunting careers, are unable to help her—they in fact need to understand her suffering so that she can be set free. It helps establish a key element of the Winchesters' moral struggle that runs throughout the entire series: in order to protect humanity, they sometimes have to kill creatures who suffer and are therefore sympathetic, which in turn weakens their own humanity.

Though Constance displays elements of a Woman in White and a Vanishing Hitchhiker, her tale most strongly incorporates that of La Llorona (the weeping woman). According to Domino Renee Perez, Constance clearly is La Llorona: "the bogeywoman of Mexican and Chicano folklore" who is doomed to walk the face of the earth for murdering her children (154). She is not explicitly portrayed as Mexican in the episode, but the core elements of the La Llorona tale are certainly in place. Instead of simply adapting any one of these legends to form the plot of an episode, *Supernatural* blends the most important, and most familiar, elements together to craft its own unique narrative. Mikel Koven and Gunnella Thorgeirsdottir state that "*Supernatural*'s monsters are artificial fusions of many folkloric and cultural variants" (192). By combining popular elements of these well-known legends, the series recontextualizes them for the viewer while also acknowledging their folk and Gothic origins. In this fashion, *Supernatural* routinely presents narratives that are unique and intriguing, but also somewhat familiar because they are based on popular legends, stories that we seem to have heard before. Often, these folkloric elements allow the writers to establish narrative and cultural contexts that forward an element of familiarity before taking the narratives in unpredictable directions. This familiarity gives viewers a false sense that they know what is going to happen, based on other variants of the tale they have experienced. The narrative context makes episodes like this seem predictable at the outset, but as viewers have learned, they rarely remain so.

Supernatural is not afraid to borrow from the same legend a second time either, utilizing the ever-famous roadside ghost again during the second season episode "Roadkill" (2.16). Here, the Winchester brothers help a victim of an accident, Molly McNamara, ultimately realize that she has indeed died and is now a spirit who is frightening others. This phenomenon of the ghost who is unaware of his or her death was popularized in M. Night Shyamalan's *The Sixth Sense* (1999), and has since become a popular trope in ghost-based dramas. The confusion over who is actually being haunted in ghostly tales, and who is doing the haunting, is explored by Dani Cavallaro in *The Gothic Vision* (2002), who points out that it is often unclear "exactly where the sense of menace originates" (1). In general, *Supernatural* depicts ghosts in a dark fashion, relating the message that anything of paranormal origin is, at the very least, suspicious, which is not at all surprising, given the Winchesters' history with the paranormal. In "Roadkill," it does not take them long, however, to ultimately do what is right and to help Molly realize that she is the one menacing others. Ultimately, the Winchesters' goal is not necessarily to destroy monsters, but to preserve humanity. Unfortunately, that often leads to the destruction of their antagonists, even ones who are portrayed sympathetically. In this particular episode, the ghost herself is frightened and is unaware of the impact she is having on others, and Sam and Dean quickly realize that helping the ghost is the best course of action.

Regardless of who is more frightened, the ghost or her unintended victims, fear is still the driving force behind many spectral tales. Part of the desire to believe in the supernatural, particularly ghosts, may be our desire to overcome fears we perceive as real. According to Joe Grixti, people tend "to fear the very strange, especially when it is closely associated with the familiar" (198). Ghost stories on the small screen often play upon universal fears: the fear of death, the fear of losing a loved one, and the fear of ghosts and the supernatural. In this regard, confronting ghosts on the screen can help viewers deal with real-world anxieties about death. If, as Keith Durkin indicates, America is a death-denying society, and its popular media is rich in "thanatological content," then America's current cultural obsession with ghosts is quite logical (1: 47). As such, a number of *Supernatural* episodes have incorporated ghosts as antagonists, another example of how the series creatively reimagines real-world fears and anxieties.

Unlike many episodes that contribute to the show's overall mythology though, *Supernatural*'s treatment of ghosts is usually confined to a single episode, resolving the ghostly conflict within the hour. These episodes provide a sense of closure and, in the case of "Roadkill," even acceptance of one's fate. An exception to this utilization of ghosts has occurred in more recent seasons, as the ghostly presence of beloved character Bobby Singer periodically appears.[1] Obviously, the Winchesters struggle with Bobby's death, and that struggle extends across multiple seasons. Though they typically resolve ghostly conflicts within a single episode, often destroying the otherworldly entities, or sometimes helping these spirits find rest, letting Bobby go has been more difficult. Bobby's ghostly presence also contributes to Sam and

Dean's moral dilemma: they are typically willing to destroy ghosts in order to protect humanity, but they are unable—or unwilling—to do so with Bobby.

The Season Two episode, "Playthings" (2.11), builds on the vengeful spirit motif by employing a traditional haunted house setting. As Lorna Jowett and Stacey Abbott point out, "The gothic, in its most recognizable manifestations, exhibits rich surface detail, distinctive iconography (that may include iconic monsters) and consciousness of its detachment from the 'real' or from realism" (107). All of these elements are present in this episode, which is self-contained and does not connect to the larger mythology of the series, but which certainly connects to the longstanding Gothic tradition of haunted houses.

After two mysterious deaths occur at the Pierpont Inn in Cornwall, Connecticut, Sam and Dean visit, determined to figure out who, or what, is responsible. When they arrive, Dean comments on the Gothic nature of the house. Within the old house itself, there are a number of antique items, including a large collection of dolls which, when bad things happen to them, also occur to people inside the inn. These elements elevate the episode above a stereotypical haunted house tale and provide a rich context for the multigenerational haunting that unfolds over the course of the episode. In addition to folkloric and Gothic traditions, this episode also makes a number of references to the iconic haunted hotel films *The Shining* (1980) and *Psycho* (1963), which also follow the Gothic/horror tradition. By referencing these popular films, *Supernatural* once again uses familiar narratives to help build its context, adapting those narratives in order to create a unique episode. Sam and Dean are given Room 237, which is a direct reference to the movie version of *The Shining*, Stanley Kubrick's film adaptation of Stephen King's 1977 novel. The similarities do not end there. The young girls portrayed in this episode, Tyler and Maggie, are dressed in a nearly identical fashion, reminiscent of the ghostly twins from the Overlook Hotel. Also, the bar scene, in which Dean talks with the caretaker Sherwin, is evocative of, but much more benign than, the bar scene in *The Shining*, in which the tormented protagonist Jack Torrence descends deeper into alcoholism and evil. These references help establish not only the haunted history of the inn itself, but also point to a wider history of haunted hotels in popular culture. *Supernatural*'s use of the familiar creates the expectation of predictability, allowing the writers to surprise viewers when the narrative unfolds in unexpected ways.

In addition to *The Shining* similarities, an even stronger popular cultural reference is the grandmother kept in the attic, a scenario reminiscent of the classic film *Psycho*. However, key differences are present. In *Psycho*, the woman in the attic is the corpse of Norman Bates's mother, who he had killed at some earlier time. In this episode, the grandmother, Rose, is incapacitated because of a stroke and ends up sacrificing herself in order to save her daughter and granddaughter from the vengeful spirit of her deceased sister, Maggie. Instead of being the victim, Rose is a hero. The presence of an older, motherly figure returning from the dead is a relatively common folklore motif, indexed by Baughman as motif 323 (146). Though Rose is not technically dead, her incapacitation serves as a pseudo-death from which she briefly returns in order to summon Maggie to her and away from her granddaughter, Tyler. *Supernatural* uses these iconic horror films, which themselves rely on Gothic imagery, in order to establish a similar atmosphere for viewers while also adding an element of cultural familiarity.

Wendigos and Zombies

Ghosts are not the only type of creature the Winchesters find themselves battling. Over the course of its long run, the brothers have defeated a variety of other creatures, including vampires, witches, werewolves, and even a rather nasty leprechaun, all of which have mythic backgrounds. By populating their universe with characters with actual folkloric origins, the creators of *Supernatural* tap into existing cultural fears and beliefs, lending an air of authenticity and familiarity to the tales being shared. The series has focused a number of episodes on cannibalistic monsters, including the notorious wendigo, and the ever-popular zombie. Though these two creatures have evolved from different folkloric roots, their narratives share some common elements that *Supernatural* has explored at various times throughout the series.

The show's second episode "Wendigo" (1.2) featured the iconic crypto-zoological character, which comes from Native American traditions and is associated with cold winter climates. According to lore, a wendigo is created when a person succumbs to eating human flesh. During this episode, Sam and Dean investigate the disappearance of hikers in the middle of a Colorado forest, learning that there have been similar reports of disappearances at twenty-three year intervals. They eventually kill the creature, not with silver as the lore would suggest, but with the use of flare guns.[2] Yet the question at issue is not which version of the tale is most closely related to its folkloric origins, but why supernatural-themed programs focus on the creature. To answer this, it is important to consider what is at the core of the wendigo tale: a loss of humanity, which is best illustrated by resorting to cannibalism, one of society's greatest taboos. In this regard, the wendigo tales share a common element with zombie films, which have achieved broad popularity in recent years. In the typical zombie narrative, the consumption of flesh is the defining difference between the living and the undead. Even though surviving characters may be willing to commit any number of atrocious acts against each other, as the television series *The Walking Dead* (2010–) clearly illustrates, people simply do not eat each other. Like the modern zombie, the wendigo represents the decline from human to monster. Unlike the zombie, however, the wendigo's origins are entirely folkloric. The cannibalistic zombies that are popular now are largely derived from George A. Romero's classic film *Night of the Living Dead* (1968), which created its own context and largely ignored much of the Haitian folk roots of zombie lore. The wendigo fits into the folk narrative structure that *Supernatural* employs, yet it touches on the same popular themes of most zombie narratives.

This does not mean, however, that *Supernatural* intentionally shied away from popular zombie narratives. In fact, the series has incorporated them often and has stayed relatively true to their folk roots, avoiding overly simplified portrayals often seen in other zombie tales. As Kyle William Bishop indicates, "zombies are more than just mindless monsters bent on the destruction of humanity and global social culture; they are also important … creatures, embodying both folkloristic and ideological beliefs and traditions" (37). By adapting the creatures in unique ways, the series creates zombies with unique identities, but with enough connections to lore to maintain familiarity. The series' first foray into zombie lore occurred in the Season Two episode "Children Shouldn't Play with Dead Things" (2.4), the title of which is derived from the 1972 cult zombie film bearing the same name. Again, *Supernatural* employs a familiar cultural reference to craft its own, unique story. Angela Mason, the daughter of a professor of ancient Greek, is reanimated by a love-struck graduate assistant. Though the episode invokes the name of one of the genre's classic entries, this tale does not include some of the key elements common to zombie narratives. Though she does murder her ex-boyfriend, Angela does not turn cannibalistic—she simply cuts his throat. Also, the traditional "shoot 'em in the head" mentality that has become a staple of zombie narratives does not work here. In fact, Angela is ultimately killed by being impaled in her coffin by a silver stake, a technique usually reserved for the destruction of vampires.

"Dead Men Don't Wear Plaid" (5.15) is perhaps the most straightforward of *Supernatural*'s attempts at a classic zombie tale, but again it manages to present a significant variation on the theme. The episode begins with a corpse, the remains of a man named Clay Thompson, digging his way out of a grave in Sioux Falls, South Dakota. He makes his way to the home of Benny Sutton, who he kills off screen. It turns out that Clay wanted revenge for Benny shooting him in the back five years earlier. At this point in the episode, aside from Clay exacting his revenge on Benny, the zombies appear harmless. In fact, nearly twenty have returned from the dead and resumed their lives with their families. This includes the wife of *Supernatural*'s patriarchal figure, Bobby Singer. In the traditional zombie narrative, familial bonds are rendered meaningless as the mindless zombie horde consumes anyone it encounters. In this episode, however, Bobby's wife does not consume—she bakes pies. This bit of irony does not last long. The zombies do eventually devolve into the more familiar, mindless, cannibalistic creatures that populate traditional narratives.

What is interesting about *Supernatural*'s portrayal of zombies is how the writers use familiar themes and elements to craft a unique variant. The creatures' isolation from humanity is not what makes these zombies horrifying— at least not at first. The fact that they are so familiar and seemingly normal is what is most frightening and dangerous. Familial bonds are often problematic in zombie narratives, as *Night of the Living Dead* illustrates. In this film, a major character named Barbara is rendered incoherent by the death of her brother, while the Cooper family squabbles constantly as their daughter slowly dies and becomes a zombie, eventually killing and eating her mother. This same familiarity leads Sheriff Jody Mills to welcome her dead child back into her life, only to have him turn cannibalistic and kill, and partially eat, her husband Sean. Also, though the zombies of Sioux Falls do eventually resort to eating people, leading Sam to round up a posse to hunt them down, it is their initially benign nature that creates the conflict in the first place. Fortunately, Bobby resists the urge to give in to this familiarity and kills his wife before she turns.

Supernatural explores the zombie theme a number of other times, albeit in different ways that usually retain some common element of zombie lore. In "It's the Great Pumpkin, Sam Winchester" (4.7), zombies are brought to life by a witch's spell and the summoning of Samhain, and they again are dispatched by being impaled in their graves. Also, the Season Five story arc focuses on the Croatoan virus, which transforms those infected into mindless, murderous creatures, even though they are not cannibalistic in nature. This scenario features the popular zombie trope that a disease is at the center of the bizarre resurrection. Cannibalistic zombies also return in the Season Seven episode "How to Win Friends and Influence Monsters" (7.9), in which the Leviathan creates a food additive that turns people into mindless killers.

Clearly, *Supernatural* has incorporated zombie lore a number of times, with much of the show's inspiration drawn from popular culture variants as well as traditional folklore, but the eighth season contains a pair of episodes that reach deeper into myth to explore the nature of the undead. "Everybody Hates Hitler" (8.13) features the art of necromancy and the legendary character from Jewish folklore, the Golem, a creature that has been brought to life after being fashioned out of clay, or some other base matter. Traditionally, a golem is not technically a zombie, but Victor Frankenstein's Creature is seen as a variation of this being, popularizing the notion that a golem is a reanimated corpse. "Remember the Titans" (8.16) reaches even deeper into myth, when a zombie-like character by the name of Shane turns out to be

Prometheus, the famed Titan from Greek mythology who is fated to die and come back to life every day. Versions of the myth do vary, but portraying Prometheus as a zombie is indeed an unusual interpretation. In most versions of the myth, Prometheus, who is famed for tricking Zeus and giving fire to man, was sentenced to have his liver eaten every day by an eagle. Again, *Supernatural*'s integration of narrative themes takes familiar folkloric characters—from Haitian zombies to Greek Titans—and adapts them in an original fashion to build its own Gothic mythology.

Vampires

Along with ghosts, vampires are perhaps the most common creatures within the Gothic tradition and are indexed by Baughman as folklore motif number 251 (140). Unsurprisingly, they make an appearance on *Supernatural* more than two dozen times, and in varying fashions. From the blood sucking, violent nests of murderous creatures led by the Alpha Vampire to Dean's loyal friend Benny Lafitte, vampires have appeared in every season of the series, and while they bear some resemblance to folklore and the Gothic, they have been reimagined to fit the larger context of the series. As Cavallaro notes, "images of the vampire summoned by the Gothic vision indicate that this monster is a context-bound fantasy which alters through time…. Not all vampires are alike; some are portrayed as enemies, others as intimate friends or even lovers" (181). *Supernatural*'s vampires, while holding on to some traditional elements, likewise vary greatly, not only from those found in lore and literature, but from each episode in which they appear. By building off of the traditional lore, the writers once again appeal to that which is familiar before reshaping it for dramatic purposes.

The series' first foray into vampire lore occurs during the first season episode "Dead Man's Blood" (1.20), in which the brothers encounter a nest of vampires who prey upon tourists. Like traditional vampires, these creatures feed on human blood, eschew daylight, and are able to turn others into vampires. Sam and Dean eventually use arrows soaked in dead man's blood to take down most of the creatures. Notably absent are the more traditional ways of killing a vampire, including a stake through the heart, decapitation, or exposure to sunlight. The source of the lore regarding dead man's blood is apocryphal, but it has found its way into major, recent cultural adaptions, including Anne Rice's book series *The Vampire Chronicles* (1976–2014) and episodes of the television series *The Vampire Diaries* (2009–). Using blood on the tips of arrows to destroy the creatures is a development unique to this series, once again illustrating *Supernatural*'s tendency to adapt traditional lore in nontraditional ways.

Supernatural not only makes changes to the lore to suit its dramatic needs, it even varies its treatment of the creatures themselves the next time they make an appearance. "Bloodlust" (2.3) paints a completely different picture of vampires, depicting the creatures as fearful of being hunted by people like the Winchesters and fellow hunter Gordon Walker. The vampires here are relatively benign—though they possess the ability and urge to kill humans, they have chosen a more peaceful existence, feeding solely on cattle. Sam is kidnapped by the group in an effort to stop the hunters from destroying them but that seems to fuel the passions of Gordon, who uses the familiar dead man's blood to torture the gang's matriarch Lenore in order to illustrate her monstrous nature. Here, the hunter Gordon is the real monster of the piece, and the vampires are the victims, illustrating that monstrousness is not entirely the domain of supernatural creatures. This idea has become increasingly important in recent seasons of *Supernatural*, particularly as it pertains to the fates of Sam and Dean themselves.

Perhaps the most important vampire in the *Supernatural* universe is Benny Lafitte, who surfaces at the beginning of Season Eight and who serves as a recurring character over the next three seasons (albeit in Season Ten, he appears only as a hallucination). Benny is a vampire who Dean meets in, and eventually rescues from, Purgatory. In many ways, Benny is a traditional vampire in that he has fangs, drinks blood, possesses superhuman strength and speed, and is affected by those elements that affect vampires in the context of the series. However, he is cast in a nontraditional role as a reformed vampire fighting against other monsters and serving as a surrogate brother for Dean, a relationship that causes tension between the Winchester brothers. This friendship between Dean and Benny is eventually put to the test in the Season Eight episode "Taxi Driver" (8.19). When Sam becomes trapped in Purgatory, Dean enlists Benny to save him. However, this requires the ultimate sacrifice: Dean must kill Benny so that he can return to Purgatory in order for Sam to escape. Benny's loyalty to Dean never wavers, and after returning to Purgatory, he holds off three vampires so that Sam can escape. Though he is considered a "monster," his sacrifice allows him to experience redemption, and his death is one of the noblest ones of the series.

Though *Supernatural* employs many elements associated with traditional vampire lore, others are nowhere to be found.[3] Notably absent are the large, European castles: the vampire nests in *Supernatural* are usually decidedly urban in nature. Despite this and other changes, the characters stay true to their Gothic roots. The discrepancy between folkloric and modern depictions of vampires is noted by William Hughes: "Many of the attributes and restrictions which today characterise the fictional vampire are derived not directly from folklore, but from eighteenth century behavioural studies of the peoples of Eastern Europe, published for a western European readership" (242). This linking of mythical vampires to actual people with flawed, human behavior is reflected in *Supernatural*. Even when the vampires are "good," as is the case with Lenore and Benny, they are still unnatural "others" capable of atrocious acts. While they may choose to commit these violent acts only to save those they care about, that does not prevent them from being "unhuman." Yet, as humans and hunters, Sam and Dean exhibit much the same motivation and behavior. This illustrates a core, recurring conflict within the series: monstrosity and evil exist on many levels and in many forms, both human and nonhuman. Sometimes the lines get blurred, making everyone, potentially, a monster.

Welcome to Fairy Land

Many creatures in the *Supernatural* universe have folkloric origins, but the third season episode "Bedtime Stories" (3.5) specifically explores the dark side of children's fairy tales. This episode directly incorporates modern variants of a number of classic fairy tale characters, including the Three Pigs, Snow White, Cinderella, Hansel and Gretel, and Little Red Riding Hood. Such adaptations are not only common in the *Supernatural* universe, but in the development of modern narratives in general. Noted fairy tale scholar Jack Zipes states that "the oral and literary traditions conspired and colluded to reach out to other forms of art to propagate their wonder and fairy tales" (x). *Supernatural* has propagated and adapted a number of creatures from lore during its lengthy run, but its treatment of fairy tales, particularly in this episode, strikes a balance between comedic and horrific. This blending of these two seemingly disparate views is characteristic of the Gothic fairy tale in general. Lucie Armitt acknowledges that the "inter-relational reading of a fairy-tale and Gothic modes may appear anomalous" (268), but further exploration reveals that the two are quite commonly linked together. Armitt specifically points out the Gothic motifs and malevolent structures in works like "Hansel and Gretel" and "Little Red Riding Hood" (268): two tales that feature prominently in this episode.

"Bedtime Stories" is particularly clever in that it introduces popular fairy tales as a major storyline, yet it simultaneously rejects them as unbelievable. In fact, Sam has to convince Dean that the murders taking place parallel popular fairy tales. Dean assumes that all fairy tales have happy endings, but Sam explains how fairy tales originally consisted of sex, violence, and cannibalism before being "sanitized." Though Dean reluctantly accepts Sam's premise that fairy tales are being acted out, he mocks his brother for his knowledge of fairy tales. In order to defeat the menace, the Winchesters, particularly Dean, have to accept the notion that fairy tales are indeed real.

Perhaps the problem is that Dean simply is incapable, at this stage of his life, of completely comprehending the meaning of the tales he is experiencing. Bruno Bettelheim states, "All good fairy tales have meaning on many levels: only the child can know which meanings are of significance to him at the moment" (169). The irony here is that everything they have faced in other episodes fits the definition of being unbelievable, yet the fairy tales everyone knows are harder for Dean to believe than others. Growing up, Dean's life was anything but a fairy tale with a happy ending, making his failure, or inability, to believe quite logical. While he is willing to accept the presence of menacing creatures in his own world, Dean seems unable to understand a world in which stories end with "happily ever after." According to Olga Reimann, "The hero continually and distinctly feels the contradiction between two worlds, that of the real and that of the fantastic" (cited in Todorov 26). Dean's disbelief is likely rooted in the fact that childhood tales are very well known to him, but the happy ending has never been part of his real world. For this reason, he actually finds them more unbelievable. While he readily accepts the existence of malevolent creatures hinted at in obscure tomes, something very familiar is more difficult for Dean to accept. Ironically, the series uses folklore, fairy tales, and myths to add an element of familiarity for viewers, yet the main character automatically rejects the possibility that fairy tale creatures can be real because they are too familiar. Though Dean initially rejects the idea of fairy tales being real, that does not stop him from confronting them head on, especially when they take a dark turn, which makes them, in turn, part of the world he understands.

The rejection of fairy tale lore is humorously depicted in "Clap Your Hands If You Believe" (6.9). Once again, it is Dean who is put in the position of rejection of fairy tale lore by killing a fairy. In this particular instance, Dean is attacked repeatedly by a tiny ball of light while David Bowie's "Major Tom" plays in the background. In one of the series' most humorous moments, Dean leads the small creature into an open microwave and turns it on, destroying the fairy in seconds. Even while fighting malevolent forces, the integration of fairy tale characters allows for comic relief. This episode is also noteworthy because it features another folkloric character, a leprechaun, which is a type of fairy. Naturally, *Supernatural* adapts this character in a unique fashion, having him forced to count every grain of salt that is spilled in front of him. Traditionally, like many other supernatural characters, leprechauns do avoid salt, but lore does not present any compulsions to count the individual grains. *Supernatural's* adaption of fairies and leprechauns, though unique (for example, crop circles serve as fairy rings), does incorporate the key element of fairy lore: mischief. As a result, this episode blends familiar lore with comedy to create one of the more lighthearted episodes of the series.

While *Supernatural*'s debt to folkloric and Gothic traditions is hard to ignore, it is also important to note the complexity and diversity these various elements bring to the overall mythology of the series. In exploring this mythology, it is necessary to examine the origins of the specific elements that *Supernatural* has employed. Mikel J. Koven believes that "to understand *how* popular film and television uses folklore motifs, we must dig deeper to see what happens when such motifs are recontextualized within the popular media text" (70). *Supernatural* draws upon not only the Gothic tradition, but also folklore, fairy tales, and cultural elements that people are not only familiar with, but comfortable with as well. The series cannot definitively be identified as following in the lines of any particular genre, because it draws from multiple genres in imaginative ways. It then bends them to its own dramatic purposes, creating a unique mythology that is simultaneously familiar yet foreign.

Notes

1. A similar storyline from Season Nine involves Kevin Tran's ghost. Kevin returns as a ghost in order to ask Sam and Dean to rescue his mother. After they are reunited, Kevin remains a ghost and leaves the Bunker with his mother. As with Bobby, Sam and Dean find it difficult to "let go" of Kevin, largely out of their own guilt over being the cause of his death.

2. *Supernatural* is not the only series to dedicate an episode to the wendigo. *The X-Files*' first season includes the episode "Shapes," which features this legendary creature. The short lived series *Fear Itself* (2008) also shared its grizzly version of the creature in "Skin and Bones."

3. The show also reinterpreted Gothic's most famous vampire by portraying Bram Stoker's Dracula as a comic figure in "Monster Movie" (4.5).

Works Cited

Armitt, Lucie. "Gothic Fairy-Tale." *The Handbook to Gothic Literature*. Ed. Marie Mulvey-Roberts. New York: New York University Press, 1998. 268–269. Print.

Baughman, Ernest W. *Type and Motif-Index of the Folktales of England and North America: Indiana Folklore Series Number 20*. Bloomington: Indiana University Press, 1966. Print.

"Bedtime Stories." *Supernatural*. Writ. Cathryn Humphris. Dir. Mike Rohl. Perf. Jensen Ackles and Jared Padalecki. CW Network, 1 November 2007. Television.

Bettelheim, Bruno. *The Uses of Enchantment: The Meaning and Importance of Fairy Tales*. New York: Vintage, 1976. Print.

Bishop, Kyle William. *American Zombie Gothic: The Rise and Fall (and Rise) of the Walking Dead in Popular Culture*. Jefferson, NC: McFarland, 2010. Print.

Cavallaro, Dani. *The Gothic Vision: Three Centuries of Horror, Terror, and Fear*. New York: Continuum, 2002. Print.

Durkin, Keith F. "Death, Dying, and the Dead in Popular Culture." *Handbook of Death and Dying: The Presence of Death*, 2 vols. Ed. Clifton D. Bryant. Thousand Oaks, CA: Sage, 2003. 43–49. Print.

Grixti, Joe. "Ambiguous Shades: Consciousness and the Images of Fear." *British Journal of Educational Studies* 31.3 (October 1983): 198–210. Print.

Hughes, William. "Vampire." *The Handbook to Gothic Literature*. Ed. Marie Mulvey-Roberts. New York: New York University Press, 1998. 240–245. Print.

Koven, Mikel J. *Film, Folklore, and Urban Legends*. Lanham, MD: Scarecrow Press, 2007. Print.

Koven, Mikel J., and Gunnella Thorgeirsdottir. "Televisual Folklore: Rescuing *Supernatural* from the Fakelore Realm." Ed. Stacey Abbott and David Lavery. *TV Goes to Hell: An Unofficial Road Map of* Supernatural. Toronto: ECW Press, 2011. 187–200. Print.

Jowett, Lorna, and Stacey Abbott. *TV Horror: Investigating the Dark Side of the Small Screen*. New York: I. B. Tauris, 2013. Print.

MacAndrew, Elizabeth. *The Gothic Tradition in Fiction*. New York: Columbia University Press. 1979. Print.

Perez, Domino Renee. "The Politics of Taking: La Llorona in the Cultural Mainstream." *The Journal of Popular Culture* 45.1. (2012): 153–171. Print.

Schlosser, S. E. "White Lady." *American Folklore*. n.d. Web. 18 June 2015.

Todorov, Tzvetan. *The Fantastic: A Structural Approach to a Literary Genre*. Trans. Richard Howard. Cleveland: Case Western Reserve University Press, 1973. Print.

Zipes, Jack. "Grounding the Spell: Fairy Tale Film and Transformation." *Fairy Tale Films: Visions of Ambiguity*. Ed. Pauline Greenhill and Sidney Eve Matrix. Logan: Utah State University Press. 2011. ix-xiii. Print.

PART 3

Gothic Women:
Heroes and Victims

Coloniality
and the Chicana Gothic
Travelling Myths in the Pilot

LEOW HUI MIN ANNABETH

In *"This Land Was Mexican Once,"* her against-the-grain history of Napa and Sonoma, Linda Heidenreich presents a fascinating historical anecdote from 1841, about the wife of a Californiano soldier named Enrique Licaldo. After Licaldo is killed in battle, his wife—whose name does not survive—attempts to drown their newborn child, and then dies of a fever. This story, Heidenreich says, was likely "a fiction" propagated well into the twentieth century by the family of General Mariano Guadalupe Vallejo, who adopted the child (103). She reads its ideological function as a reification of General Vallejo's authority over the land and its inhabitants, embodied in the role of family patriarch (106–07). But more interesting to me is the statement with which Heidenreich prefaces her story: she asserts that "Llorona stories have been told, by women and men, from the time of the conquest. Often the context of the stories is conquest, colonization, and violence against subaltern peoples. And so it should not be surprising that we would find a Llorona tale in the North" (103). By choosing to present this story as a Llorona story, Heidenreich makes a deliberate and independent historiographical decision. There is no indication in her text that the Vallejos ever cast the Licado tragedy in the mode of the Llorona narrative tradition. Inasmuch, then, as Heidenreich claims that "it should not be surprising," I insist that we ask what it means to "find a Llorona tale *in the North*" (103, emphasis mine).

One such tale is attempted in the first episode of *Supernatural*, which premiered on 13 September 2005. "Pilot" introduces elements that define the aesthetic of the series, at least initially: the road-trip format, the small-town hauntings, the travelling duo of battle-scarred brothers. At the same time,

"Pilot" brings into play a tension that lingers throughout the series, grounded in the assumptions that the show makes about white American masculinity and narratives of American national identity.

Supernatural's pilot episode is an aggressive representation of failed maternity, one in which the murders of Sam's mother and girlfriend bracket the monster-of-the-week plot about a matricidal ghost who kills men on a lonely stretch of Californian highway. The show's development of this plot reveals the antagonist to be a combination of two specific ghost stories—the Vanishing Hitchhiker, who appears in some iteration across the world, and La Llorona, who for reasons of history is embedded in the cultural politics of her native Mexico and the American Southwest.

In this essay, I argue that the narrative tensions of the early episodes of *Supernatural* are inherently linked to colonial contestation of land and nation. An assertion of belonging is met with the assimilationist tendencies of white-imperialist American masculinity. This extends to the appropriation and integration of immigrant folkloric narratives into the Americana of urban legend. In *Supernatural's* "Pilot," a dialectic emerges between two strains of the Gothic: a frontier narrative that comes to dominate the entire structure of the television series, and a Chicana heritage built on Indigenous and immigrant resistance to a project of complete Americanization. Then, to speak of "a Llorona tale in the North," as Heidenreich does, necessarily re-situates "the North," or Anglo California, within a larger history—along the lines of Emma Pérez's project of bringing the concept of diaspora into the borderlands.

Imperial California

To adequately define the Gothic is an impossible project, although that does not mean that it has not been attempted before. The Gothic, whether as a genre or as an aesthetic, is notoriously difficult to pin down. Can it be conjured by the physical landscape of the castle or the moor? Is it evoked by the plot elements of hauntings or incest? Or does it make itself known by its cultural politics, its ambivalence over the dangers of unrestrained sexuality and the intrusion of the foreign, the continental, the Catholic, into a quaint English domesticity?

These questions are significant in their import because they relate to the translation of the Gothic into the setting of *Supernatural* and similar media. Teresa Goddu points out in her introduction to *Gothic America* (1997) that the category of the American Gothic forces the critic to consider the question of *America* as a nation. Capitalizing on the Gothic's thematic concerns of moral corruption and decay, it challenges the American nation narrative through its relationship with time and historiography. More to the point, the American Gothic "tells of the historical horrors that make national identity possible yet must be repressed in order to sustain it" (10). "Just as *gothic* unsettles the idea of America," she adds, "the modifier *American* destabilizes understandings of the gothic" (4).

Although the southern United States has been the principal object of attention when it comes to the Gothic in America—and with good reason, since its "historical horrors," thanks to the narrative promulgated in schools, are the most prominent in the American racial imagination—there is no room for self-absolution or exceptionalism. Mark Busby identifies the manifestation of the Gothic on the frontier of the American West as related to a transformation between the Old World and the New; specifically, "a changed consciousness that results from violence in the wilderness" (86). Settler colonialism exchanges the idea of Europe for a U.S. imperialist vision of modernity. Given the preoccupation of the Gothic with situations of liminality since its emergence in the eighteenth century, the term Frontier Gothic becomes doubly apt. Geographically remote, the castle on the moor or the rural Italian convent are, to the English imagination, also located on the frontiers of civilization. The role of place in the Gothic is inseparable from the role of ideology; that is to say, the Gothic setting is intrinsically and inextricably ideological.

It is in this vein that we get to Heidenreich's question of the apparition of La Llorona in the North. In the pilot episode of *Supernatural*, Sam Winchester is a pre-law student at Stanford University, when his estranged brother Dean drags him out on the road to search for their missing father in the small town of Jericho, California. The title of Heidenreich's history book is telling, a quote from Gloria Anzaldúa: *"This Land Was Mexican Once"*: the setting is the remnants of empire.

The empire is intrinsic to the concept of the Gothic, whose preoccupation is with Otherness. And as such, scholars have striven to show, the postcolonial is embedded in the Gothic; its most prominent and well-known manifestation is in Charlotte Brontë's *Jane Eyre* (1847), where the body of Bertha Mason, the madwoman in the attic, incarnates not merely colonialism but also its abject institutions of slavery and anti-Blackness (Meyer 254).[1] Another example provided by William Hughes and Andrew Smith comes from another Brontë sister—Emily's Heathcliff in *Wuthering Heights* (1847), whose "dark skin and unknown origins" (Hughes and Smith 2) have been ascribed to ancestry with the lascars who are also colonial subjects migrating to the metropole.

There is a direct connection between the postcolonialism of the former British Empire and Chicana critical thought. Emma Pérez's *The Decolonial Imaginary*, for example, directly finds inspiration in the work of Homi K. Bhabha (x, xvi). In recognizing the influence of postcolonial criticism on Chicanismo, this lineage bears out Robert Stam and Ella Shohat's nuanced observation that "all of the Americas are postcolonial in the sense of having achieved independence from European colonialism, even if Britain and the United States exercised hegemonic power in Latin America" (274). Stam and Shohat go on to declare:

> But either all the colonial-settler states are postcolonial or none of them are. More precisely, they all form a palimpsestic mélange of temporalities and chronotopes, mingling the colonial (in relation to indigenous peoples), the post-colonial (in the sense of postindependence), the neocolonial (in the political economy of North-South domination), and the paracolonial (in that colonialism does not explain everything) [274].

It is precisely this relationship that is at play in *Supernatural*'s "Pilot" and only alluded to. Reading Cherríe Moraga's infanticide play *The Hungry Woman: A Mexican Medea* (1995), Tanya González has proposed the category of "Chicana Gothic" as a genre (2007; 2010), one wherein the archetypes of La Llorona and La Malinche are re-appropriated by feminist Chicanas to signify "bad" motherhood as a rejection of colonial and Chicano patriarchal oppression.[2]

Bad Mothers and the Chicana Gothic

La Llorona is a potent image in Chicana aesthetics, and has been rede-ployed by Chicana writers to make new, varied political points always closely linked to maternity and rupture from children. Moraga, for example, refers to undocumented Mexicana mothers as "a kind of contemporary Llorona, refusing the separation of families compounded by globalization" (138). But González objects to the critics for whom "when ghosts or supernatural occur-rences appear in these texts [like Moraga's], the first association made is with Latin American magical realism" ("The (Gothic) Gift of Death" 45). And no wonder: the relapse into postmodern gloss runs the risk of doing what Filipino cultural theorist E. San Juan, Jr., dismisses as "compensat[ing] for the subal-ternity of people of color by eulogizing their 'hybrid,' 'in-between,' decentered situation" (7). To San Juan, this marks a lazy contentment with the insuffi-ciency of the postcolonial narrative, and the salvific potential of cosmopoli-tanism and fragmentation. González's interpretation of Moraga also exposes this approach to postcolonial storytelling as glossing over the deep and inescapable atrocities of colonial violence (47); and her sympathies are clearly with a more contentious and oppositional mode of storytelling.

Doris Sommer's work on the trope of inter-ethnic romance as a nation-alist narrative deepens the problematization of hybridity that San Juan and González provide. While San Juan and González's complaint is with hybridity as a postmodernist aesthetic of the narrative, Sommer's argument that the Latin American "Boom" novels like Gabriel García Márquez's were popular outside Latin America because they were "consistent with the First World's taste for the postmodern" is coupled with an analysis of their literary heritage in earlier romance novels. In these precursors, Sommer identifies a trend in which romance between lovers from competing national factions "provides a model for apparently non-violent national consolidation during periods of internecine conflict" (75). Romance and the bourgeois family, Sommer argues, offer the opportunity to situate national unity not just economically or polit- ically, but fundamentally in biology itself (81). This derives from the ideal- ization of colonial mestizaje, which is seen as the historical origin of modern Latin America (81); furthermore, these nationalist romances are compelled to present their inter-ethnic unions as mutually reciprocated and consensual (87), which conceals, if only partially, the racial and sexual violence of mes- tizaje (91).

To sidestep this baggage in Moraga's unambiguously ethnic-nationalist writing, González suggests that *The Hungry Woman* is not in the same genre as postmodern postcolonials whose work is consumed by approval and can- onization, but instead in alignment with Gothic texts by American women of color, such as Toni Morrison's *Beloved* (1987) (54). In such stories, the cen- tral plot element of infanticide, which renders the women of color protago- nists thoroughly monstrous, is rehabilitated as a desperate act of resistance against a racist and patriarchal order.

Supernatural's "Pilot" offers no such sympathy to its villain. Although the female ghost of "Pilot" is revealed to have killed her children in a fit of madness after learning of her husband's infidelity, with the heroic Winchester brothers there is no generosity for this madness, just as Brontë gives no quar- ter to Bertha Mason's penchant for arson and murder in the Rochester bed- chamber. Instead, the ghost seeks to imitate the husband she so despises, seducing her victims before killing them, and thus committing to a quest of showing that every man is ultimately unfaithful. At the culmination of "Pilot," La Llorona tries to ply these charms with Sam, but is foiled by his resolute dedication to his fiancée Jessica. She is foiled once more when she is shot by Sam's bad-boy brother Dean, whose lechery is a source of humor in his early characterization and who fans and critics have noted is not merely patronizing in his attitude toward women (Stabile 87), but also violently misogynistic and obsessed with the word *bitch* (Freund §1.5). It is hard not to see here a contrast being drawn not only between chastity and promiscuity, but between female and male sexuality as well. In the violence that Dean enacts upon her body, La Llorona is presented with the proof she has been seeking: that the masculinity she encounters is invariably aggressive and accorded an exemp- tion from the specter of monstrosity attached to her.

In this way, Moraga's Chicana feminist reading of La Llorona, in its opposition to patriarchal control over women's reproduction, is surprisingly also central to the thematic underpinnings of "Pilot," which is about women being disposable sex objects and bad mothers. The Woman in White who haunts Jericho is a bad mother for committing infanticide, yes, but Mary Winchester, Sam and Dean's mother, is implicitly also a bad mother for being murdered by a demon in the infant Sam's nursery—she is a failed mother because her death removed her from motherhood. Similarly, La Llorona's project of seduction and murder justifies her destruction at the Winchester brothers' hands; and the episode closes with Jessica's murder, parallel to Mary's, as the impetus of Sam re-entering the lifestyle of a hunter.

The misogyny of *Supernatural* is further sanctified by being performed on the white bodies of Mary and Jessica, which imbues their deaths with a spiritual quality and provides the men in their lives with aspirational motivation, as opposed to—as with the appearance of the villainous Woman in White—a resentful urge to destroy. But the manifestation of La Llorona in between those two repulsive murders complicates a dynamic that might otherwise be legible principally through the lens of gender. With her existence acting as an aberrant representation of femininity that interrupts Mary and Jessica's purity, she ensures that "Pilot" is underlain with the very violence that the Chicana Gothic addresses.

Assimilating Im/Migrant Tales

Enrique Ajuria Ibarra, a scholar of the Mexican Gothic, observes in "Ghosting the Nation: La Llorona, Popular Culture, and the Spectral Anxiety of Mexican Identity" that La Llorona "is a folk figure that has even been embraced by popular visual culture in the United States" (132). Offering *Supernatural*'s "Pilot" as an example, he writes that "despite her modernization and her location in a more American environment, this ghost still features distinctive folk traits: a specter that is both guilt-ridden and a victim of her husband, a vengeful spirit that represents a moral warning, a ghost that is found by a river and is clearly of Hispanic roots" (132).

But *is* the specter shown in *Supernatural*'s "Pilot," as the argument claims, "clearly of Hispanic roots?" In the series, La Llorona is detached from the Mexican land of California and repackaged as a generic "woman in white"— a ghost whose very name, which recollects the eighteenth-century English Gothic romances, indicates the differing expectations of fragile maternity laid upon white femininity, as opposed to (in this case) Latina or Indigenous femininity. The classic Americana of *Supernatural*'s narrative and plot devices like the road trip and the Colt revolver, as well as the white American origins of antagonists like Hook Man and Bloody Mary, conceal a foundational narrative of land, space, and hauntings that is marked by colonialism and people-of-color diasporas—which is conjured up in later episodes by the appearances of jinni and rakshasas.

Multiple migrations are present in the narrative of the Frontier Gothic. There is of course the move—physical and ideological—of the English colonial arrival in the United States, which brings along the convention of the Gothic. In "Pilot," another form of move that is built into the plot is the northward migration of La Llorona across the colonial border. But just as the central tenet of the Frontier Gothic involves the transformation of colonized land into the western civilization that is its past and its objective, *Supernatural's* narrative embarks on a similarly assimilatory approach to ethnicity and ethnically marked folklore, in its interaction with other travelling stories. "Pilot" cannot be viewed in detachment, but as part of a larger narrative trajectory that interacts with other Indigenous and immigrant stories.

I mentioned earlier in this essay that the portrayal of La Llorona in "Pilot" is divorced of any overt racialization. The character is played by an actress of color, Sarah Shahi, who is Persian American, but given the (married) name of Constance Welch. This ethnic ambiguity, a deliberate playing with race, does recall the American Gothic's fundamental fear of miscegenation and Black citizens passing as white. At the same time, the name of La Llorona is never uttered, and the plot chooses to emphasize the gendered aspects of the story—infidelity and infanticide—rather than its racial elements.

Moraga has, as González points out, recuperated the trope of infanticide as a feminist act in *The Hungry Woman*. Moraga's own reading of La Llorona is similarly one of Indigenous resistance: in her essay collection *A Xicana Codex* (2011), she envisions La Llorona as a force generated at the moment of imminent colonial violence: "'¡Ay, mis hijos! We have to go! Where can I take you?' The mythic cry of La Llorona, the 'Weeping Woman,' was said to have been first heard in the dark of night in the streets of Tenochtitlán, just before the arrival of the Spanish into México" (138). This genealogy that Moraga creates for La Llorona, as a self-professed Xicanadyke feminist, is—tellingly—a variant of the narrative that eschews collapsing the character with sexual colonization; her maternity predates conquest and rape, and assumes a protective nature. Nonetheless, such a re-imagination could not exist except as a feminist response to a dominant narrative that already connects the folkloric figure with sexual colonization, consensual or not.

Although "Pilot" takes place on colonized land, with a central antagonist whose narrative is so closely tied to the experience of colonialism, there is no inkling of that tension in *Supernatural's* representation of La Llorona. Nonetheless, colonialism cannot be extricated from the conversation. The show's second episode, "Wendigo," takes an Indigenous narrative of demonic cannibalism and has the Winchester brothers destroying the titular creature to save a group of lost white hikers. As in "Pilot," the patriarchy and whiteness of settler colonialism are upheld through the literal destruction of monsters who stand in for Indigenous bodies.

The manipulation of Indigenous stories to serve colonial ends is also at work in *Supernatural*'s representation of immigrant folklore. The show's concept is perhaps at its strongest when it addresses the urban legends that have become a staple of Americana, such as Bloody Mary—urban legends that are distinctively American, and have achieved global recognizability *as American* through the export of media products like *Supernatural*. Before the series story arcs turned to outright Christian fantasy, though, it also dabbled in monsters of the week of distinctly immigrant origin in racialized ways, without acknowledging the role of race in its narratives. For example, in the second season of *Supernatural*, the rakshasa is described as belonging to "a race of ancient Hindu creatures" ("Everybody Loves a Clown," 2.2), and the script leaves it at this biographic detail, despite the questions that such a throwaway phrase must raise (what does *race* mean for a racialized myth, or what constitutes a *Hindu creature*?).[3]

More than that, these stories that *Supernatural* takes as its wobbly foundation are immigrant stories that are forcibly assimilated and americanized. The jinn in "What Is and What Should Never Be" (2.20) is deliberately made threatening by being covered in henna-like tattoos, and yet, as a character, his supernatural powers are limited to the American cultural stereotype, seen in Disney's *Aladdin* (1992) or much earlier in *I Dream of Jeannie* (1965–1970), of the wish-granting genie. Similarly, the rakshasa of "Everybody Loves a Clown" is a villain who has been merged with the spectacle of the circus and the American horror archetype of the clown.

Besides the veneer of Orientalism, these stories have been subjected to capricious additions and revisions in adherence to an arbitrary vision of an American horror story. Such a narrative decision on the part of the show's producers is at odds with an overlooked aspect of postcolonial folklore: its organic hybridity in the retellings of diasporic peoples. Nasario García provides an ethnographic note on La Llorona in one of his compilations of Southwest oral histories: she walks the countryside in rivers and arroyos, and "is also likely to have appeared in the inner city along a primary canal (*acequia madre*), a drainage ditch (*renaje*), or a cement water channel" (294). Mobile, even omnipresent as she may be, the Llorona whom García chronicles is a woman whose connection to water is not random; she walks the waterways of her people. This is a feature of schoolyard tales in Albuquerque, and she meanwhile defends the honor of Chicanas in Los Angeles. Immigrants and diasporic subjects pass on and mutate stories in accordance with a contextual logic absent from the contrived plots into which studio executives can appropriatively jam racialized folklore.

Conclusion

According to Busby, the Frontier Gothic narrativized the expanding boundaries of the U.S. settler-colonial state as a zone of contention, where an Anglo-American effort in the New World superseded European values and conquered Indigeneity to form a nation. Like that Frontier Gothic, the television series *Supernatural* eventually eschews the Indigeneity of its first two episodes—its Llorona episode and its wendigo episode—and progresses through a shaky grasp of people-of-color immigrant stories before ending up with a Christian fantasy involving deeply masculine, if questionably heterosexual, white men as protagonists.

However, colonialism lingers and haunts the discourse of *Supernatural* just as it does the stories. Indeed, *Supernatural's* evasion of colonial violence may be said to provide a conducive vehicle for its manifestation; as Hughes and Smith remark, Gothic hauntings "may emerge where the colonial context is at best oblique or distorted…. Gothic postcolonialism is, in this respect not merely protean but also truer to the naked ambitions of power and ascendancy that lie behind the project of Empire" (2). Furthermore, to return to the theme of the Chicana Gothic, the two refrains of the Woman in White in "Pilot" are: that she wants to go home and that she cannot go home. In short, this is the existential question of the postcolonial subject in diaspora— even when the diaspora is, as with La Llorona, situated on her native land.

In her criticism of Helena María Viramontes's novel *And Their Dogs Came with Them* (2007), which Annemarie Pérez has also classified as a work of the Chicana Gothic, Mary Pat Brady writes: "Haunting refutes linear temporality; it mocks it. If linear temporality suggests 'there is no going back,' haunting suggests the effervescence of a denser 'now' that is endowed with a more complex temporal structure of flows, swirls, and connections" (186). Although La Llorona's appearance in *Supernatural* was very probably not intended to introduce anti-colonial and feminist resistance at the outset of the television project, her presence is an inherently resistive one when contrasted against the thematic elements that "Pilot" actually chooses to foreground—the masculine vocation of hunting, the vulnerable mortality of mothers and wives, and the active agency of the Winchester brothers at the cost of certain other characters'. By appearing "in the North," La Llorona cannot but gesture toward the "flows, swirls, and connections" that make up the fabric of the Winchesters' America.

The contradictions and (post)colonial questions invoked by the conventions of the Gothic in *Supernatural* are not restricted to this one popular supernatural drama. *The Vampire Diaries*, which has run on The CW since 2009, is set in a fictional town populated by, as the name suggests, vampires, and also werewolves and ghosts. In the narrative sequences that take place during the Civil War, race is conspicuously absent from the conversation; the show strenuously maintains the farce of calling a Black witch, Emily Bennett, a "servant," and pretends that the vampire Pearl and her daughter Anna—played by Kelly Hu and Malese Jow—would have been perfectly fine as socialites in nineteenth-century Virginia.

More recently, over on Fox, *Sleepy Hollow* premiered in 2013 and is set, as the name once more suggests, in the rural New York town of Sleepy Hollow, where demons and the dead rise from the underworld to gestate the Apocalypse. *Sleepy Hollow* has the still-rare distinction of co-starring Nicole Beharie as an African American police lieutenant, alongside the white time traveler Ichabod Crane. The conceit of the show is that Crane, like numerous other characters, hails from eighteenth-century colonial America and fought the British for independence. Yet, despite Crane's early expression of satisfaction at learning from a contemporary Black woman that the institution of slavery was abolished, the history-minded fantasy shies away from addressing a colonial history of race that extends into the present day.

That these three television series, which are tied together by their shared use of the Gothic, take place in very disparate geographical settings is an intriguing fact. It offers the opportunity for a future investigation of how, precisely, the Gothic makes racism manifest depending on a spatially-specific subgenre: the Frontier Gothic in *Supernatural*'s California, the Southern Gothic in *The Vampire Diaries*' Virginia, and so forth. What is evident, though, is that in every case the surface of the shows' plots hides a depth of unspoken folklore that passes through retellings with a resistive essence intact. "Pilot" concludes with the violent exorcism of a woman who has already had her origins exorcised. But *Supernatural* makes one point clear: even with its supernaturally deadly Colt revolver, which was forged on the night the Mexican army reclaimed the Alamo, some things are unkillable.

Notes

1. I am aware that numerous house styles, including this publisher's, recommend the lowercase for the terms *black* and *white*, on the basis of the argument that both are adjectives that describe colors. Like many, however, I intentionally capitalize *Black* as an ethno-political identity label that demonstrates the social construct of race to carry a historical force that goes beyond color. As Malaika Jabali has recently written, "Blackness was an imposition. It was forced onto the Ashanti and Fulani and Hausa and Yoruba and Igbo people by Europeans to justify African enslavement…. Blackness was created precisely to be an immutable trait that could not be formed through adoption" ("Shaun King Is Not Rachel Dolezal: What the Media Gets Wrong About Race in America," *For Harriet*, 29 August 2015, http://www.forharriet.com/2015/08/shaun-king-is-not-rachel-dolezal-what.html). Meanwhile, I leave *white* in the lowercase for the simple fact that the social and legal institution of whiteness has, by design, made itself more mutable in who it encompasses and more securely defined by who it excludes. It possesses no similar unity as a concept that would, to me, warrant the value of capitalization.

2. Let me here state that although my essay begins with a conversation on the Chicana Gothic and the centrality of La Llorona to Chicana aesthetics, I wish to be clear that I am providing not a commentary on Chicana art but on a white American response to Chicana cultural politics. I write as a non-American, Southeast Asian (Singaporean) Chinese, who is non-white but also does not identify as a person of color. I am under no impression that three years in California qualifies me to speak with authority on the cultural significance or antecedents of La Llorona or Chicanismo, only with an individual reading of the circumstances of "Pilot."

3. Xenophobia has a long tradition within the Gothic genre. For more on how the Gothic appropriates race, see H. L. Malchow's *Gothic Images of Race in Nineteenth-Century Britain* (1996).

Works Cited

Ajuria Ibarra, Enrique. "Ghosting the Nation: La Llorona, Popular Culture, and the Spectral Anxiety of Mexican Identity." *The Gothic and the Every Day: Living Gothic.* Ed. Lorna Piatti-Farnell and Maria Beville. London: Palgrave Macmillan, 2014. 131–151. Print.

Brady, Mary Pat. "Metaphors to Love By: Toward a Chicana Aesthetics in *Their Dogs Came with Them.*" *Rebozos de palabras: An Helena María Viramontes Critical Reader.* Ed. Gabriella Gutiérrez y Muhs. Tucson: University of Arizona Press, 2013. 167–191. Print.

Busby, Mark. "Sam Shepard and Frontier Gothic." *Frontier Gothic: Terror and Wonder at the Frontier in American Literature.* Ed. David Mogen, Scott P. Sanders, and Joanne B. Karpinski. Rutherford, NJ: Fairleigh Dickinson University Press, 1992. 84–93. Print.

"Everybody Loves a Clown." *Supernatural.* Writ. John Shiban. Dir. Phil Sgriccia. Perf. Jensen Ackles and Jared Padalecki. CW Network, 5 October 2006. Television.

Freund, Katharina. "'I'm glad we got burned, think of all the things we learned': Fandom Conflict and Context in Counteragent's 'Still Alive.'" *Transformative Works and Cultures* 4 (2010). Web.

García, Nasario. *Brujerías: Stories of Witchcraft and the Supernatural in the American Southwest and Beyond.* Lubbock: Texas Tech University Press, 2007. Print.

Goddu, Teresa A. *Gothic America: Narrative, History, and Nation.* New York: Columbia University Press, 1997. Print.

González, Tanya. "Chicana Gothic? The Aesthetics of Violence and the Environment." National Association of Chicano and Chicana Studies Association. Seattle. 9 April 2010. Conference Presentation.

_____. "The (Gothic) Gift of Death in Cherríe Moraga's *The Hungry Woman: A Mexican Medea (2001).*" *Chicana/Latina Studies* 7.1 (2007): 44–77. Print.

Heidenreich, Linda. *"This Land Was Mexican Once": Histories of Resistance from Northern California.* Austin: University of Texas Press, 2007. Print.

Hughes, William, and Andrew Smith. "Introduction: Defining the Relationships between Gothic and the Postcolonial." *Gothic Studies* 5.2 (2003): 1–6. *Ingenta-Connect.* Web.

Meyer, Susan L. "Colonialism and the Figurative Strategy of *Jane Eyre.*" *Victorian Studies* 33.2 (1990): 247–268. *JSTOR.* Web.

Moraga, Cherríe L. *A Xicana Codex of Changing Consciousness: Writings, 2000–2010.* Durham: Duke University Press, 2011. Print.

Pérez, Emma. *The Decolonial Imaginary: Writing Chicanas into History.* Bloomington: Indiana University Press, 1999. Print.

San Juan, Epifanio, Jr. "Transforming Identity in Postcolonial Narrative: An Approach to the Novels of Jessica Hagedorn." *Post Identity* 1.2 (1998): 5–28. Print.

Sommer, Doris. "Irresistible Romance: The Foundational Fictions of Latin America." *Nation and Narration*. Ed. Homi K. Bhabha. London: Routledge, 1990. 71–98. Print.

Stabile, Carol A. "'Sweetheart, This Ain't Gender Studies': Sexism and Superheroes." *Communication and Critical/Cultural Studies* 6.1 (2009): 86–92. *Taylor & Francis*. Web.

Stam, Robert, and Ella Shohat. *Race in Translation: Culture Wars around the Postcolonial Atlantic*. New York: New York University Press, 2012. Print.

Wearing the Woman in White
The Doomed Lives and Afterlives of Women

E. J. NIELSEN

Supernatural is a show that, in the best Gothic tradition, is built upon the doomed bodies and restless spirits of its female characters. The series' pilot episode sets up this running theme by featuring a trifecta of Women in White beginning with Mary Winchester, whose fiery death at the hands of the demon Azazel is the primary catalyst for John, Dean, and Sam Winchester's journey as demon hunters. At the center of that episode's narrative is the case of a woman who, betrayed in love, has taken her own life and the lives of her children, and is thus cursed to walk the Earth killing unfaithful men. The episode ends with the death of Sam's girlfriend Jessica, who suffers the same fate as Mary, and whose death will once again prove a catalyst for Sam's re-entry into both hunting and the Winchester family unit.

Throughout the course of the show's run, women involved with the Winchesters have often suffered gruesome fates, whether it is the psychic Pamela Barnes having her eyes burned out by an angel prior to being killed by a demon, or hunters and family friends Ellen and Jo Harvelle sacrificing themselves in an attempt to stop Lucifer. Human antagonist Bela Talbot is dragged to Hell by hellhounds, an obvious foreshadowing of Dean's own fate at the end of Season Three. More recently, hacker and fan-favorite Charlie Bradbury sacrificed herself for the Winchesters near the end of Season Ten. Non-human women rarely fare better, with the two longest surviving supporting characters being the male-bodied angel Castiel and the male demon Crowley. However, as is also not uncommon in the Gothic tradition, death is rarely the end for the women of *Supernatural*. Their afterlives are frequently marked by further violence and additional issues of consent, as their bodies are taken over by supernatural forces who threaten the main male characters. Although it is worth acknowledging that male characters, too, are sometimes subject to demonic possession, these motifs still play out primarily in the narratives of the series' female characters.[1]

Bronwyn Calvert's essay "Angels, Demons, and Damsels in Distress: The Representation of Women in *Supernatural*" acknowledges *Supernatural's* poor treatment of its female characters, but problematizes a simple reading of consistently underserved women by placing it in the larger context of the show's focus on the two main characters, Dean and Sam Winchester, as well as on broader series themes. Any other character, Calvert argues, "whether angel, vampire, demon, or would-be action heroine, will always have to exist on [the brothers'] terms" (104). Thus, in order to fairly evaluate whether there is a bias in the show's treatment of male versus female characters, it is reasonable to ask how characters other than Dean and Sam are treated by the narrative relative to each other and whether that appears to be shaped collectively by their respective genders.

As Helene Meyers points out, "Gothic misogyny certainly takes the form of figuring women as 'wounded creatures who were born to bleed' … however, it also functions through the positioning of women as dangerous, even demonic threats" (449). As demonstrated through the portrayals of nineteenth-century characters who shift from human to supernatural/monstrous beings, such as Lucy Westenra and Mina Harker in Bram Stoker's *Dracula* (1897), or even human figures, such as Bertha Mason in Charlotte Brontë's *Jane Eyre* (1847) or Catherine Earnshaw in Emily Brontë's *Wuthering Heights* (1847), female Gothic characters often fall into what Kelly Hurley defines as "abhuman" categories, namely a "not-quite-human subject, characterized by its morphic variability, continually in danger of becoming not-itself, becoming other" (66). As an expansion of Hurley's discussion of this "morphic variability," the use of human "vessels" in *Supernatural* frequently positions female characters in both roles, helpless victim and dangerous monster, forcing them to exist in a constant state of "abhuman" liminality. Although male characters on the show can also take on the role of angelic or demonic vessel, as I will demonstrate in this essay, they do so less often and within a very different framework, one that allows them a greater degree of agency and narrative importance, if not always absolute consent.

Vessels and Meatsuits

Dean and Sam, in addition to being the show's twin loci, are also the pre-eminent "vessels" of *Supernatural* in their role as what Dean evocatively calls "angel condoms" for Michael and Lucifer ("Sympathy for the Devil," 5.1). Nevertheless, it is the doomed women of the show who most frequently find themselves in the role of vessels in various forms, their bodies possessed by outside forces, their appearances stolen, and their restless spirits denied peace, without even the dubious comfort of narrative centrality.

Vessels on *Supernatural* are humans possessed by supernatural entities, most commonly angels or demons. Vessel-hood is an inherently liminal (and, indeed, abhuman) space, as it exists between the self and the occupying other. A vessel is neither alive nor dead but instead is a sort of reverse Schrodinger's box in which the state of the container can only be determined once the "cat" is removed. An angelic vessel does not need to eat or sleep; the body exists in an unchanging and ageless stasis, capable of enduring or recovering from conditions far beyond what a human would survive. A vessel occupied by a demon, conversely, seems to exist in a different form of stasis wherein injuries are ignored rather than healed, at least for the duration of the possession. Death of the angel or demon, while these entities possess the vessel, usually kills the vessel as well, as any injury dangerous enough to kill such an entity would likely also be fatal to a human. Expulsion of an unwanted possession by the vessel or others is difficult but may sometimes be accomplished through the use of sigils, rituals, or, very rarely, by sheer force of human will. If the human has been heavily wounded and not healed, however, they run the risk of dying immediately following the exorcism. Reapers, ghosts, Leviathans, Eve, and some other creatures from Purgatory have also been shown to use or require vessels.

Within the *Supernatural* universe, humans are unique in having a soul and a body, both of which render them vulnerable to possession or other harm and may lead to their objectification and commodification within the supernatural realm. Souls are sold, traded, and used for currency as well as for their battery-like raw power, while bodies are fragile but necessary "meatsuits" whose component parts may also have value, such as the bone of a nun used to kill Leviathans, or the dead man's blood that weakens vampires. While the existence of human souls as a primary distinguishing factor from supernatural creatures is a staple in the Gothic genre, the commodification of body parts is a more recent development, seen not only in *Supernatural* but in other examples of the genre, such as *Buffy the Vampire Slayer* (1997–2003) and *True Blood* (2008–2014). This commodification creates a situation wherein humanity's worth is perceived by angels or demons as being located primarily in their *objective* value as usable bodies or souls, outside, of course, of their value as prey for many other supernatural creatures.

Use of a vessel is apparently necessary for many supernatural creatures to manifest on the human plane of existence. Angels may only possess "willing" living vessels, though the ways in which they can obtain consent do not necessarily contain full disclosure of the terms and conditions of vessel-hood and may involve threats of bodily harm to the vessel or others. Only some humans can function as successful angelic vessels, and the ability to house a particular angel may run in certainly familial bloodlines, as demonstrated in Castiel's connection to the Novak family. In the Winchesters' case, this means their family trees have been manipulated for generations, much like cattle, in order to create the perfect "brains and brawn" combination of traits that allows them to house Michael and Lucifer. Humans unable to handle the possession may die instantly or be slowly eaten away from the inside. Demons, in contrast, can apparently possess any human body, living or recently dead, willing or otherwise, unless the bodies in question have some form of anti-possession mark on or near them. This difference may be partially explained by the fact that while angels are, as Castiel explains, non-human "waves of celestial intent" ("The Third Man," 6.3) whose true forms may be "the size of the Chrysler building" ("Family Matters," 6.7) and are thus always going to be a bit of an awkward fit, demons were all once human. Once the human is possessed, his or her personality and consciousness are sublimated by the possessing entity, who may choose to suppress the human's awareness entirely, allow them some measure of awareness, or give them a front row seat to what their body is doing without their control. These people may not even be aware that they are being possessed.

Supernatural often makes viewers hyper-aware of the nature of female vessels *as vessels* in a way that is generally untrue of the male vessels.[2] There is no backstory given for Crowley's signature human vessel, for instance, or for any of Alistair or Azazel's, or any idea how Raphael, Bartholomew, Uriel, or, perhaps most enigmatically, Zachariah, were able to persuade humans to let them use them as "meatsuits." The angel Gadreel's unnamed first vessel apparently has so little to do that he chooses to hang around with the rogue angel Metatron until he can be re-worn by Gadreel, even though there is no reason for either to imagine that Gadreel will require the use of that vessel's body again. In contrast, Josie Sands is given an entire episode to explain how she offered herself as a sacrifice to save Henry Winchester and became the vessel for the Knight of Hell, Abaddon. Likewise, the angel Hannah's storyline includes encountering the husband her vessel Caroline Johnson has left behind, as well as her subsequent abandonment of said vessel to allow Caroline and her husband to reunite, the only happy ending for an angel or demon vessel that we are shown.

Rather than emphasizing the humanity of the female characters, this treatment creates an emphasis on the use of female bodies *as* vessels and thus also as *victims*, while their possession simultaneously transforms them into something non-human or monstrous. This is made even more explicit when we are actually introduced to women only moments before they become unwitting vessels, as with the unnamed girl thrown into a crevasse by dragons and then possessed by Eve in "Like a Virgin" (6.12), or the comatose patient who serves as the second onscreen vessel for the demon Ruby in "I Know

What You Did Last Summer" (4.9). In both cases, these women become the equivalent of the stereotypical female character killed in the first five minutes of a horror film to introduce the impending danger to the audience, as their human existence is predicated entirely on becoming a vessel. In all cases this focus on their prior humanity renders their status as one of both liminality and victimhood. As characters on the show have themselves noted, the use of human bodies as vessels by supernatural beings ("meatsuits" and "angel condoms") embodies issues of consent, violation, and bodily autonomy, but it is female bodies that are consistently used to demonstrate those inherent consent issues of vessel-hood and of its abhuman duality as victim/monster. As Hurley says, "Gothic materiality," i.e., the horror of a body that is merely a fleshy shell separated from its proper soul, "is a condition which might overtake any human subject … but which is particularly compatible with the condition of femininity" (118). Once "occupied," the women's bodies become both objects and threats that must be violently eliminated by the male hunters, no matter the cost to the human souls still trapped within. While *Supernatural* may lack, for instance, the insistent patriarchal undertone of Lucy Westenra's double murder in *Dracula* as wholly necessary for saving her soul, the repeated violence enacted upon possessed female bodies implies much the same thing in order to keep the viewer firmly on the Winchesters' side.

In addition to *Supernatural*'s propensity to give us the appearance of—but not the context for—their female bodies prior to possession, the now objectified bodies of possessed women are also far more likely to be used by demons specifically to harm or betray the vessel's loved ones and others around them. This is most graphically illustrated when the demon Lilith possesses the young daughter of the Fremont family in "No Rest for the Wicked" (3.16), choosing to remain within the family home in order to hold the rest of the Fremonts hostage, torturing and killing them for her own amusement. Lilith later possesses Ruby's first vessel while impersonating Ruby in an effort to trick the Winchesters. Both Kevin Tran's mother Linda ("What's Up, Tiger Mommy?," 8.2) and girlfriend Channing ("We Need to Talk about Kevin," 8.1) are possessed by demons in order to get to Kevin or to persuade him to cooperate with Crowley. In "First Born" (9.11), the Knight of Hell Abaddon possessed Cain's wife Colette in an attempt to get him to rejoin the Knights of Hell, or, failing that, to kill Colette in revenge. And in "Born Under a Bad Sign" (2.14), "Meg" possesses Sam Winchester and uses his body in an effort to destroy or at least discredit the Winchesters, murdering people and being a danger to those around "Sam." The fact that the loci of these threats can be found within the female form itself is nothing new within the Gothic tradition, which often treats the female body as "intrinsically pathological" (Hurley 120).[3] The death of those persons being used as vessels usually seems to be a side effect rather than an intended consequence of the experience. The entities dwelling within, however, rarely seem overly concerned with the maintenance or care of the bodies they are using, either, in the case of angels, because they are able to heal damage to their forms, or, in the case of demons, because they can abandon a body should it become too damaged to function. Still, the "sacrifice" is one of the vessel's body/identity and not directly of its life, even if that is the end result commonly enough to make these things functionally synonymous.

Just as the physical bodies of women are used without their consent to trick and betray others, supernatural entities are more likely to use the appearance of deceased female characters in order to manipulate male characters. In terms of the viewer's experience within the medium of television, there is no *visual* difference between seeing a possessed living character and seeing the stolen appearance of a spirit, thus making the latter function as a metatextual form of spirit possession wherein the appearance itself is an "object" of use. Lucifer seems especially fond of this technique, taking the form, and, initially, the identity of Nick's dead wife in order to convince him to allow Lucifer to possess his body in "Sympathy for the Devil" (5.1), and then, as Nick's body decays, appearing to Sam as his deceased girlfriend Jessica in "Free to Be You and Me" (5.3) as part of a campaign to persuade Sam to agree to be his new vessel. Lucifer later utilizes Nick's appearance while taunting Sam and then Castiel with hallucinations, but he does not pretend to *be* Nick. Eve, still occupying the unnamed virgin sacrifice, chooses to take on Mary Winchester's form both to emphasize her own status as the Mother of Monsters and to taunt Dean and Sam in "Mommy Dearest" (6.19).

Sacrifice and Manipulation: Meg Masters and Josie Sands

Sacrifice is, of course, a constant theme in *Supernatural* and detailing the many ways in which characters have or are willing to sacrifice themselves or others would be a book unto itself. However, there is a subset of sacrifices that again skews female: sacrifices that require the life of a specific type of creature and, more importantly, those that are not narrowly avoided or later undone by the narrative, as has been the case for both Winchester brothers throughout the series. Lilith must be and is killed for Lucifer to be freed ("Lucifer Rising," 4.22). Dr. Eleanor Visyak is the creature of Purgatory killed to open the way there ("The Man Who Knew Too Much," 6.22). The only surviving nephilim, Jane, is killed by Castiel so that her heart can be used as part of a ritual to seal Heaven ("Clip Show," 8.22). We are given no indication that Jane has ever been a danger to others, while Dr. Visyak has been an ally and romantic interest of Bobby Singer. In contrast, the male cambion Jesse

Turner, who is considered just as much of an "abomination" as a nephilim and is shown to be dangerously powerful, manages to escape ("I Believe the Children Are Our Future," 5.6). An attempt to sacrifice Abaddon by "curing" her and returning her humanity, part of a ritual to seal Hell, fails and the Winchesters instead end up "curing" Crowley instead. Crowley, who as a human sold his soul to a demon for a larger penis, will eventually regain his power and throne as King of Hell while still retaining enough humanity to be an occasional, if dubious, ally of the Winchesters. There is no such potential in the *Supernatural* narrative for Abaddon; she is simply destroyed.

Death is, of course, rarely the end in *Supernatural*. During the Rising of the Witnesses, the original, human Meg Masters is one of the spirits raised by the demon Lilith to attack Dean. While Meg died following an exorcism, the actual cause of death was the injuries previously inflicted upon her by the Winchesters. As Bobby Singer points out, "That girl's body is broken. The only thing keeping her alive is that demon inside. You exorcise it—that girl is going to die" ("Devil's Trap," 1.22). It is in this episode that Meg makes clear she was aware of the demon's possession and of the injuries inflicted upon her body while possessed. This possession and her subsequent death, which Meg specifically ties to the fatal injuries inflicted by Dean and Sam, led to her sister's suicide. The demon, adding further insult to injury, also "cut off [her] hair and dressed [her] like a slut." Of course, Meg's dangerous and wounded spirit, which like her body has been used without her consent, must then be vanquished by Bobby and the Winchesters with a spell in "Are You There, God? It's Me, Dean Winchester" (4.2). Meg's story is perhaps one of the most explicit examples of the physical violation and of the loss of self and of bodily autonomy that is inherent in demonic possession. This loss of self is carried over symbolically through the narrative as the unnamed demon who possesses Meg continues to use "Meg Masters" as an alias even as she occupies other bodies.

Josie Sands's possession is perhaps the most brutal of anyone's, male or female, within the ten seasons of *Supernatural*. While the Knight of Hell Abaddon is referenced as possessing both male and female vessels, as seen in her willingness to take over Henry Winchester and his grandson Dean, Abaddon is only shown while possessing female bodies: Colette, the Mother Superior, Larry Ganem's wife, and of course, Josie Sands. She is further coded as female by referring to herself as "Queen of Hell." Abaddon is so fond of Josie's body that she returns to it multiple times and even re-creates it upon its destruction. The fact that Josie is a rare female Men of Letters candidate who ends up possessed by a demon just prior to her initiation and who then proceeds to destroy the entire organization seems like an implicit authorial rebuke of the idea of the Men of Letters going "co-ed," especially as Josie begs for the possession in an attempt to save the man she loves: "I could be more useful to you. People underestimate a woman" ("Mother's Little Helper," 9.17). She is then used to destroy the entire Men of Letters organization from the inside, culminating in the death of Henry Winchester, the man she originally sacrificed herself to save. While possessed, she is shot in the head and body, still inhabited by both Josie and Abaddon, and is cut into tiny pieces that are then scattered. As Dean evocatively describes: "The demon trap in your noggin is gonna keep you from smoking out. We're gonna cut you into little steaks and bury each strip under cement. You might not be dead, but you'll wish you were" ("As Time Goes By," 8.12). No other demon, including Azazel, the killer of Mary Winchester, Jessica Moore, and John Winchester, is treated to such an inherently sadistic method of defeat. Such abnegation of Josie's body is, of course, not unknown within the broader Gothic tradition, being especially reminiscent of the brutal staking and beheading deemed necessary to ensure the complete death of the undead Lucy Westenra, as well as the unnamed vampire brides in *Dracula*, or the rending apart of the female creature's body by Victor Frankenstein prior to animation. In fact, Mel Brooks's film *Young Frankenstein* (1974) is explicitly referenced by Dean after the brothers decide to sew Josie's body back together, Abaddon and Josie still trapped within ("Clip Show," 8.22).

After her body is reassembled and sewn back together, her flesh ends up doused in Holy Oil and set on fire in "Sacrifice" (8.23). It is only at this point that Abaddon flees Josie's body, meaning that at least until then Josie's soul was still present at some level of consciousness. Given that Abaddon is an incredibly violent and cruel Knight of Hell, it is completely reasonable to consider that "she" may have forced Josie to experience or endure at least some of the physical torture that her body was undergoing, as well as the psychological torment of being used to destroy both the organization she devoted herself to and the man she loved, in a similar manner to what Meg was forced to endure during her possession.

The excessive violence visited by the Winchesters upon the bodies and spirits of Meg Masters and Josie Sands during their possessions is treated in the show as being both appropriate and necessary, especially in the case of the powerful demon Abaddon. Both women have abhuman and monstrous bodies that *must* then be brutally destroyed by the male characters in order to render them safe. Meg, even after a discussion of how she might have been saved if the Winchesters had exorcised her prior to or in place of fatally wounding her, a discussion accompanied by expressions of guilt by Dean and Sam, is still referred to by Dean as someone they "*couldn't* save" (4.2, emphasis mine). Josie never regains control of her body, but does appear in an old Men of Letters recording, which Sam and Dean come across after they have chopped her body up and hidden the pieces. This film, instead of reminding the brothers of Josie's humanity, identity, or victimhood, leads to their decision to "put

Humpty Dumpty back together again" ("Clip Show," 8.22), so they can use her still-possessed body to cure Abaddon. Likewise, human Meg is seen just prior to dying of her wounds, when she thoughtfully thanks the Winchesters for freeing her and gives them information on the demons ("Devil's Trap," 1.22). Her spirit then appears as a witness during the Apocalypse ("Are You There, God? It's Me, Dean Winchester," 4.2). These scenes, by emphasizing the lost humanity of both vessels, foreground the gratuitousness of the specific physical violence used by the Winchesters and the fact that such violence, due to the nature of vessels, cannot be inflicted upon the demons without simultaneously being inflicted upon Josie and Meg. Both women are brutally abused, first mentally by the demons and then physically by the heroes, for having bodies that demons are able to possess. This is, of course, part and parcel of the broader Gothic tradition, where male heroes find themselves inflicting untold violence on female characters to "save" them in a larger, metaphysical sense, and *Supernatural*'s narrative, like many of those before it, focuses not on the pain of the woman being destroyed but on the effect of her destruction upon the man or men doing the deed.

Abaddon is fond enough of using Josie as a vessel that the Knight of Hell has other demons enact a ritual to recreate Josie's body so that she can possess it again, the second time in the narrative that Josie's body is recreated or reassembled so that it can be used by others ("Devil May Care," 9.2). It is never made clear whether, within the rules that govern demonic possession, Josie's soul was once again trapped within her body at this time, as she and Abaddon are now treated as one and the same entity. Abaddon, and to an indeterminate extent Josie as well, are finally put to rest only when Dean Winchester stabs Josie's body repeatedly with the First Blade ("King of the Damned," 9.21). Unfortunately, since Josie technically consented to demonic possession, her soul may have been consigned to Hell either the first time Abaddon abandoned her burning vessel or after Abaddon's final destruction. What is at stake for the overarching narrative is Abaddon, and the viewer is left to wonder what, if anything, was left of Josie Sands by the time Abaddon and the Winchesters were finished with her. In a further ironic twist, Abaddon's ambition to become Queen of Hell is ultimately frustrated, and she is forced to stand by while Crowley (whose identity and vessel are both male) retains the title of king.

As Kelly Hurley states, "When the male subject is confronted with the fact of his own liminality, his own abhumanness, his own bodily fluctuability, he will attempt to keep this fact at bay by insisting that only the female body is chaotic and abominable, never his own" (123–24). It is the women of *Supernatural*, then, whose bodies and spirits most frequently occupy the liminal spaces between life and death and between possession and free will, and who are most frequently used to embody the thorny issues of consent on the show.

These women are simultaneously innocent victims and destructive monsters whose punishment for their otherness is enacted upon their possessed bodies, and whose destruction is then used to advance the plotline of the show's male characters. This tendency in *Supernatural* is part of a much larger tradition within the Gothic that utilizes women as dispensable fictional devices used to show the negative effects of coming too close to something evil. These female types are placed within their respective narratives not with the ultimate goal of being proactive and independent but, instead, to be rescued or killed (sometimes one and the same) by the male hero. We can only hope that the promised "peace when you are done" will someday apply to the wayward daughters as well as to our wayward sons.

NOTES

1. Delineating every exception to the themes presented is beyond the scope of this essay, but a few major examples include the extensive backstory of Jimmy Novak, vessel for the angel Castiel, and the periodic possession of the bodies of John, Dean, and Sam Winchester.

2. While gender presentation in *Supernatural* is a potentially complicated and thorny issue given the nature of many of the beings in question, for purposes of this essay, beings will be referred to by the gender they use to refer to themselves or are most commonly referred to by others.

3. While there are certainly in-show examples of entities pretending to be *male* characters, such as the Trickster's impersonation of Bobby ("Mystery Spot," 3.11), the extended impersonation of Dean and Sam by Leviathans in the seventh season, or even the sibling ghouls impersonating Adam and Kate Milligan ("Jump the Shark," 4.19), these tend to differ from the impersonation of women in that they do not necessitate the presence of, use of, or harm to the original male character or body, instead existing independently because they do not use the actual humans in question as vessels, but instead are merely assuming their appearance.

WORKS CITED

"Are You There, God? It's Me, Dean Winchester." *Supernatural: The Complete Fourth Season*. Writ. Sera Gamble and Lou Bollo. Dir. Phil Sgriccia. Perf. Jensen Ackles and Jared Padalecki. Warner Bros., 2009. DVD.

"As Time Goes By." *Supernatural: The Complete Eighth Season*. Writ. Adam Glass. Dir. Serge Ladouceur. Perf. Jensen Ackles and Jared Padalecki. Warner Bros., 2013. DVD.

Calvert, Bronwyn. "Angels, Demons, and Damsels in Distress: The Representation of Women in *Supernatural*." *TV Goes to Hell: An Unofficial Road Map to* Supernatural. Ed. Stacey Abbott and David Lavery. Toronto: ECW Press, 2011. Print.

"Clip Show." *Supernatural: The Complete Eighth Season*. Writ. Andrew Dabb. Dir. Thomas J. Wright. Perf. Jensen Ackles and Jared Padalecki. Warner Bros., 2013. DVD.

"Devil's Trap." *Supernatural: The Complete First Season*. Writ. Erik Kripke. Dir. Kim Manners. Perf. Jensen Ackles and Jared Padalecki. Warner Bros., 2006. DVD.

"Family Matters." *Supernatural: The Complete Sixth Season*. Writ. Andrew Dabb and Daniel Loflin. Dir. Guy Bee. Perf. Jensen Ackles and Jared Padalecki. Warner Bros., 2011. DVD.

Hurley, Kelly. *The Gothic Body: Sexuality, Materialism, and Degeneration at the Fin de Siècle.* Cambridge: Cambridge University Press, 1996. Print.

Meyers, Helene. "Misogyny." *The Encyclopedia of the Gothic Vol. 2.* Chichester: Wiley-Blackwell, 2013. 448–450. Web.

"Mother's Little Helper." *Supernatural: The Complete Ninth Season.* Writ. Adam Glass. Dir. Misha Collins. Perf. Jensen Ackles and Jared Padalecki. Warner Bros., 2014. DVD.

"Sympathy for the Devil." *Supernatural: The Complete Fifth Season.* Writ. Eric Kripke. Dir. Robert Singer. Perf. Jensen Ackles and Jared Padalecki. Warner Bros., 2010. DVD.

"The Third Man." *Supernatural: The Complete Sixth Season.* Writ. Ben Edlund. Dir. Robert Singer. Perf. Jensen Ackles and Jared Padalecki. Warner Bros., 2011. DVD.

"What's up, bitches?"
Charlie Bradbury as Gothic Heroine

ASHLEY WALTON

Although significant female characters existed before her, Charlie Bradbury is unlike any other woman on *Supernatural*. She undermines gender
expectations, defies the commonly-held hunter lifestyle, and saves the Winchester brothers on numerous occasions. Before Charlie, *Supernatural* had a
few strong female recurring characters, but each of them fall into unsophisticated tropes and lack the backstory, personhood, and character development
of Charlie.

Supernatural's recurring female characters share one core similarity:
they all die. There are a few exceptions, but most of the characters are not
developed enough for their deaths to impact the day-to-day of the Winchesters. As Mary Borsellino states (referencing the first season but applicable to
the show at large): "There are strong female characters in a number of the
episodes (though the ratio of them to the generic, simpering damsels leaves
a lot to be desired), but they are never the ones to solve the mystery, kill the
monster, or help the helpless" (108). Indeed, the first few seasons of *Supernatural* follow a formula in almost every episode: attractive woman gets into
trouble, Sam and Dean show up, and the boys save the damsel. It's strange
that in each case, it's rarely a man who needs help, and it's never an elderly
woman—supernatural forces seem to specifically target attractive and mostly
single women.

Some of the more complicated women of *Supernatural*, such as mothers
and hunters Mary Winchester and Ellen Harvelle, Meg the lovable demon,
and Bela the femme fatale, vacillate between heroism and regression, which
is standard for Gothic heroines.[1] In fact, it's as though *Supernatural* mirrors
the treatment of women in Gothic and horror as a whole, most notably through
Charlie Bradbury. In many ways Charlie breaks the mold for female depic-

114

tions on the show, and she even defies some definitions of Gothic heroism. Although she eventually meets the same fate as the other *Supernatural* women (and most women in horror) Charlie's character pointedly deconstructs female tropes the show repeatedly reinforces, and she makes strides toward a more positive representation of women in horror at large.

A Brief Overview of Gothic Females

The Gothic has a complicated relationship with female characters. Born out of the eighteenth century, the time period marked a shift in familial and organizational structures as men were drawn to the workplace and women increasingly stayed at home. Gender roles were "insistently codified even as they were insistently resisted" (Heiland 3). Gothic literature explored these attitudes toward gender, creating stories and characters that re-inscribed tropes on the one hand and defied them on the other. According to Helen Hanson, "Gothic heroines tended to both appease and free themselves from patriarchal dominance" (5), and "it's not uncommon for the female gothic heroine to oscillate between victim and heroine" (60).

Many Gothic stories feature women as one of the main characters, but it's easy to see these roles as simultaneously progressive and regressive. In the eighteenth century, women's writing started to become popularized in what Ellen Moers coined the "Female Gothic," which she says is "the work that women writers have done in the literary mode that, since the eighteenth century, we have called the Gothic" (90). Some literary scholars have expanded the definition to include any Gothic literature that explores female roles (Heiland). Ann Radcliffe, one of the most well-known Female Gothic writers, encouraged women to empower themselves within the domain of the home, finding a place and a voice within the structure of patriarchy (Heiland 81). Jerrold Hogle notes that "Ann Radcliffe allows her heroines independent property and the ultimate freedom of choice within the fervent worship of their fathers and an avoidance of all direct political action," instating the Gothic tradition of hesitating "between the revolutionary and conservative" (13).

As contemporaries of Radcliffe, William Godwin and Mary Wollstonecraft further questioned the place of women in society and whether patriarchal structures could be abolished altogether. According to Donna Heiland, both Godwin and Wollstonecraft "exposed British society as a mechanism for the production of gothic lives, and both explored the difficulty of escaping those lives in novels structured around the disturbing and often uncanny patterns of repetition" (81). Godwin and Wollstonecraft's legacy was left in the hands of their daughter Mary Shelley, who posed even more radical ideas about how social injustice shapes individuals and society. Aware of her mother's groundbreaking treatise "A Vindication of the Rights of Woman" (1792), Shelley wrote, "If I have never written to vindicate the rights of women, I have ever befriended and supported victims to the social system," which most readers agree includes Victor Frankenstein's creature itself (Gilbert and Gubar, *Feminist Theory* 71).

Influenced by Wollstonecraft and Shelley, the Brontë sisters began publishing Gothic romances, and in particular, Charlotte Brontë captivated Victorian readers with *Jane Eyre* (1847). Drawing on Gothic themes—including secrets, mysterious estates, coincidences, and eerie atmosphere—Brontë created a new type of female protagonist, one that the author described as "poor, obscure, and little" but also smart, independent, and thirsty for knowledge (Gilbert and Gubar, *Feminist Theory* 75). *Jane Eyre* also included a female character that would become a trope explored by many other writers, labeled by Sandra Gilbert and Susan Gubar as "the madwoman in the attic," after Rochester's wife who lost her mind and was hidden away. Ultimately, *Jane Eyre* addresses female anxieties of the nineteenth century and also re-inscribes female roles as either the "monster" or the "angel."

Since the foundation was laid by pivotal authors of the eighteenth and nineteenth centuries, the Gothic tradition has taken many forms. Films, television shows, movies, and comic books explore Gothic themes and tropes, including Gothic heroines. In recent years, the horror genre has stemmed from the Gothic, inscribing and creating new tropes, such as the female slasher victim depicted in *Halloween* (1978) and *Friday the 13th* (1980). Another trope is the Final Girl, a term coined by Carol Clover (35) to describe the girl who usually gets away after everyone else has been killed, seen in *The Texas Chainsaw Massacre* (1974), *Halloween*, *Alien* (1979), *Friday the 13th*, *A Nightmare on Elm Street* (1984), and *Final Destination* (2000). These female horror tropes have been used so many times that when a horror narrative includes a female character, the narrative is immediately part of an intertextual conversation. This intertextuality has given birth to meta-horror, such as *Scream* (1996) and *The Cabin in the Woods* (2012), which feature typical female victims and the Final Girl, but they also offer overt commentary on the plot and tropes of the genre. In addition, Gothic-horror meta-commentary *Buffy: The Vampire Slayer* (1997–2003) takes the teenage blonde girl alone in the graveyard and makes her the thing that monsters fear, rather than the other way around. *Buffy* has in turn influenced films like *Hostel 2* (2007) and *You're Next* (2013), which include a Final Girl who becomes the hunter.

When it comes to women in horror, creators and viewers are usually hyper-aware of context and intertextuality. A television show seated in Gothic horror does not start with a clean slate, but rather one that is already rich with history. Because audiences approach a horror narrative with expectations regarding plot, theme, tone, and tropes, the narrative can play with these expectations. A horror piece may fulfill some tropes, self-consciously avoid others, and deliberately complicate some. It's the intertextual conversation—the fulfillment and avoidance of meeting expectations of the genre—that can make horror narratives particularly engaging.

Given *Supernatural*'s overt and subtle references to Gothic and horror tropes, characters, and plots, it's easy to read its treatment of women as being in conversation with previous horror and Gothic stories. In the first few seasons of *Supernatural*, its treatment of women seems to re-inscribe tropes, recognizing the female victim narrative as being a genre signifier. The problem is that it's difficult to see how the show offers any commentary, complication, or critique of this treatment. It's simply a restatement of what's been done before. Mary Borsellino says, "This can be explained by the fact that it is, after all, the hero's prerogative to save the day, and Sam and Dean—the heroes of *Supernatural*—are both male. But the masculinity the characters attempt to embody is one that reinterprets tropes introduced into the post-modern horror genre by *Buffy*, and the ways in which *Supernatural* seeks to recontextualize these images is distressingly easy to read as an attempted regression away from the frontiers *Buffy* opened up" (108–09).

In many ways, Charlie defies the overt regression that Borsellino points out. Charlie is more fleshed-out than any other female—and many of the male characters—on *Supernatural*. At first she seems like an endlessly happy female in a male narrative, but as her character arc progresses, she shows multi-faceted complexity, and it's clear she's one of the most self-actualized characters on the show. However, in true Gothic fashion, Charlie hesitates between the revolutionary and the conservative. She's allowed a complex and satisfying identity, but in the end, she meets the same clichéd fate of all the strong *Supernatural* women who have come before her.

Charlie Deconstructs Sexist Language

Charlie is the first female character to meta-commentate on the treatment of women in *Supernatural*, and by extension, in the horror/Gothic genre. Plenty of genre meta-commentary can be found before Charlie's presence, but she offers a fresh perspective from a female protagonist as she deconstructs sexist language and re-appropriates language usually used by male characters.

In one instance, Charlie deconstructs sexist language when Dean and Sam excitedly show her the magical Bunker left to them by the Men of Letters. Charlie speaks her mind, saying, "Too bad they got wiped out. Though, that is what they get for the sexist name" ("Pac-Man Fever," 8.20). Charlie's reference to the men who started "Men of Letters" overtly calls out their sexism for excluding women in their title. However, since the people who actually named the society are the writers of *Supernatural*, her comment offers a wink to the viewers who recognize they have been watching a male-slanted show for eight seasons. To some extent, Charlie's calling attention to the show's sexism makes the affront more forgivable, because the writers also write Charlie, and therefore, seem to be acknowledging their surface-level sexism.

Throughout the show, Charlie disrupts the usual use of female-gendered pejoratives. In every episode she says something to the effect of "What's up, bitches?" or "Later, bitches" or "Arrivederci, bitches!" ("The Girl with the Dungeons and Dragons Tattoo" [7.20], "LARP and the Real Girl" [8.11], "Pac-Man Fever"). The only other time a character affectionately uses the term "bitch" is when Dean derogatorily says it to Sam. Somehow, it has more power coming from Charlie because of her gender. Even though the term has been somewhat reclaimed by women, it's still uncommon for women to lovingly use the term to refer to men. Usually, it's a pejorative to describe men as weak or overly sensitive. But Charlie recontextualizes the term, using it affectionately and playfully.

Charlie also spins lines typically offered by male characters. For example, in "LARP and the Real Girl," when she learns that a fairy is being held against her will, Charlie says, "Gilda, my name is Charlie Bradbury, and I'm here to rescue you." The phrase is borrowed from *Star Wars: A New Hope* (1977), when Luke tells Leia, "I'm Luke Skywalker. I'm here to rescue you." It's not the first phrase that Charlie borrows and gender-bends from *Star Wars*. On two separate occasions, both her male coworker and a fellow LARPer tell her they love her, and she responds, "I know." The interaction is borrowed from a famous scene in *Star Wars: The Empire Strikes Back* (1980) when Leia tells Han Solo she loves him, and he confidently responds, "I know." The gender-swap in these interactions allows Charlie to be the one with the power and confidence in the exchange, rather than the damsel in distress, the bystander, or the passive object.

Charlie Undermines Gender Expectations

Charlie undermines stereotypical gender expectations in many ways. First, she's a character engrossed in "geeky" pop culture.[2] When Dean asks Charlie if she has any tattoos she can use to flirt with a guard, he says, "All tattoos are sexy." Charlie responds, "Mine is Princess Leia in a slave bikini straddling a 20-sided die" ("The Girl with the Dungeons and Dragons Tattoo"). Sam and Dean look at each other and decide maybe that's not *the* "sexy tattoo" to help them through this situation. Of course, there are many women who love "geek" culture as much as Charlie, but it's still a male-dominated space, and other female characters on the show don't exhibit such passion for their hobbies, besides the fans at the *Supernatural* convention, depicted as over-the-top, hysterical fangirl stereotypes who are out of touch with reality.

In addition to being engrossed in "geek" culture, which is usually gendered male, Charlie's profession undermines gendered tropes. In popular media, computer technologists, gamers, and coders are usually males. Not only does Charlie practice the art of computer programming, but she is also widely-accepted to be the best at it—by her peers and Dick Roman himself, leader of the Leviathans, who tells her: "Your spark—it's one in a million … 'cause I can feed every fact in your brain to someone else, and they still wouldn't be able to be you" ("The Girl with the Dungeons and Dragons Tattoo"). Whether keeping the company of hunters, angels, scientists, computer programmers, or super-villains, Charlie Bradbury is always regarded as the smartest person in the room.

Not only does Charlie comfortably inhabit male-centered spaces, but she undermines gender expectations with her sexuality itself. In "The Girl with the Dungeons and Dragons Tattoo," Sam and Dean assume Charlie to be heterosexual when they ask her to flirt with a security guard, because why wouldn't she be? It seems that every other female in the *Supernatural* universe until the seventh season has been heterosexual. Not only is Charlie a lesbian, she's comfortable bringing it up. She flirts with women, kisses women, and comments on trying to pick up women. As such, Charlie disrupts *Supernatural*'s overwhelming heteronormativity. Catering to fans, *Supernatural* hints and teases homosexual subtexts between various characters, but there aren't any overtly and outwardly homosexual characters, besides the couple cosplaying as Sam and Dean at a *Supernatural* convention, whose sexuality is mostly used as a punchline at the end of the episode, with Dean shivering from the incestuous implications. Charlie is our first depiction of guilt-free homosexuality that isn't simply the vehicle for a punchline or a discreet nod to fan slashfic. As such, she also completely avoids the typical heteronormative female role as potential love interest to the Winchesters.

Charlie Steers Her Narrative

Most of the *Supernatural* characters only exist insomuch as they orbit Sam and Dean Winchester. Typically, the show focuses on monster-of-the-week scenarios and utilitarian characters. Usually, the show does not pause on personality details or glimpses of supporting characters' lives. As noted by Patricia Brace, "In general, important women in the lives of Sam and Dean fall into three broad categories: mothers, lovers, and monsters" (84). This closely aligns with Sandra Gilbert and Susan Gubar's observations of the

Female Gothic. They note that typically, women in nineteenth-century stories were either confined to the "angel" narrative or the "monster," and even women writers tended to gravitate toward these tropes rather than attempt to "kill the aesthetic ideal through which they themselves have been 'killed' into art" (17).

In "The Girl with the Dungeons and Dragons Tattoo," Charlie is introduced with character details that aren't afforded to most characters on the show. She wears bright colors (including a pink Princess Leia t-shirt), she drives a yellow scooter, she dances to "Walking on Sunshine" in the elevator by herself, and her cubicle at work is splashed with action figures and comic book pages. We are even given details into her personal life: she breaks into Super-PACs for fun, and she picks up women at reproductive rights benefits. Her vibrant personality is impossible to ignore, and she peppers her dialogue with pop-culture references that include allusions to Harry Potter, *Lord of the Rings*, *War Games*, *Battlestar Galactica*, Indiana Jones, and *Star Trek*. In fact, when Charlie is present, she gets some of the best-written lines on the show, which are usually reserved for Sam, Dean, or Castiel. Prior to Charlie, we've only seen women in terms of their roles: hunters, thieves, demons, victims, or mothers. And we certainly haven't been given details like their taste in books and movies. We're given enough detail to understand how the women fit the larger narrative, but we do not linger to learn about their personalities, tastes, and passions. That changes with Charlie.

Not only does Charlie have a personality, she has goals, a drive, and a narrative separate from the Winchesters. Most of the female characters feel like pit stops for Sam and Dean, or fuel for their raison d'être. However, Charlie makes decisions that do not involve Sam or Dean. In "Slumber Party" (9.4), she decides to leave the Winchester narrative completely. She explains she's leaving because she wants more than the life of a hunter: "I was raised on Tolkien, man…. Where—where's my quest?" In other words, Charlie's reason for leaving does not revolve around hunting or the Winchesters—she wants adventures of her own. Unlike Sam and Dean, she is not defined by being a hunter. Yes, she hunts, but she's also a geek, a gamer, a reader, a hacker, a LARPer, and more. She wants to venture outside of the Winchesters' scope of experience and see what horizons can be discovered. Her gumption and drive take her to a whole other dimension, where even the Winchesters haven't visited, making her narrative arc truly unique in the *Supernatural* universe and even a rarity in Gothic horror, wherein most women are helplessly acted upon rather than action-oriented (Hanson 49). Before leaving the Winchesters for Oz, Charlie asks, "You gonna be all right without me?" This may sound like an ironic question coming from any other female character on the show, but coming from Charlie, it seems sincere. After all, she has personally saved the day (and their lives) several times.

Charlie Saves the Day (Repeatedly)

It's rare for a female character in *Supernatural* to save the day. Because the Winchester brothers are the heroes, they are typically the characters to solve the puzzles and save the victims. As mentioned earlier, Mary Borsellino has commented on the general ineffectiveness of *Supernatural's* female characters. Of course, Borsellino made this statement when only three seasons of the show had been aired, so the show obviously had a long road ahead of it. But even as the story continues through the first six seasons, Borsellino's remarks hold true. It's rare to find female characters who have an impact on an episode arc—let alone a season arc. In fact, in most of the episodes, the female victim who the Winchesters try to help could die, and it wouldn't affect the outcome of the show or the episode—other than the Winchesters being sad and feeling guilty. This changes when Charlie comes along, at least until Charlie's presumed final episode.

Charlie saves the Winchester brothers on at least three separate occasions. The first time, she serves a vital role in saving the entire world. When we meet Charlie in "The Girl with the Dungeons and Dragons Tattoo," she learns monsters are real, discovers the dark intentions of Leviathans, and risks her life when she holds her own against the Big Bad of the season. When confronted with the new, the scary, and the supernatural, she meets each challenge head-on and does things she's never done before, including breaking into a building and stealing information from a dangerous monster. This is virtually unprecedented because most of the women Sam and Dean come across simply ask for help and hide, or they're already indoctrinated in the ways of hunting. But Charlie is coming into this world fresh—and she quickly learns to not only adapt and save herself but to save everyone else.

The second time Charlie saves the Winchesters is in "LARP and the Real Girl," and this time Charlie does all the saving single-handedly. The usual Winchester episode arc is flipped on its head when, instead of the Winchesters swooping in and saving the girl, Charlie saves herself, a damsel in distress, and saves the boys while she's at it. In fact, the Winchesters aren't the ones to solve the episode puzzle (as per usual). Instead, Charlie discovers that they're dealing with a fairy being held against her will by Boltar. And right on cue, Charlie reassures the fairy that she's there to rescue her, stealing the line usually reserved for male action stars. Most importantly, Charlie destroys the book that's holding the fairy hostage—just before Sam and Dean are about to be killed. Before doing so she says, "I'm the one who saves damsels in distress around here," just in case there was any question about who was saving the day. Charlie even steals the end-of-episode kiss, typically reserved for the heterosexual couple at the end of an adventure story.

When Charlie saves the day the third time, it's again without the help of Sam or Dean, and she kills the Wicked Witch of the West with the help of Dorothy ("Slumber Party"). While Sam and Dean are possessed by the evil witch's magic, it's up to Dorothy to physically hold them at bay, while Charlie hunts down the witch and kills her by stabbing her with a ruby slipper—weaponizing a symbol of femininity and using it as a source of power, rather than a cage of societal expectations. After killing the witch, Charlie confidently quips, "Ding dong, bitches," calling attention to the fact that it's Charlie who saves the day and Charlie who gets the snarky hero line after killing the villain.

Charlie Accepts Herself

While Sam and Dean attempt to navigate dichotomies within themselves, Charlie transcends such strident thinking and instead accepts all the parts of herself. Sam and Dean's lives are determined by black and white, binary categories. Their entire reason for hunting—and living—is their ability to separate "good" from "evil." In most circumstances in the show, this is fairly straightforward. There are some outlier cases, such as Benny Lafitte, the brotherly vampire, but for the most part, good and evil are easily labeled and separated.

Supernatural's clear boundaries between "good" and "evil" make it difficult for Sam and Dean to process some of their own qualities. Both characters become easily distraught and self-flagellating when faced with personal dilemma because for them there are only two options, and if they're doing one thing that may be incidentally evil, then they must be personally evil. This is why, when confronted with personal moral dilemmas, Sam and Dean concur that there's something wrong with them or that the world would be better off without them, rather than recognizing the truth: that there is good and evil in us all, and that's what makes the world both frightening and comforting.

Aside from the categories of "good" and "evil," the Winchesters live by other dichotomies, such as straight/queer, male/female, and self/other. Again, for the most part, these categories are presented in a tidy way. However, in any context, seemingly oppositional forces are not so easily upheld. Jerrold Hogle suggests: "The reason that Gothic others or spaces can abject myriad cultural and psychological contradictions, and thereby confront us with those anomalies in disguise, is because those spectral characters, images, and settings harbor the hidden reality that oppositions of all kinds cannot maintain their separations, that each 'lesser term' is contained in its counterpart" (11). The only way to move toward personal "wholeness" or what psychologist Carl Jung calls "individuation," is to accept all the parts of the self—even those parts that seem to contradict one another or the parts that seem "lesser"—to become a well-functioning whole. For Dean and Sam, that means embracing and acknowledging both the good and bad within themselves, and it means acknowledging both the masculine and feminine qualities within themselves and seeing both as essential, despite their adherence to stereotypical, blue-collar masculinity and Dean's aversion to what he calls "chick flick moments." Throughout the series, the Winchesters fail to move toward wholeness. In fact, the only character on the show who seems to have achieved a sophisticated sense of self is Charlie.

At first, Charlie may seem like a deceptively simple character. Her unyielding optimism and upbeat attitude could be interpreted as saccharine, untrue to real life, or playing into the trope of the subservient female character with the smile on her face, rain or shine. However, Charlie is more than her surface-level smiles. She has literally met the dark side of herself, and she doesn't suppress it or hate herself for it—she recognizes it, accepts it, and moves on.

In "There's No Place Like Home" (10.11), Charlie's self is divided into two halves: "Good Charlie" and "Dark Charlie," which deconstruct the dichotomy of good and evil. Good Charlie can't hurt a fly, seems to utterly lack a sex drive, and can't do what she does best—hacking—because it's "bad." On the other hand, Dark Charlie is snarky, focused, and ultra-violent—Dean calls her a ninja and Good Charlie admits, "She is a badass." As Sam and Dean dig into Charlie's history to try to help her two halves become whole again, the brothers find an old psychiatrist's file that says Charlie suffered from "anti-authority disorder, clinical depression, and violent outbursts" as a teenager. This unveils a different side to Charlie, who's usually unrelentingly positive in the face of evil, cracking jokes and forcing hugs.

Although Dark Charlie hurts Sam and Dean, looks for trouble, and even kills someone, Good Charlie acknowledges that she needs her other half. Good Charlie says, "Let me just tell you, being good is really annoying." She can't hack into anything or hit on the female bartender—there's a vital part of Charlie's selfhood that's missing. Good Charlie admits, "I keep calling her 'she' but she's me." Dean disagrees, but he misses the point. Dark Charlie is part of Charlie, just as much as Good Charlie is part of Charlie, and it's only by merging the two that Charlie can be made whole again.

Once Charlie is back to herself, she makes simple and profound statements that summarize the moral of her narrative for the episode. When Sam asks Charlie about Dark Charlie, she says, "I just got to keep moving forward. We all do." She doesn't wrack herself with guilt, tell them that the world would be better off without her, or go on a suicide mission. She acknowledges that the only thing she can do is accept herself and move on. Charlie also tells Dean that she forgives him for beating up Dark Charlie, and by extension, her. When Dean tells her he can't forgive himself, Charlie replies, "I know. Kind of your move. How's that working out for you, huh?" The implication is that if Charlie can accept both the good and the bad within herself, forgive herself for beating up Sam and Dean, and becoming a murderer, Dean should be able to follow in her footsteps toward wholeness.

Conclusion

Given all the strides that Charlie's character makes, it's disappointing that she meets a similar demise to the other female characters on *Supernatural*. Mary Borsellino concludes, "You can take the girl out of the grave, but in the end *Supernatural* always puts her right back in her place, six feet under" (116). Unfortunately, that seems to be the case with Charlie. While many of the main male characters can visit Heaven, Hell, and Purgatory and still rise from the dead, Charlie's bones are burned—signifying that she won't be coming back.

Most disappointing is the way in which Charlie dies, losing her wits and regressing to the stereotypical female horror victim and not unlike nineteenth-century Gothic heroines, playing second-fiddle in a patriarchal narrative. In "Dark Dynasty" (10.21), Charlie separates herself from the group—even after Sam and Dean repeatedly warn her not to do so—violating rule number one for staying alive in a horror narrative. Without thinking ahead and knowing that the Stynes are looking for her, she goes back to her hotel room, where she is cornered in the bathroom and killed in the shower—much like many female horror victims that have come before her, starting with *Psycho* (1960). For all of Charlie's progressive qualities, her death unfortunately fulfills many stereotypical portrayals of female horror victims.

While her final scene invokes regressive tropes, Charlie Bradbury dies a heroine. Right before her demise, she single-handedly cracks the codex to translate the *Book of the Damned*, ultimately freeing Dean from the curse of the Mark of Cain—a task that no other character could do, even the powerful witch Rowena. In an attempt to avoid her fate, Charlie could have listened to Dean's pleadings over the phone and given her codex notes to the Stynes, but she remains true to her convictions, simply telling Dean with her last words, "I can't do that," using her final moments to send her notes to Sam. Indeed, Charlie's final act is to save the day—and presumably Dean's life—one last time. In true Gothic form, Charlie could be labeled a sacrificial angel or a progressive hero, but either way, she meets her fate off-screen—no snarky hero line or struggle shown. Jerrold Hogle says: "No other form of writing or theatre is as insistent as Gothic on juxtaposing potential revolution and possible reaction—about gender, sexuality, race, class, the colonizers versus the colonized, the physical versus the metaphysical, and abnormal versus normal psychology—and leaving both extremes sharply before us and far less resolved than the conventional endings in most of these works claim them to be" (13). Charlie's final scenes seem to firmly place her in the position of a complicated, hard-to-define as revolutionary or regressive Gothic heroine. Perhaps disappointingly, she doesn't die fighting with her katana in hand or spouting her spitfire quips. However, she does die a hero—one who sacrifices herself for the Winchesters—but also one who complicates and adds to the portrayal of women in *Supernatural*, horror, and popular culture.

Notes

1. In "Buffy the Vampire Slayer, Jo the Monster Killer: *Supernatural*'s Excluded Heroines," Mary Borsellino discusses the contentious characterization of hunters Ellen and Jo Harvelle. Though originally conceived as strong female figures, both characters ultimately follow the fates of other women on the show.

2. In addition to Charlie Bradbury being engrossed in geek culture, it's significant that Felicia Day plays the character. Author of *You're Never Weird on the Internet (Almost)* (2015) and founder of the YouTube Channel and multimedia production company Geek & Sundry, Felicia Day is self-regarded and mentioned in popular media as "the queen of geeks." She has earned that title in part due to her web series *The Guild* (2007–2013), which she wrote, starred in, and produced, loosely basing the series on her own experiences as a gamer. Because of her reputation, Felicia Day brings depth to Charlie Bradbury in a way that no other actor could.

Works Cited

Borsellino, Mary. "Buffy the Vampire Slayer, Jo the Monster Killer: *Supernatural*'s Excluded Heroines." *In the Hunt: Unauthorized Essays on Supernatural.* Ed. Leah Wilson. Dallas: Benbella, 2009. 107–118. Print.

Brace, Patricia. "Mothers, Lovers, and Other Monsters: The Women of *Supernatural*." *Supernatural and Philosophy: Metaphysics and Monsters … for Idjits.* Ed. Galen A. Foresman. West Sussex, UK: Wiley Blackwell, 2013. 83–94. Print.

Clover, Carol. *Men, Women, and Chain Saws: Gender in the Modern Horror Film*, 2d ed. Princeton: Princeton University Press, 2015. Print.

"Dark Dynasty." *Supernatural.* Writ. Eugenie Ross-Leming and Brad Buckner. Dir. Robert Singer. Perf. Jensen Ackles and Jared Padalecki. CW Network, 6 May 2015. *Hulu.* Web. 8 May 2015.

Day, Felicia. *You're Never Weird on the Internet (Almost).* New York: Touchstone, 2015. Print.

Gilbert, Sandra, and Susan Gubar. *Feminist Literary Theory and Criticism: A Norton Reader.* New York: Norton, 2007. Print.

_____. *The Madwoman in the Attic: The Woman Writer and the Nineteenth-century Literary Imagination*, 2d ed. New Haven: Yale Nota Bene, 2000. Print.

"The Girl with the Dungeons and Dragons Tattoo." *Supernatural.* Writ. Robbie Thompson. Dir. John MacCarthy. Perf. Jensen Ackles and Jared Padalecki. CW Network, 27 April 2012. *Netflix.* Web. 28 March 2015.

Hanson, Helen. *Hollywood Heroines: Women in Film Noir and the Female Gothic Film.* London: I. B. Tauris, 2007. Print.

Heiland, Donna. *Gothic and Gender: An Introduction.* Oxford: Blackwell, 2004. Print.

Hogle, Jerrold E. "Introduction." *The Cambridge Companion to Gothic Fiction*. Ed. Jerrold E. Hogle. Cambridge: Cambridge University Press, 2014. 1–20. Print.

Jung, Carl Gustav. *Psychological Types: Or the Psychology of Individuation*. Trans. Godwin Baynes and B.C. Cantab. London: Kegan Paul, Trench, Trubner & Co., 1946. Print.

"LARP and the Real Girl." *Supernatural*. Writ. Robbie Thompson. Dir. Jeannot Szwarc. Perf. Jensen Ackles and Jared Padalecki. CW Network, 23 January 2013. *Netflix*. Web. 28 March 2015.

Moers, Ellen. *Literary Women*. Garden City, NY: Anchor, 1977. Print.

"Pac-Man Fever." *Supernatural*. Writ. Robbie Thompson. Dir. Robert Singer. Perf. Jensen Ackles and Jared Padalecki. CW Network, 24 April 2013. *Netflix*. Web. 29 March 2015.

"Slumber Party." *Supernatural*. Writ. Robbie Thompson. Dir. Robert Singer. Perf. Jensen Ackles and Jared Padalecki. CW Network, 29 October 2013. *Netflix*. Web. 29 March 2015.

"There's No Place Like Home." *Supernatural*. Writ. Robbie Thompson. Dir. Phil Sgriccia. Perf. Jensen Ackles and Jared Padalecki. CW Network, 27 January 2015. *Hulu*. Web. 29 January 2015.

PART 4

Gothic Others: Monstrous Selves

"We've all been demons"
Postmodern Gothic and the Fragmented Self

Jessica Seymour

One of the most interesting things about watching *Supernatural* is seeing the characters grow and change over the series. These personality changes reflect the postmodern Gothic convention of the fragmented self, which changes or splits characters' personalities, and harkens back to the literary traditions of Dr. Jekyll and Mr. Hyde. Frequently, characters fragment into darker, more murderous versions of themselves. *Supernatural* also explores the opposite personality change by examining antagonists who grow and become more empathetic and "human" through prolonged interaction with the Winchesters. The demons Crowley and Meg, and the angels Gabriel and Balthazar are each irrevocably changed when they interact with the Winchesters—although this is not always necessarily a good thing for the characters.

According to Heinz Kohut's theory of self psychology, the self is a psychological structure, with the "structure" suggesting stability across time. It's the individual's experience of selfhood. When this structure becomes unstable the self becomes fragmented. Kohut's ideas extended Donald Winnicott's idea of the "true" and "false" self; the "true" self is based on spontaneous authentic experience, while the "false" self acts as a façade—usually as a defensive response or learned behavior. Kohut argued that it is more rewarding to identify the damaged remnants of the self, to understand the structure of an individual's self even when the structure becomes unstable, than to identify with an external personality or false self that does not have the support of a psychological structure. Essentially, the "true" self, no matter how damaged, is structurally the same regardless of the various forms it takes. The self can be fragmented, but remains the self.

Kohut's discussions of the structure of the self are particularly interesting when considering Robert Louis Stevenson's *The Strange Case of Dr. Jekyll and*

Mr. Hyde (1886). Rather than reinforcing the idea of a coherent identity, Stevenson challenges the concept by offering the reader a portrayal of an incoherent identity built around two separate individuals. Dr. Jekyll and Mr. Hyde are separate identities that exist in the same body. Hyde represents the suppressed aspects of Jekyll's personality, with the implication being that Hyde is the "true" self while Jekyll is the "false," socially conditioned façade. Although Hyde's characteristics do not appear when Jekyll is in control of the body they share, Jekyll feels guilty over the crimes committed when he wears the Hyde persona. In this way, the two personalities behave as a fragmented self because each personality carries the sins and self-loathing of the other; structurally, they come from the same space but they react in different ways.

Often, the concept of the fragmented self comes into play when considering portrayals of gender in Gothic texts. According to Carol Margaret Davison's analysis of the Victorian Gothic and gender, the Gothic genre lends itself particularly well to engagement with the concept of gender, particularly during the Victorian era, because of its "ability to tap deep-seated, sometimes repressed, desires and anxieties, coupled with its fixation on literal and symbolic transgressions" (126). This ability also suits Gothic texts when examining mental illness and disassociation. The fragmented self comes into play here because mental illness is framed as a secondary or "false" self that exists in opposition to the healthy self; the mentally ill self is an unhealthy doppelgänger to be removed or suppressed (Dawson 52). It is the disruption of expectations—the dismissal of the expected behaviors of the characters—as an expression of the fragmented self that is the focus of this essay.

The postmodern Gothic disrupts the idea of binary opposition—male/female, healthy/unhealthy—by creating a fragmented self which remains in a state of permanent flux. Ordinarily, the fragmented self depersonalizes aspects of identity (Dawson 52). It takes subconscious behaviors such as aggression and sexual deviance and externalizes them by associating them with a different self. This externalizing of the darker aspects of the self is discussed in Maria Beville's *Gothic-Postmodernism: Voicing the Terrors of Postmodernity* (2009), where she writes that

> the dark underside of humanity is put on display with all its hate, greed and prejudice laid bare…. Gothic discourse can subsequently be seen as giving a voice to this dark side of what could be termed our collective unconscious, firmly establishing it as an intrinsic part of our social consciousness. Although terrifying and horrible, this darker side is something that we must all accept and come to terms with, and this, arguably places the Gothic as a site of discourse in an essential role in contemporary social philosophy [42].

The important point to note here is that, while the darker aspects are externalized through the monstrous figures in a text, they are meant to serve as a reminder of the human responder's own potential toward monstrosity. The fragmented self divorces characters from their darker aspects while simultaneously making these darker aspects known—both to the characters and the audience.

In *Supernatural*, as a postmodern Gothic work, the fragmented self is hyper-personal. When characters become evil, soulless, demonic, or otherwise inhuman, they carry the sins of their dark selves (or their Hyde personas) when they change back to their original state. Their original psychological structure fractures, heals, and fractures again, but their Hyde doppelgänger remains a part of their identity. No character is completely the same after their change, and in some cases characters' personalities are irrevocably altered because they feel they must atone for the crimes their Hyde persona committed.

"It's human, more or less"

"Human" is considered the default state of selfhood in the *Supernatural* universe—with nonhumans representing the false, fragmented human self. Most nonhuman creatures in *Supernatural* were either originally human (vampires, demons, vengeful spirits, etc.) or feed off of humans as parasites (shifters, ghouls, etc.). In *Supernatural*, the human/nonhuman binary is present but indistinct, particularly when the characters become fragmented through continued exposure to other races or species. There are certain traits that are constructed as "human" traits—such as romantic love, compassion, a desire for autonomy and personal growth. Nonhumans, in contrast, exhibit traits such as sexual lust, blood-lust, and a lack of conscience. Nonhumans even have their own unique afterlife; while humans go to either Heaven or Hell when they die, nonhuman monsters are sent to Purgatory.

Hunters like Dean and Sam Winchester claim that there is a clear distinction between the human and the nonhuman, and in many genres these two states of being would act as a binary. In the postmodern Gothic, however, binaries are blurred and warped, and so humanity and inhumanity become located on a spectrum, and where a character sits on the spectrum becomes context-dependent. When Sam loses his soul in Season Six, he technically remains human but does not behave in a particularly human manner; in contrast, when he is addicted to demon blood during Seasons Three and Four, he becomes less human physically, but exhibits extremely human characteristics—jealousy, fear, a desire to protect his loved ones, and a certain level of self-assurance tempered with self-doubt. As Dean notes, Sam's fragmented self becomes increasingly difficult to categorize as the series progresses, and therefore difficult to categorize within Dean's absolutist worldview.

As the characters in the *Supernatural* series engage with members of other species (humans engaging with nonhumans, and vice versa) they learn and grow, but *fragmentation* occurs when characters are violated by the other group because in that case the characters have very little power over the resulting changes to their personality. These changes are therefore framed as unwanted and unnecessary. The *Supernatural* narrative does, however, make a distinction between the positive change from human to nonhuman (Jekyll to Hyde) and the negative change from nonhuman to human (Hyde to Jekyll).

Many human characters become their worst selves after contact with nonhumans. Sam's psychic abilities are a result of being fed demon blood as a child, and later he loses his soul after being rescued from the Cage. This change makes him a more efficient hunter, but a far less empathetic person, and this story arc concludes with the attempted murder of Bobby Singer. Dean's decision to take the Mark of Cain (after being manipulated by the demon Crowley) leads to his change into a demon in Season Ten. Dean's demonic self is characterized as a mixture of humorous and horrifying, and his change back to a human does not ease the murderous impulses that the Mark gives him. Charlie Bradbury, arguably the least violent character in the series, has her personality split in Season Ten after she returns from Oz. Her Hyde persona embodies her desire for vengeance and she subsequently murders the drunk driver who killed her parents.

In each case, the human characters find themselves questioning how the change during their Hyde phase reflects their Jekyll personality, and the resulting character development leads to a fragmented self. Similarly, nonhuman characters must question how much their fragmenting selves reflect their "true" nonhuman selves. Angels are an interesting nonhuman entity; they do not begin as human, but they are idealized by humans and are not considered monstrous (at least at the beginning of Season Four when they are introduced to the *Supernatural* mythology). Angels can be considered monstrous (from the malicious manipulation of humans by Zachariah, to the parasitic attachment of Tamiel) and clinically unemotional (as Castiel is when we first meet him). Neither of these are considered particularly human traits, and it is the abandonment of these perceived negative traits and the development of more human characteristics that signals their shift toward humanity.

"What are you, Castiel?"

Castiel has gone through a remarkable number of personality changes over the course of the series. He occupies a liminal space between angel and human, exhibiting traits for both. Apart from his slow fall from grace, he was a vessel for Leviathans, a god, lost his memory (Season Seven), was brainwashed (Season Eight), and temporarily became human (Season Nine). These frequent and significant changes have left a lasting impression on the character and his portrayed personality, and by the end of Season Ten he bears the characteristics of his various selves as a single, fragmented self who is neither completely human nor nonhuman. However, Castiel tries to retain as many human characteristics as possible.

Although angels are portrayed in *Supernatural* as unemotional and detached (immediately after their introduction) it is shown that this is a trained trait, not ingrained, as angels consistently demonstrate their ability to feel emotions and act on them regardless of whether they are connected to Heaven through their "grace." When Anna Milton removes her grace to become human, she does so because she claims that she couldn't feel anything in her angel state, but when she takes her grace back in "Heaven and Hell" (4.10), she still maintains an emotional connection with the Winchesters and, later, Castiel. Castiel's developing ability to feel emotions results from his continued interaction with the Winchesters.

Castiel begins the series as an angel of the lord, but his portrayal in the series is very different from the typical angels of popular culture: "Read the Bible. Angels are warriors of God. I'm a soldier.... I'm not here to perch on your shoulder" ("Are You There, God? It's Me, Dean Winchester," 4.2). He follows orders without question and although he is more sympathetic to humans than other angels he is still, as Dean puts it, a "dick." Castiel's characterization includes human and nonhuman characteristics. He is pragmatic, but optimistic; he is willing to kill, but is clearly uncomfortable with Uriel's methods of "purification"; he protects Dean, and threatens him: "You should show me some respect. I dragged you out of Hell. I can throw you back in" (4.2). It is his exposure to the Winchesters that leads to his rebellion against the other angels in Heaven and his fall from grace. It is established in "Heaven and Hell" that rebellion is the angels' "murder one" when Castiel and Uriel are sent to kill the now-human Anna. The fact that Castiel later asks Anna for guidance in his own rebellion demonstrates the extent to which Castiel is betraying his own kind for the sake of the Winchesters and the humanity they represent.

Castiel becomes more "human" over the course of the series; although he is clearly sympathetic to humanity in a way that other angels are not, there is a clear progression in his emotional range as he and the Winchesters interact more frequently. One of the main identifying traits of angels is their desire to follow orders. They are taught to view personal autonomy with suspicion. Angels who exercise autonomy and defy their holy orders, such as Uriel, are generally portrayed negatively (unless their defiance is fueled by a desire to protect or join humanity, like Anna, in which case the portrayal is more positive). When Castiel and Uriel are ordered to follow Dean's instructions in

"It's the Great Pumpkin, Sam Winchester" (4.7), Castiel does not warn Dean that this is happening or try to force his decision because this would skew the results of the experiment. At this point in the series, Castiel is a good angel, and a good soldier, because he does not try to exercise autonomy. Through continued exposure to "Team Free Will," however, Castiel begins to recognize the power he has as a free agent and eventually chooses to fall from grace.

Unlike Sam, Dean, and Charlie, Castiel begins the series as a nonhuman, which brings up some interesting questions about where Castiel sits on the Jekyll/Hyde spectrum because Castiel himself represents a fragment of Jimmy Novak. Jimmy is a human whose body is used as a vessel for Castiel because angels cannot take physical form on Earth. Jimmy's ability to act as a vessel for Castiel (and specifically Castiel, as it seems only certain vessels can be used for certain angels) indicates that they share some core values and traits in order to be compatible, so it is reasonable to consider Castiel to be an extension of Jimmy's character. Castiel, like all angels, required consent before he could inhabit Jimmy's body, but as the show progresses, viewers get the impression that if Jimmy had known what Castiel planned to do he would not have consented so easily. Although Castiel justifies his use of Jimmy's body by saying that Jimmy was "devout" and prayed to be used as a vessel ("Lazarus Rising," 4.1), the fact remains that while Castiel wears Jimmy's face he causes significant damage in Jimmy's personal life and, eventually, condemns Jimmy to a lifetime of torment and eventual death when his body is destroyed at the end of Season Five (only to be brought back again). In this way, Castiel acts as a Mr. Hyde figure despite the fact that he is not actively evil.

Castiel develops more emotional engagement as the series progresses, but his fragmented self—the disrupted psychological structure upon which his self is constructed—is a result of violations or manipulations of his character. In Season Six, he is manipulated into working with Crowley. He convinces himself that this is the right thing to do, but it disrupts his sense of self because it forces him to recognize how far he is willing to go to defeat the angel Raphael. His body is then used by the Leviathans to enter the world in Season Seven, but not before he gets a boost of power that briefly makes him a god. This creates a massive personality change and a subsequent aspect of guilt. Although he is not really "himself" when the Leviathans take his body, he carries the responsibility of his actions at that time because even though his self has been fragmented, it is still *his* self, his consciousness remains intact.

When Castiel loses his memory and later takes on Sam's psychosis in Season Seven (which is recounted in the fittingly entitled episode "The Born-Again Identity," 7.17) and is brainwashed in Season Eight, he is again forced to become another version of his self (a "false" self), which he then incorporates into his idea of his own selfhood. The subsequent fragmented self that Castiel embodies is more "human" because, since he has worn so many personalities, he has learned to embody the human traits such as romantic love, compassion, a desire for autonomy, and personal growth. He tells Jimmy Novak's daughter Claire in "The Things We Left Behind" (10.09) that he has discovered there is no "righteous path … just people trying to do their best in a world where it's far too easy to do your worst." He has abandoned his angelic self-assurance and adopted a fragmented human stoicism in an imperfect world.

This physical and mental dislocation from who he was and who he has become makes Castiel a particularly interesting character from a postmodern perspective. There is a fluidity to the character, born from years of fragmentation, and this has led to an expression of selfhood that is constantly in flux but always "true." His fragmented self can change and adapt to suit the needs of the characters around him. He is a brother to the angels, but he also acts as an honorary brother to the Winchesters, forcing him to alter his "brother" persona as needed to accommodate the expectations of these different families. His physical self remains largely separate from these mental selves and the expectations different characters have of him. This is similarly the case for the Novak family—physically, he looks like Jimmy Novak, but he behaves so differently that the physical and mental dislocation of the character is particularly jarring for those characters who knew Jimmy before Castiel took possession of his body. The angels and Death can feel the physical changes wrought upon his vessel, but Sam and Dean insist that he remains Castiel no matter how many times his self fragments. As two characters who are similarly a conglomeration of fragmented selves, Sam and Dean are in a good position to judge Castiel's continued selfhood.

Castiel's Hyde persona has evolved into a Jekyll, and this is ultimately framed within the narrative as a good change. Castiel is not the only angel who evolved from a Mr. Hyde to a Dr. Jekyll, but his evolution is the most structurally interesting because of the fragmentation of his character. Other angels who change do not fragment quite so violently as they make their way from nonhuman to human.

"I'm officially on your team, you bastards"

Balthazar and Gabriel are interesting characters in the *Supernatural* universe because they are not entirely antagonistic, but they do fill the role of antagonist in a number of episodes. They are not malicious in the sense that their intention is to amuse themselves, with harm to humans being a byproduct of their amusement. As was the case with Castiel, Balthazar and Gabriel occupy vessel bodies and as a result could be considered Mr. Hyde figures.

Their vessels are not named (and as a result dehumanized and objectified) and the various humans who encounter Balthazar and Gabriel in the early stages of their respective character arcs are primarily used for entertainment. It is only through repeated interaction with the Winchesters that Balthazar and Gabriel, like their fellow angel Castiel, become more compassionate toward humanity and their Mr. Hyde personalities develop into Dr. Jekylls.

Gabriel hides on Earth by pretending to be the Trickster who delights in tormenting humans. He adheres to a moral code, only attacking those humans who he feels deserve it, but he cannot be considered "good" by the standards of human characters because he kills humans for fun. In "Tall Tales" (2.15), he claims that he does not kill the Winchesters—despite the fact that they frequently try to kill him—because he likes them. Later, during the Season Five episode "Changing Channels" (5.8), the audience learns that the Trickster is really the archangel Gabriel, and that he had taken an interest in Sam and Dean because they are vessels for the archangels Michael and Lucifer. He does not, however, care about the safety of other humans or the world as a whole, saying, "Heaven, Hell, I don't care who wins, I just want it to be over" (5.8). After a discussion with the Winchesters and Castiel, however, he begins to reconsider his priorities—and who he really cares about in the grand scheme of things.

It is difficult to argue that Gabriel's self is fragmented, because his psychological structure is not disrupted or attacked in the way that the humans Sam, Dean, and Charlie, and the angel Castiel, are disrupted. In fact, I would argue that this is less of a fragmentation and more of a restoration. Gabriel's self is fragmented when he meets Sam and Dean in Season Two. He behaves as a nonhuman, but he embodies the opposite nonhuman traits that angels embody. It appears that he has done everything possible to distance himself from his angelic past, and this has disrupted his psychological structure by forcing an archangel (a soldier for Heaven and a brother to thousands of angels) into the persona of Trickster (a decadent, sexual being who desires immediate amusement). Engaging with the values of humans, and to an extent the fragmented, humanized Castiel, allows Gabriel to heal and realign his priorities so that he can choose to fight for the humans in "Hammer of the Gods" (5.19).

In one of his final scenes of Season Five, Gabriel fights Lucifer to give the Winchesters time to escape. During this fight, he allies himself firmly with humanity, telling Lucifer that he wants to be on the side of the humans because "they're flawed. But a lot of them try. To do better, to forgive" (5.19). Although the humans are "flawed," they are held in the *Supernatural* narrative to be the ideal state of selfhood. By allying himself with humanity, Gabriel heals his fragmented self and prioritizes the human traits of compassion (he saves the goddess Kali and sends her away with the Winchesters) and personal growth.

Balthazar begins his narrative arc as a similarly fragmented angel who is rebelling against his angelic self. Balthazar is an interesting case among the angel characters because he is introduced to the audience as an angel but exhibits several human characteristics, including fear, joy, and sexual desire. He has a sense of humor and enjoys playing with humans in a similar way to Gabriel in his Trickster persona. He explains during "The Third Man" (6.3) that his desire to hide from other angels and enjoy his rebellion was triggered by seeing Castiel rebel with minimal consequences. His psychological structure has been disrupted, and Balthazar is a fragmented version of his original self. It is important that Balthazar waited until after another angel rebelled, because it demonstrates his character's desire for self-preservation—a nonhuman trait, as many of the (good) human characters are more self-sacrificing as a rule. This shows that, although Balthazar exhibits human characteristics, he is still very much a dick (to borrow Dean's words) and nonhuman in every sense that matters.

Balthazar is shown intentionally putting human characters in danger, particularly the Winchesters who make good "marmosets" to distract other angels with ("The French Mistake," 6.15). Despite this, he chooses to ally himself with Castiel almost immediately. He works with Castiel to fight Raphael, even going back in time to save the *Titanic* in "My Heart Will Go On" (6.17) in order to get more souls for Castiel's war machine. Despite his alliance with Castiel (and by extension, Castiel's values), Balthazar distances himself from the potential to be considered human. When Dean reprimands him for his nonchalant attitude to the potential dangers to descendants of the *Titanic* survivors, Balthazar responds: "Oh, sorry, you have me confused with the other angel.... I don't care" (6.17). He separates himself from the more humanized Castiel at the same time that he is allied with him.

Despite this, Balthazar does eventually join the Winchesters against Castiel in "Let it Bleed" (6.21). Although he claims that this switch is not because he has a "shred of decency," he clearly has a moral center because it is the knowledge that Castiel has allied with the demon Crowley that leads him to turn on his fellow angel. He does not agree with this decision, and he also doesn't agree with the potentially dangerous plan to have Castiel ingest the souls of Purgatory. Later, Balthazar refers to Castiel as his friend in "The Man Who Knew Too Much" (6.22). It could be argued that his decision to turn against Castiel could have been motivated by a desire to protect Castiel from going past the point of no return. When Castiel turns on Balthazar and kills him, the camera zooms in on Balthazar's shocked, saddened face. As he dies, Balthazar uses the name Castiel's friends use—"Cas"—to indicate the depth of Castiel's betrayal and Balthazar's belief that they were friends before Castiel (literally) stabs him in the back.

Like Gabriel, Balthazar allies with humanity against his fellow angels because "human" is the ideal state of selfhood in *Supernatural*, and by choosing to ally with the humans these angels have evolved from their fragmented state of selfhood to a state with a more secure psychological structure. Both of the angels die almost immediately after allying with the humans, but they die as Dr. Jekyll rather than Mr. Hyde.

"Not all demons are the same"

In the beginning of *Supernatural*, there are no good demons. If angels occupy a liminal space, bearing traits of human characters and nonhuman characters, then demons are typically portrayed as occupying a singularly evil space. There are exceptions, notably Casey from the episode "Sin City" (3.4), who claims to have never killed anyone and begs her lover to spare Dean Winchester, but the general rule of demonic characterization in the series is that they are irredeemably evil. Redeemed demons are difficult to accept (and trust) for viewers of the *Supernatural* series since Ruby's betrayal in "Lucifer Rising" (4.22). Both the characters on the show and the viewers are suspicious of any demon who seems to have changed their personality and motivations, because as numerous story arcs have proved, such a change is usually only temporary or illusory.

Two demons, however, occupy the liminal space between good and evil by embodying several human traits and eventually allying themselves with the humans: Meg and Crowley. Although neither of these characters can be considered completely "good," they do good things and help the Winchesters in repeated interactions with the brothers. Meg grows closer to the Winchesters through their mutual interest in defeating Crowley, while Crowley is forced to become more human as part of the Winchesters' attempts to close the Gates of Hell in Season Eight, and becomes addicted to the feeling of being human as a result. While both demon characters behave more compassionately as a result of their developing humanity, their change in personality is framed as having an ultimately negative effect on these characters but a positive effect on the narrative as a whole.

As was the case with the angel characters, the demons can exist in the human world by taking human vessels (which they derogatively call "meat-suits"). Demons were originally human souls who were twisted by Hell until there is very little humanity left in them. Because of this, the demon characters embody a Mr. Hyde persona when they are introduced to the audience, because they are their worst selves. These selves have fragmented so badly that their psychological structure is unrecognizable. Meg's fragmented self is healed and humanized through her interactions with the Winchesters and Castiel, while Crowley's self is fragmented further as a result of his adopting human traits.

Meg is initially motivated by loyalty to a cause—Lucifer's cause. When Lucifer is trapped in the Cage, she transfers her energy and zeal into killing those who betrayed him, which allies her with the Winchesters and Castiel because they have the same goals. In this case, she is still motivated by vengeance, which is a human trait, but not a particularly commendable one. At first, her alliance with Sam, Dean, and Castiel is tenuous and she still makes morally repugnant choices, such as planning to leave her meatsuit (a budding actress) to be torn apart by hellhounds in "Caged Heat" (6.10) in order to give the Winchesters a chance to capture Crowley. Although she is ultimately unable to do this, the fact that she had planned to is telling of her character's priorities and moral code.

After Castiel takes Sam's memories from the Cage in "The Born-Again Identity" and becomes mentally traumatized in the process, Meg watches over Castiel in the psychiatric ward because he is still a valuable asset. However, her time with Castiel, caring for him and protecting him, clearly has an effect on Meg. She remains with Castiel or in his vicinity for the remainder of the season and ultimately leads the charge against Dick Roman and the Leviathans in "Survival of the Fittest" (7.23). Her interactions with Castiel (based in a romantic subplot between the two) allow her to see human traits and exhibit some of her own.

In her final episode, "Goodbye Stranger" (8.17), Meg had progressed from completely evil, to "kind of good." She claims to miss the Apocalypse because it was a simpler time, when her decisions were free of moral consequences. While she is imprisoned by Crowley, she is frequently tortured and deliberately sends the demons to kill innocent humans to give herself time to devise an escape. When Sam exhibits disgust that Meg would allow people to be killed, Meg replies sarcastically: "Hi, I'm Meg. I'm a demon" (8.17). Regardless, later in the episode she sacrifices herself to Crowley to give the Winchesters and Castiel time to obtain the Angel Tablet and escape.

This is in direct contrast to her earlier "sacrifice" in "Caged Heat," where she only stayed to fight because she couldn't abandon her meatsuit. In "Goodbye Stranger," she makes a conscious decision to defend the Winchesters, sending Sam to warn Dean and Castiel while she distracts Crowley, with the knowledge that she may not survive the confrontation. She is also not surprised or even upset to see the Winchesters abandoning her at the end of the episode. This is justified by a hinted romance between Meg and Castiel, who Meg refers to as her "unicorn" (a reference to her earlier discussion with Sam, when she refers to his ex-girlfriend as a unicorn because she was special enough to make Sam consider giving up his life as a hunter), and her desire to kill Crowley and avenge Lucifer is framed as secondary to that romance. Castiel replaces her former mission for Lucifer and gives her something new to believe in and fight for. Her compassion and possible romantic love humanizes her in her final moments.

While Meg reclaims her humanity and heals her conflicted self, Crowley remains fragmented and simply becomes *more* fragmented through his interactions with the Winchesters. When he was human, Fergus Roderick MacLeod sold his soul and was sent to Hell. During his time there, his psychological structure was damaged and he reinvents himself as Crowley. Unlike Meg, who simply assumed the identity of the first girl she possessed and didn't have a "demon" name of her own, Crowley builds his identity and sense of self around his divided psychological structure. This essentially renders his fragmented self as a new "true" self, as he is quite comfortable in this identity. His interactions with the Winchesters violate this identity when they forcibly inject him with human blood in an attempt to "cure" his demonic self and return him to the ideal human state.

The audience first meets Crowley in "Abandon All Hope" (5.10), as the King of the Crossroads. While he is King of the Crossroads, he punishes demons who try to take advantage of loopholes in the contracts they make. Initially his alliance with the Winchesters is a marriage of convenience, yet despite being a demon, he is remarkably honest, and always keeps his bargains. Also, like Meg, Crowley displays more loyalty than the average demon and is not prone to betraying the people he makes deals with, particularly the Winchesters.

Regardless, Crowley is still a demon. When Sam and Dean need a demon to cure as part of the ritual to close the Gates of Hell, they capture Crowley and begin to periodically inject him with human blood. Crowley initially finds this laughable, but after an altercation with Abaddon, a Knight of Hell, Crowley has a brief monologue where he becomes increasingly upset when Sam doesn't share a sense of camaraderie with him, saying: "We just shared a foxhole, you and I…And still you're gonna do me like this?" ("Sacrifice," 8.23). Just as Balthazar was shocked and saddened when Castiel betrayed him, Crowley is shocked and saddened when Sam goes back to injecting Crowley with human blood despite their brief alliance against Abaddon. This is a very human response and confirms that the blood is working to bring out long repressed emotions in Crowley. Later, he appears to be considering how he will live a human life and then willingly bares his neck so that Sam can inject him with the next dose of blood.

Sam is interrupted before he can completely cure Crowley, but Crowley has already been irrevocably changed. He has been infected with humanity. Early in Season Nine, Crowley escapes the Winchesters and becomes addicted to human blood; he takes human victims and injects himself with their blood and watches sad movies. The human blood gives him the ability to feel empathy, which disrupts his psychological structure and fragments his sense of self. He was a happy Mr. Hyde, and now he is a vulnerable Dr. Jekyll.

"You have that thing, that spark that makes humans so special"

Supernatural approaches the fragmented self through a number of characters (with humanity acting as the ideal state of personhood) and calls into question how personal identity can be constructed and shaped by the world around us. As each of the Mr. Hyde figures discussed above become more "human," they also become more vulnerable. Balthazar and Gabriel are killed within moments of openly allying with the Winchesters/humanity, Meg dies protecting the brothers from Crowley, and Crowley's blood addiction weakens his hold over the masses of Hell and leaves him susceptible to manipulation. Crowley's most "human" trait is arguably the affection he feels for Dean and his son Gavin MacLeod, which leaves him open to the manipulations of Abaddon ("King of the Damned," 9.21), Dean ("Brother's Keeper," 10.23), and even his own mother (and what does it say about the state of Dean's fragmented self that he is less trustworthy than the King of Hell?). In *Supernatural*, humanity appears to be a dangerous state of being when it is not naturally a part of someone. When a human character fragments, there is a clear negative result—both in the narrative and in the character. When a nonhuman character becomes more human, there is a clear negative result to the character, but generally speaking a positive result to the narrative. It seems that even if being human is not always safe, it is always *good*—if not for the character, then for the rest of the world.

Works Cited

"Are You There God, It's Me, Dean Winchester." *Supernatural: The Complete Fourth Season*. Writ. Sera Gamble. Dir. Phil Sgriccia. Perf. Jensen Ackles and Jared Padalecki. Warner Bros., 2009. DVD.

Beville, Maria. *Gothic-Postmodernism: Voicing the Terrors of Postmodernity*. Amsterdam: Rodopi, 2009. Web.

"Changing Channels." *Supernatural: The Complete Fifth Season*. Writ. Jeremy Carver. Dir. Charles Beeson. Perf. Jensen Ackles and Jared Padalecki. Warner Bros., 2010. DVD.

Davison, Carol Margaret. "The Victorian Gothic and Gender." *The Victorian Gothic: An Edinburgh Companion*. Ed. Andrew Smith and William Hughes. Edinburgh: Edinburgh University Press, 2012. 108–123. Print.

Dawson, Conor Michael. "The Fractured Self: Postmodernism and Depersonalization Disorder." *Aigne* 1 (2011): 51–65. Web.

"The French Mistake." *Supernatural: The Complete Sixth Season*. Writ. Ben Edlund. Dir. Charles Beeson. Perf. Jensen Ackles and Jared Padalecki. Warner Bros., 2011. DVD.

"Goodbye Stranger." *Supernatural: The Complete Eighth Season*. Writ. Robbie Thompson. Dir. Thomas J. Wright. Perf. Jensen Ackles and Jared Padalecki. Warner Bros., 2013. DVD.

"Hammer of the Gods." *Supernatural: The Complete Fifth Season*. Writ. Andrew Dabb and Daniel Loflin. Dir. Rick Bota. Perf. Jensen Ackles and Jared Padalecki. Warner Bros., 2010. DVD.

Kohut, Heinz. *The Restoration of the Self*. New York: International Universities Press, 1977. Print.

"Lazarus Rising." *Supernatural: The Complete Fourth Season*. Writ. Eric Kripke. Dir. Kim Manners. Perf. Jensen Ackles and Jared Padalecki. Warner Bros., 2009. DVD.

"Let It Bleed." *Supernatural: The Complete Sixth Season*. Writ. Sera Gamble. Dir. John F. Showalter. Perf. Jensen Ackles and Jared Padalecki. Warner Bros., 2011. DVD.

"The Man Who Knew Too Much." *Supernatural: The Complete Sixth Season*. Writ. Eric Kripke. Dir. Robert Singer. Perf. Jensen Ackles and Jared Padalecki. Warner Bros., 2011. DVD.

"Sacrifice." *Supernatural: The Complete Eighth Season*. Writ. Jeremy Carver. Dir. Phil Sgriccia. Perf. Jensen Ackles and Jared Padalecki. Warner Bros., 2013. DVD.

Stevenson, Robert Louis. *The Strange Case of Dr. Jekyll and Mr. Hyde*. 1886. New York: Dover Thrift Edition, 1991. Print.

"The Things We Left Behind." *Supernatural: The Complete Tenth Season*. Writ. Andrew Dabb. Dir. Guy Norman Bee. Perf. Jensen Ackles and Jared Padalecki. Warner Bros., 2015. DVD.

Winnicott, Donald W. "Ego Distortion in Terms of True and False Self." *The Maturational Process and the Facilitating Environment: Studies in the Theory of Emotional Development*. New York: International Universities Press, 1965. 140–157. Print.

"Sympathy for the Devil"
The Neutralization of Traditionally Evil Figures

SAMANTHA J. VERTOSICK

There is something about villains that draws audiences to them—the audience either loves them, or loves to hate them. Regardless, one of the most fascinating aspects of evil characters tends to be their inevitable tragic backstories. A tragic backstory garners empathy, and sometimes even sympathy, for the villain or, perhaps, puts the reader in a place where he or she must grapple with either feeling sorry for said characters or continue to condemn them for their treatment of the hero. Hit television series *Supernatural* puts the viewer in these positions countless times throughout its ten-plus seasons. More specifically, what *Supernatural* does is take a traditionally evil figure or character and write them in a way that forces the viewer to both sympathize with and admire the character. *Supernatural* has made a name for itself in its distinctive and often controversial show content—no other show has put characters such as Baldur, Osiris, and Metatron, to name only a few examples, into a modern-day setting. In a show that often relies on its main characters, Sam and Dean Winchester, to define what is "good" and what is "evil," and then to subsequently vanquish said evil, there is a surprising amount of sympathy to be found for traditionally demonized figures. The neutralization of characters such as Lucifer, Cain, Crowley, and Death in turn blurs the moral conscious of the viewer as much as Sam and Dean Winchester's own skewed moralities. Despite this, what *Supernatural* is doing isn't exactly new, and in fact follows a traceable literary tradition of having "sympathy for the devil."

Lucifer: "God wanted the devil!"

When considering *Supernatural*'s sympathy toward their "devils," it is perhaps best to start by taking a look at the epitome of devils, Lucifer.

143

Although the exact origins of the biblical Satan are unclear, "most scholars agree that in the writings of the third/second centuries BCE are the first examples of a character who is the archenemy of Yahweh and humankind" and that "the New Testament is probably more responsible for standardizing 'Satan' as the name for the archenemy of God in Western Culture" (Avalos 679). The actual name "Lucifer" was not popularized until the Middle Ages, when two New Testament traditions merged.[1] This is where the idea emerges that Lucifer—an imitation of "an angel of light"—and his minions could take possession of bodies to cause evil deeds.[2] From this union also comes the tale of Michael and Lucifer struggling over the body of Moses (Avalos 679)— a brotherly struggle *Supernatural* viewers know all too well.

While there is no sympathy to be found for Lucifer in these biblical tales, there are countless other textual sources where Lucifer can be viewed as a tragic figure, such as in John Milton's *Paradise Lost* (1667).[3] The tale is a familiar one—Satan is cast into Hell for attempting to lead a rebellion against God after becoming envious of the Son of God and humankind. Stanley E. Fish best summarizes the predicament as the reader falling with Eve since they are "repeatedly asked to choose between the interpretation which comforts" and "the interpretation which is true"; a choice that is made difficult by "the lure of Satan's scientism" or rationality (261). Through Milton's Satan, the "readers, too, are continually challenged to choose and to reconsider their most basic assumptions about freedom, heroism, work, pleasure, language, nature and love" (Lewalski and Maus 1830).

Bill Ellis, in his book *Lucifer Ascending: The Occult in Folklore and Popular Culture* (2004), cites the allure of Lucifer or Satanism as a vehicle "for protest against existing adult or institutional social structures" and as such, "especially attractive to adolescents who are going through the process of internalizing these structures," which harkens back to Milton's own Satan in his questioning of existing structures (223). Yet the attraction of Lucifer in the show *Supernatural*, which has a wide demographic of viewers, does not solely lie in the possibility of the character being a proxy for rebellion even if that is his ultimate motivation. Lucifer's attraction instead rests in his tragic backstory, which neutralizes the character by eliminating the possibility of him being completely evil.

While the first mention of Lucifer occurs in Season Three, it is in Season Four where the viewer hears Uriel tell the story of Lucifer's fall. The series writers also treat the heavenly feud as what otherwise might be considered a run-of-the-mill family squabble. This again brings Lucifer and his brother archangels "down to earth," so to speak. For example, in "Hammer of the Gods" (5.19), Lucifer and Gabriel's conversation sounds very much like an everyday family quarrel, with no apocalyptic repercussions whatsoever. Gabriel expresses his love for his brother, but tells him that he must put his jealousy behind him. Lucifer's tale is almost identical to that of the Lucifer found in *Paradise Lost* and ironically, it is the angel Anna Milton who kills Uriel, a supporter of Lucifer ("On the Head of a Pin," 4.16). At the end of Season Four, Lucifer is freed from "the Cage" in Hell and must find a vessel to inhabit, which is where his tragic backstory is first given a human element.

In an episode fittingly titled "Sympathy for the Devil" (5.1), the audience is first given a glimpse at Lucifer's soon-to-be vessel, Nick. Nick is a recent widower who lost his wife and child during a home invasion. Lucifer intensifies Nick's grief by causing him to hallucinate about the murders, but it is in the form of Nick's deceased wife that Lucifer is able to convince Nick to agree to become his vessel in exchange for promised retribution. While Lucifer utilized trickery to get Nick to accept, one cannot help but still feel sorry for Lucifer's vessel—no matter what Lucifer does, his vessel Nick has already suffered a great deal and a part of him still exists within Lucifer.

Matters are only complicated when it is revealed that Sam is meant to be Lucifer's vessel and Dean is destined to be Michael's ("Free to Be You and Me," 5.3). In a theme common to *Supernatural*, the conflicts of the two brothers reflect those of Sam and Dean, not only to bridge the gap between the brothers and the "monsters" they hunt, but also to further complicate the plot by garnering sympathy for the show's antagonists. As Lucifer predicted, Sam eventually agrees to let Lucifer occupy his body in what would be a failed attempt to throw Lucifer, and himself by default, back into the Cage; in other words, Sam literally becomes the monster Dean and he have hunted for so long. In an epic showdown at Stull Cemetery, Sam is able to throw himself back into Lucifer's Cage, only to have Michael, who is occupying Sam and Dean's half-brother Adam's body, follow him into the Cage and get locked up as well. The fight between Michael and Lucifer has then been reduced to a fight between brothers—and brothers the audience is more than familiar with at that. The quarrel between two epic entities has thus been neutralized into a Winchester family fight that ends in tragedy with Sam and Adam locked in Lucifer's Cage.[4] Fans appear to further forget that Lucifer is the actual devil in their admiration for his witty quotations and one-liners, much like the Satan of *Paradise Lost* who tempts the reader with his rationality; but when Lucifer is finally caged, problems for the Winchesters do not end there. As typical of any monarchy, with the old king gone, a new one must take his place.

Crowley, or, the Devil You Know

Although there are hoards of demons on *Supernatural*, Crowley is undoubtedly the most well-known on the series and beloved so much, his actor was promoted from guest star to season regular. Crowley, like Lucifer, is revered in the fan community for his wit, charm, memorable one-liners, and even his handsome looks. His appearances on *Supernatural* span over ten years and at least eight seasons, giving him an impressive run so far. Much like Castiel, Crowley's relationship with the Winchesters can be best described as an on-again, off-again relationship.

Crowley's history on *Supernatural* could take an entire book to chronicle, but like many other traditionally evil characters on the show, his initial malevolent demeanor is softened through his backstory and interactions with the Winchesters. Perhaps it is best to begin with Crowley's origins. While Crowley's name may be an obvious nod to English occultist Aleister Crowley (1875–1947), *Supernatural's* Crowley has more in common with a demon by the same name in Neil Gaiman and Terry Pratchett's *Good Omens: The Nice and Accurate Prophecies of Agnes Nutter, Witch* (1990). Show creator Eric Kripke has even previously admitted at the 2007 San Diego Comic-Con that Neil Gaiman's work heavily influences *Supernatural* (Boris par. 16).[5] In the "Dramatis Personae" of *Good Omens*, Gaiman and Pratchett's Crowley is described as "an Angel who did not so much Fall as Saunter Vaguely Downwards," much like *Supernatural's* own Crowley (8). The Crowley of *Supernatural* fame is not explicitly said to be an angel, but he does possess powers that set him apart from other demons, causing speculation about his exact origins. He also fits the description of *Good Omens* Crowley, in that both demons may be of Hell, but they maintain their own moral beliefs, going as far as working with angels to accomplish their goals.

Both Crowleys team up with an unlikely ally to oppose Lucifer and stop the Apocalypse from happening—*Good Omens*' Crowley partners with the angel Aziraphale while *Supernatural's* Crowley is seen teaming up at times with the angel Castiel and the Winchester brothers throughout the series. As mentioned earlier, Crowley is not only neutralized by his connections to the docile Crowley of *Good Omens*, but through his own backstory and interactions with the Winchesters. His fascinating backstory alone is enough to establish Crowley as a humorous, yet pitiful character.

In Season Six, it is revealed that Crowley was originally a seventeenth-century Scotsman named Fergus MacLeod who had a troubled relationship with his son Gavin and sold his soul to become more well-endowed ("Weekend at Bobby's," 6.4). These facts serve to lessen Crowley's threat as a demon or the King of Hell in that he is made more understandable through his very human, half-comic flaws. Crowley is only made more relatable as the series goes on; the entirety of Season Ten focuses on Crowley's troubling relationship with his manipulative mother Rowena, a witch, and a doomed, but hilarious "bromance" with the new Demon Dean Winchester.[6] Throughout his backstory and the development of new relationships, the King of Hell is domesticated in a way that almost makes him a hero in the saga that is *Super-*

natural. If not for his mixed loyalties and the hinting of a more aggressive Crowley returning in Season Eleven, an argument could be made that Crowley is one of the protagonists of the show due to the attention paid to his storyline and his status as a more humanized demon.

One way in particular that Crowley is "humanized" is in the Season Eight finale, when the Winchester brothers are attempting to "cure," or literally humanize, demons with treatments of human blood and use Crowley as their guinea pig. The treatment must take effect because Crowley begins to lecture Sam using the HBO show *Girls* (2012–), "You're my Marnie, Moose. And Hannah, she just—she needs to be loved. She deserves it. Don't we all? You. Me? We deserve to be loved. I deserve to be loved! I just want to be loved" ("Sacrifice," 8.23). This moment is pivotal in softening Crowley and sets into motion the events of Seasons Nine and Ten, explaining why Crowley acts the way he does.

As a crossroads demon originally, Crowley has always been reminiscent of *Doctor Faustus*'s likeable, not-completely-evil, Mephostopheles.[7] He performs tasks, shares information, and obtains hard-to-find objects for the Winchesters in exchange for something else in a type of Faustian agreement. It is in the ninth season that Crowley assists Dean in obtaining both the First Blade and the Mark of Cain so he can kill Abaddon, a Knight of Hell. In order to obtain the Mark of Cain, Dean and Crowley must first find Cain, the Father of Murder, himself.

Cain, the Unable

The most popularized version of Cain is clearly the one found in the Bible's book of Genesis. Cain and Abel are said to be the children of Adam and Eve, with Abel most commonly being the younger brother, sometimes a twin. Cain is a farmer who offers up a sacrifice of grain to God, while Abel, a shepherd, offers his first-born lamb. It is unknown why, but God rejects Cain's offer, which leads to Cain slaying Abel out of jealousy. When God confronts Cain about Abel's death, he pretends to know nothing, which leads to God punishing Cain "to wander earth, decreeing that the earth will no longer bear crops for him" (Hendel 97). Fearing for his life, "Cain pleads for mercy, which [God] grants by placing an unspecified sign on Cain so that no one will murder him" (Hendel 97). This is where *Supernatural* most likely draws the idea of the Mark of Cain being a literal mark on the forearm that prevents the bearer from being murdered.

Following in the suit of the traditionally evil figures before him, *Supernatural*'s Cain has a story quite different from that of his biblical counterpart. In the show, it is revealed that Cain's brother Abel was speaking to Lucifer and not God. Cain wished to save his brother's soul and offered himself to Lucifer instead in exchange for Abel going to heaven. The catch was that Cain had to send Abel to heaven himself, which he did by killing him with what would become the First Blade.[8] This act set into motion their descendants being the vessels of Michael and Lucifer, meaning that Sam and Dean are directly related to Cain and Abel. This also meant that Cain was the first Knight of Hell and bound to the Blade by the Mark of Cain placed on him by Lucifer. Even though this is just the beginning of Cain's story, he is already a much more sympathetic figure than the Cain of the Bible.

If Cain's backstory wasn't tragic enough, Cain later falls in love with a human named Colette, who absolves him of his crimes as long as he promises to discontinue his work, which he does. When the other Knights of Hell discover this, they kidnap Colette, forcing Cain to kill again until Abaddon possesses Colette in a last ditch effort to convince Cain to return to his life as a Knight. Cain tries to kill Abaddon, but only ends up killing Colette, promising her before she perishes that he will retire. Obviously, this heartrending story is much different than the one told in the Bible and sets Cain up to be deserving of empathy. Cain, like Lucifer and Crowley, is also neutralized by his connection to the Winchesters and the tragic brothers narrative so common on the show.

There are fewer references to Cain in popular literature, however. This is perhaps due to the uncertain nature of the original Cain and Abel tale. For example, although the book of Genesis claims Cain and Abel to be the children of Adam and Eve, other versions of the story say that Cain is either the son of Satan, the wicked angel Sammael, or the serpent of Eden (Hendel 97). This is not to say literary versions of Cain and Abel are non-existent, just less represented than figures such as Lucifer or that of the demon, and typically not the focus of the work in which they appear. For example, in Mike Carey's *The Unwritten* (2010), Cain appears disguised under a different name trying to alter timelines in order to undo his own story.

Another exception to Cain's general absence from literature is Lord Byron's play *Cain* (1821). Within the same vein of *Paradise Lost*, *Cain* retells the story of its titular character. Throughout the play, Cain cannot give praise to God due to dreading death, and ironically a fear of a personified Death. Cain worries that death will soon come and that he has no idea what it will be like, until Lucifer appears, shedding light on the situation and educating Cain. A fear of death is something any mortal can understand, making Byron's Cain an empathetic one as well. The ending of the play echoes the traditional biblical story, with the two brothers making sacrifices and Cain's being rejected, but Cain murders Abel for a different reason. He is disgusted that Abel must make a sacrifice of young livestock in order to win God's praise, and he reasons that if God enjoys blood so much, he can have Abel's to sate him, which only leads to Cain's banishment. This Cain differs from *Supernatural*'s in this point—Dean kills Cain in Season Ten after Dean catches him trying to murder off his own "poisoned" bloodline. While both Cains are repainted as tragic figures, Byron's Cain is motived by a fear of Death, while *Supernatural*'s character sees Death as a means to an end.

Death: Don't Fear the Reaper

Death is most likely the character on *Supernatural* with the richest literary history that is still continuously drawn upon today.[9] According to James L. Crenshaw, "The biblical concept of death is complex, like the reality it seeks to describe. Death is both natural and intrusive; it occasions no undue anxieties except in unusual circumstances … and it is the greatest enemy facing humankind" (160). Today, there are many forms of Death in literature and popular media, and most recently, these representations seek to mold Death as a benevolent figure.[10]

For example, J. K. Rowling's *Harry Potter and the Deathly Hallows* (2009) briefly personifies Death in "The Tale of the Three Brothers." The story is a fairy tale in the wizarding world that tells the story of three brothers who cheat Death. Death is angry about being cheated out of the three brothers' souls, but since Death is cunning he offers each brother a gift for having fooled him. The oldest brother chose the formidable Elder Wand in order to be the most powerful wizard in existence, the middle chose a Resurrection Stone to bring back the dead, and the youngest chose the Cloak of Invisibility to hide from Death since he knew what Death was truly after. As in most fairy tales, the youngest brother made the best choice, while the other brothers' choices ended up being their demise, which actually sounds pretty familiar in the terms of *Supernatural*. Hermione concludes the story, saying, "It was only when he had attained a great age that the youngest brother finally took off the Cloak of Invisibility and gave it to his son. And then he greeted Death as an old friend, and went with him gladly, and, as equals, they departed this life" (Rowling 409).

The Death presented in "The Tale of the Three Brothers" is described as cunning and becomes angry when he loses "victims," but at the end of the story Death is considered a friend. Death becomes a positive figure who the youngest brother does not fear, but finds comfort in and understands. *Supernatural*'s Death works in this way. In the episode "Appointment in Samarra" (6.11), Death is keen to teach Dean about the natural order of things. The entire episode is dedicated to making Dean play reaper just to learn how difficult the job is so that Dean may understand why Death can only spare one of his brothers, Sam or Adam. Despite the emotionally taxing day, Death and Dean continue to have a mutual understanding throughout the series—until Season Ten, of course.

These portraits of Death offer relief—relief that those who die and welcome Death will not be lost, sad, or disappointed, and that there is hope beyond Earthly life. Both also show that death is a part of the world's natural order. Markus Zusak's portrayal of Death in *The Book Thief* (2005) works in this sense as well. *The Book Thief* contains an even greater ratio of character death than the *Harry Potter* series and *Supernatural*, and in an unusual move, is narrated by Death himself.

Death's cunning can once again be seen in his bluntness regarding inevitability—one of the first facts he tells the audience is that, "You are going to die … [but] I'm nothing if not fair" (Zusak 13). In addition he has a vivacious attitude, stating, "I only wear a hooded black robe when it's cold … [and] You want to know what I truly look like? I'll help you out. Find yourself a mirror while I continue" (Zusak 317). Death's descriptions of himself or his attempts to address the stereotypes of Death give readers a Death that can be funny. His humor and honesty actually make the reader begin to like Death as a character, and his fondness and sympathy for humanity only makes the audience admire him more. Zusak's Death is similar to the Death found in *Supernatural*, whose humorous love for pizza and tamales also doubles as a surprisingly human quality, thus making Death more relatable in that aspect as well.

In true *Supernatural* tradition, the show's Death also shares qualities with the various personified deaths created by Neil Gaiman. Gaiman has written a Death in *Good Omens*, *The Sandman* series (1989–1996), and in *The Graveyard Book* (2008), two out of three of those Deaths being women, while *Good Omens*' Death is simply skeletal in appearance.[11] The actor chosen to portray Death, Julian Richings, fits the physical description of Gaiman and Pratchett's Death closest in his naturally very thin, almost skeletal appearance. Both *Supernatural* and *Good Omens*' Death also wear a long black coat (Gaiman and Pratchett 265). In addition to appearance, both Deaths are also the "leader" of the Four Horsemen of the Apocalypse, yet the Death on *Supernatural* is still more "human" than that of Gaiman and Pratchett's.

Supernatural's Death, in the vein of the previously mentioned "evil" characters, is also neutralized by his relationship with Sam and Dean. While he contains qualities of the aforementioned representations of Death, it is his relationship with the Winchester brothers, especially Dean, that lets the viewer see him as an ally. Death is able to gain the audience's admiration because he appears to treat the Winchesters the same way the viewer should—with understanding.

The Winchesters' relationship with Death is similar to the one shared with Crowley—Death is typically summoned to help the Winchesters in some way, just as Crowley is usually summoned only when needed. Their relationship is tense but mostly positive until the Season Ten finale "Brother's Keeper" (10.23), when Dean summons Death to kill him in an attempt to end the trouble caused by the Mark of Cain. Yet, true to the biblical story, the Mark prevents Dean from being murdered, even by Death. Death says that the only way to end this is to send Dean away and for him to kill his brother so that Sam will not try to bring Dean back. Naturally, Dean kills Death after he demands this of him—once again replaying the old Cain and Abel narrative so common to *Supernatural*.

It is unclear what the long-term repercussions of a slain Death will mean for the show's universe and the coming Darkness, but Sam and Dean have made themselves more vulnerable by losing a key ally. In works such as Kelly Sue Deconnick's *Pretty Deadly* (2014), when Death is killed, another Death must take its place, and the cycle of different Deaths is a natural thing. In Milton's *Paradise Lost*, Death is the son of Satan, and a much more malicious character than any of the aforementioned versions of Death. This Death enjoys human suffering and pain, but only fears the Son of God meant to destroy him. Perhaps this is Dean's fate—emerging from shedding the Mark of Cain as a messiah-figure for destroying Death. Regardless, the consequences of killing Death are sure to be enormous.

"Hell is empty, and all the devils are here"

In his book *Religion and Its Monsters* (2002), Timothy K. Beal suggests, "By demonizing our monsters, we keep God on our side" (6). Yet, he goes on to say that there exists space in which monsters are not just demonized, but also deified, such as the monsters seen in *Supernatural*. By only briefly discussing the circumstances surrounding Lucifer, Cain, Crowley, and Death, a viewer of the show can begin to see that this is barely skimming the surface of the "evil" figures featured on the show. There is still Azazel, Eve, Raphael, Lilith, Metatron, and of course, the Leviathans, to name a few not covered in this essay, and each of these figures comes with their own complicated narrative and motivations. Some of these narratives, like the ones discussed, also have an extensive literary history that *Supernatural* may borrow from, such as Crowley and *Good Omens*, or a history that *Supernatural* discards; think the biblical story of Cain versus the show's retelling. Whether the literary history is either embraced or rejected, these characters are still ultimately shaped to be deserving of audience empathy. The characters are also nearly always neutralized to blur the lines between what is good and what is evil, and the Winchester brothers' actions and interactions only complicate matters further. On *Supernatural*, there exists no true good and no true evil; every single figure exists on a spectrum in between the two extremes.

Nathan Stout, in "Are Monsters Members of the Moral Community?," sees Sam and Dean as the possible "bad guys" of *Supernatural*. He writes: "Sam and Dean are admirable for their consistent dedication to helping save the lives of other people, but this seems inconsistent with their apparent disregard for the lives of the moral monsters they hunt, which should leave us questioning whether or not Sam and Dean are really good.... When Sam and Dean kill with no remorse, our good guys aren't really as good as we think" (15). To respond to Stout's excellent point, perhaps the reason that *Supernatural*'s "villains" are made so relatable is to not only force the viewer to question Sam and Dean's decisions, but to question their own morals. The neutralized villain provides a mirror in which the audience can see itself more clearly by first looking at what "monstrosity" or "evil" actually is. By the standards set in *Supernatural*, one must have to try very hard to be truly evil, and viewers realize that there is constant tragedy in the job the Winchesters have chosen to do—it is not a job without heavy consequences. The neutralization of the traditionally "evil" characters on *Supernatural* demonstrates that there are two sides to every coin, and perhaps in the case of Death, that there is no need to fear the reaper after all.

Notes

1. Gustav Davidson claims the association of Satan with Lucifer is due to a misreading of Isaiah 14:12: "How art thou fallen from heaven O Lucifer, son of the morning." He points out, "The authors of the books of the Old Testament knew nothing of fallen or evil angels" (176). For the sake of looking at *Supernatural*, the two are used here interchangeably, regardless.

2. Other versions of Satan involve him as an actual dragon, or the more commonly known serpent from the Garden of Eden.

3. William Blake and Percy Bysshe Shelley viewed Milton's Satan as the true hero of *Paradise Lost* (Lewalski and Maus 1830).

4. Events beginning with Sam saying "yes" to Lucifer and ending with Sam and Adam in the Cage occur in "Swan Song" (5.22).

5. For an extended discussion of Gaiman's influence on Kripke, see Laura Felschow's "Plagiarism or Props? Homage to Neil Gaiman in Eric Kripke's *Supernatural*," in *TV Goes to Hell: An Unofficial Road Map of* Supernatural, Stacey Abbott and David Lavery, eds. (Toronto: ECW Press, 2011), pp. 230–43.

6. Some may find the relationship more problematic, but it is humorous in its use of popular culture, such as Crowley and Demon Dean taking selfies and partying together. In several scenes the two are seen hanging out at the bar, where Crowley enjoys fruity cocktails with tiny umbrellas.

7. Mephostopheles at least warns Faustus of the dangers of selling his soul and tries to sway him from making the pact since it would lead him to Hell, too.

8. Cain's story is relayed in "First Born" (9.11).

9. Lucifer (or Satan) may have more of a history or more material written about him, but it is mostly in the form of religious texts. Death, however, appears to occupy more works of general literature.

10. Crenshaw also observes, "Israel's theologians believed that God alone had

authority to terminate life" (161). This brings up a very true point that not all cultures see death or personified Death as "evil" or as a bad thing, although many old folk tales feature protagonists trying to outsmart Death. It is modern culture with major scientific and technological advances that sees death as an unfortunate end to life in a world that favors the material: "In legal terms, natural death is nowadays 'illegal,' reflecting the shifting in the perception of death as a natural life event to that of a medical failure" (Douglas 304). It is in this way that death or personified Death can be first perceived as a malevolent figure.

    11. Tessa the Reaper is based on Gaiman's Death from *The Sandman* according to *Supernatural: The Official Companion, Season 2*.

WORKS CITED

Avalos, Hector I. "Satan." *The Oxford Companion to the Bible*. Ed. Bruce M. Metzgar and Michael D. Coogan. Oxford: Oxford University Press. 1993. 678–679. Print.

Beal, Timothy K. *Religion and Its Monsters*. New York: Routledge, 2002. Print.

Boris, Cynthia. "Eric Kripke: Satan's Head Writer." *TV of the Absurd*. Ed. Cynthia Boris. TV of the Absurd, 25 July 2007. Web. 25 June 2015.

Byron, Lord (George Gordon). *The Works of Lord Byron*, Volume V. *Project Gutenberg*. Ed. Ernst H. Coleridge. Project Gutenberg, 14 Nov. 2007. Web. 16 June 2015.

Carey, Mike. *The Unwritten: Volume 1*. Art by Peter Gross. New York: Vertigo, 2010. Print.

Crenshaw, James L. "Death." *The Oxford Companion to the Bible*. Ed. Bruce M. Metzgar and Michael D. Coogan. Oxford: Oxford University Press, 1993. 160–161. Print.

Davidson, Gustav. *A Dictionary of Angels: Including the Fallen Angels*. New York: The Free Press, 1971. Print.

Deconnick, Kelly Sue. *Pretty Deadly*. Art by Emma Rios, Jordie Bellaire, and Clayton Cowles. Berkeley: Image Comics, 2014. Print.

Douglas, Cristina. "Understanding Death during Childhood: Cultural and Psychological Dimensions." *Death Representations in Literature: Forms and Theories*. Ed. Adriana Teodorescu. Newcastle upon Tyne: Cambridge Scholars, 2015. 301–322. Print.

Ellis, Bill. *Lucifer Ascending: The Occult in Folklore and Popular Culture*. Lexington: University Press of Kentucky, 2004. Print.

Fish, Stanley E. *Surprised by Sin: The Reader in* Paradise Lost. Berkley: University of California Press, 1971. Print.

Gaiman, Neil. *The Graveyard Book*. First ed. New York: HarperCollins Publishers, 2008. Print.

_____. *The Sandman*, Box ed. New York: Vertigo, 2012. Print.

Gaiman, Neil, and Terry Pratchett. *Good Omens: The Nice and Accurate Prophecies of Agnes Nutter, Witch*. New York: HarperTorch, 2006. Print.

Hendel, Ronald S. "Cain and Abel." *The Oxford Companion to the Bible*. Ed. Bruce M. Metzgar and Michael D. Coogan. Oxford: Oxford University Press, 1993. 97. Print.

Knight, Nicholas. *Supernatural: The Official Companion, Season 2*, 1st ed. London: Titan, 2008. Print.

Lewalski, Barbara E., and Katharine E. Maus. "Paradise Lost." *The Norton Anthology of English Literature: The Sixteenth Century/The Early Seventeenth Century*. Ed. Barbara K. Lewalski and Katharine E. Maus. 8th ed. New York: W.W. Norton, 2006. 1830–1831. Print.

Marlowe, Christopher. *Doctor Faustus*. 1592. Ed. Sylvan Barnet. 1st ed. New York: Signet Classic, 2001. Print.

Milton, John. "Paradise Lost." 1667. *The Norton Anthology of English Literature: The Sixteenth Century/The Early Seventeenth Century.* Ed. Barbara K. Lewalski and Katharine E. Maus. 8th ed. New York: W.W. Norton, 2006. 1830–2055. Print.

Rowling, J. K. *Harry Potter and the Deathly Hallows.* New York: Scholastic, 2009. Print.

"Sacrifice." *Supernatural: The Complete Eighth Season.* Writ. Jeremy Carver. Dir. Phil Sgriccia. Perf. Jensen Ackles and Jared Padalecki. Warner Bros., 2013. DVD.

Shakespeare, William. *The Complete Works of William Shakespeare,* 2d ed. Glasgow: Collins, 2006. 1–28. Print. Rpt. of *The Tempest.* 1623.

Stout, Nathan. "Are Monsters Members of the Moral Community?" *Supernatural and Philosophy: Metaphysics and Monsters … for Idjits.* Ed. Galen A. Foresman. West Sussex, UK: Wiley Blackwell, 2013. 7–15. Print.

Zusak, Markus. *The Book Thief,* 2d ed. London: Black Swan, 2007. Print.

"Psychotically, irrationally, erotically codependent"

Incest and the Gothic Other

MEGAN FOWLER

This essay focuses on the hints of a subtextual incestuous relationship between the two lead characters of *Supernatural*, the brothers Sam and Dean Winchester, and the various Gothic conventions and tropes this relationship embodies. This relationship will be situated within the sub-genre of the Queer Gothic, as well as numerous Gothic concepts including the uncanny, the double, and the unspeakable that plagues many Gothic protagonists. In particular, focus will be given to textual and subtextual acknowledgment of queer desire between the brothers, the brothers' relationship and lifestyle positioned as "other" in opposition to images of "normalcy" provided by the show, and the protagonists' anxiety of becoming the monstrous other that they fight, an anxiety fueled in the narrative by the peculiarity of the brothers' all-consuming love for each other.

To understand the ways in which the relationship between Sam and Dean on *Supernatural* is gothically coded, it is important to start by considering the role that sexuality plays in Gothic fiction. Gothic fiction is largely preoccupied with transgressive sexuality and sexual terror, which serves as the center of numerous Gothic tropes and texts (Haggerty 2). Unsurprisingly, this fascination largely centers on sexual behaviors that have been considered deviant or taboo in some way. Stemming from this fascination, the subtext in the Winchesters' interactions with each other follows a long tradition of incest within the Gothic. In "Gothic Sublimity," David B. Morris notes incest is the "forbidden desire to which terror always, ultimately, returns" (305). This incestuous desire shares a layer of sexual deviance from traditional hegemonic relationships with the subgenre of Queer Gothic. In *The Psychic Life of Power*

(1997), Judith Butler has drawn explicit connections between the taboo nature of queer and incestuous desire. The Winchesters' relationship, with its emphasis on family and self-sacrificial love within the context of a coded homoerotic bond, lies along this convergence between the queer and incestuous. The narrative of the show reinforces the subversive quality of the boys' bond by othering the hunter lifestyle as queer and based within an isolated, incestuous family unit in contrast to the heteronormative, traditional nuclear family.

Structurally, the series others the brothers' lifestyle as hunters of evil by frequently placing this lifestyle in contrast to depictions of "normalcy" in the show. From the pilot episode, Dean and the lifestyle he represents are configured in opposition with Sam's girlfriend Jessica, who represents a "normal, apple pie life" of marriage, a career, and a suburban home ("Pilot," 1.1). Dean's reentrance into his life pulls Sam away from the normalcy he had been attempting to build, drawing him back into a homeless, isolated, completely homosocial space. Dean is often the voice of the hunting lifestyle, becoming the voice of the queer Other whenever the brothers encounter the domestic space. He reacts with vehement disgust when confronted with the suburban subdivision being haunted in "Bugs" (1.8). Sam insists, "There's nothing wrong with 'normal,'" to which Dean replies, "I'd take our family over normal any day." Through the repeated rhetoric of "normalcy," the series defines the life Dean and Sam lead as hunters—nomadic, childless, homoerotic—through its direct contrast with societal, hegemonic expectations of domestic life, stable careers, heteronormative marriage, and children. This contrast emphasizes the subtextual eroticism of the brothers' relationship, as their bond cannot be sustained simultaneously with a heteronormative romantic relationship.

The possibility of heterosexual romance and a domestic family unit is binarily opposed to the Winchesters' relationship; one can only exist in absence of the other. The series vehemently and violently denies the possibility of potential female companionship for the brothers, as Catherine Tosenberger writes, "all of Sam and Dean's serious romantic relationships with women are doomed to failure" often via the death of the potential love interest (The Lore and Language of Incest section, para. 2). The only time the series even entertains the idea of heterosexual relationships for Sam or Dean is in the other's complete and utter absence, as seen in "I Know What You Did Last Summer" (4.9), "Swan Song" (5.22), and "We Need to Talk About Kevin" (8.1), or within the parameters of a dream reality in which the brothers' bond is nonexistent, such as in "What Is and What Should Never Be" (2.20). The series sets up the idea of Sam and Dean's lifestyle as hunters and the possibility of domestic life in a heteronormative marriage as paradoxical states that cannot coexist. This contrast with the domestic goes directly to the root of Freud's definition of the uncanny, which ripples out from the domestic into "something removed from the eyes of strangers, hidden, secret" (Freud 133).

Sam and Dean themselves become other, queer and uncanny, through their binary opposition to the tenets of heteronormative and familial normalcy. The Winchesters' bond is so all-encompassing that it leaves no room for the possibility of other partnerships; the relationship subsumes and replaces any possibility of heterosexual marriage with the queer, incestuous lifestyle the brothers build together. The excessive nature of the brothers' relationship exemplifies the Gothic preoccupation with transgressing traditional cultural boundaries.

Because of its occupation with transgressive behavior, the Gothic often serves as a foundation for explorations of excessive emotion and non-normative relationships between characters. Excess features heavily in Gothic texts, stemming from an interest in transgressive behavior and anxiety over the limitations and boundaries of societal norms (Botting 1). This excess often plays out between the romantic pairings of Gothic protagonists as well as suggestively in homoerotically charged bonds. In addition, incestuous transgression is a common theme in Gothic fiction, which frequently exceeds normative familial boundaries (Eberle-Sinatra 124). Terror in the Gothic stems primarily from the excessive; the characters who transgress traditional boundaries through these excessive dynamics fear recognition, both that others will recognize them and that they will recognize themselves. The Gothic dramatizes this anxiety through the paradoxical juxtaposition within Gothic texts of the unspeakable, the secret that motivates the paranoid terror of Gothic protagonists, and the idea of the "open secret," the recognition of this secret by the text, revealing that the secret the protagonists work so hard to conceal is repressed only within themselves. In *Supernatural*, recognition of the excessiveness of Sam and Dean's relationship ultimately manifests itself in two ways: those who know that the brothers are related comment and react to the unnatural nature of their relationship with unease, and those who do not frequently mistake their dynamic for a queer romantic one.

The idea of the open secret in the Gothic centers around the idea that the secret at the heart of most Gothic texts, primarily a sexual secret that has been repressed, is only concealed insofar as the text constructs it as being so (Rigby 52). The implications of the text make sure that the secret is never truly concealed, only repressed amongst the characters as a rhetorical means of making sex "the secret" (Rigby 52). *Supernatural* articulates a sense of the open secret through the recognition by other characters of the Winchesters' bond as transgressing hegemonically appropriate family bonds, suggesting something unnaturally erotic or incestuous between the brothers. In the sixth season, when Sam unexpectedly returns from the dead after Dean has become settled into a traditional domestic life with romantic partner Lisa, the romance between the pair immediately becomes strained and eventually dissolves altogether. Lisa tells Dean that she knew as soon as Sam reappeared in his life that their relationship was over, reinforcing the idea that the Winchesters' relationship cannot coexist with a heterosexual romance. She goes on to make an explicit analogy about how the relationship transgresses hegemonic familial boundaries, "I'm close to my sister. But if she got killed? I wouldn't bring her back from the dead" ("You Can't Handle the Truth," 6.6). Lisa recognizes Dean's past behavior as an explicit example of the ways in which Dean's closeness to Sam surpasses the traditional boundaries of familial love, moving into the realm of excessive and subversive. Lisa is not the only character to note that the brothers' relationship exceeds the commonly accepted bounds of family duty. As demonstrated in the quote in the title of this essay, the angel Zachariah suggests that the brothers' loyalty to one another is not only excessive, but also sexually charged.

In a sequence in which he is attempting to persuade the Winchesters' long lost brother Adam that they are not trustworthy, Zachariah describes Sam and Dean's relationship as "psychotically, irrationally, erotically codependent" ("Point of No Return," 5.18). His use of the term "erotic" along with the parallels he draws between the term with descriptors of monstrous and excessive behavior, insinuates the brothers' dynamic as unnatural by being explicitly sexual and incestuous in nature. Zachariah makes a point to tell Adam that the Winchesters are not his family, configuring Sam and Dean's connection as existing somewhere outside natural familial bonds. Although Zachariah is situated as a villain within the narrative, the show ultimately reinforces the sense that Sam and Dean prioritize their relationship over their familial loyalty to Adam. In the sixth season episode "Appointment in Samarra" (6.11), when given the opportunity to only save one of his brothers from Hell, Dean answers Sam without hesitation. With this scene, the series supports Zachariah's accusation by suggesting that Sam and Dean's loyalty to one another is not based solely in the tenets of family duty, but motivated by something deeper and homoerotically coded. The narrative furthers this coding through other characters equating the brothers' relationship as analogous to a romantic couple, accentuating the erotic undertone of their interactions.

Supernatural draws attention to the Winchesters' relationship with each other as sexually and romantically coded through allusions made by supporting characters in the series. Characters often compare Sam and Dean's relationship with those of real and fictionalized couples. Similarities are often drawn between the boys and outlaw couples, including Bonnie and Clyde ("Nightshifter," 2.12) and, on more than one occasion, *Natural Born Killers'* Mickey and Mallory ("You Can't Handle the Truth" and "Slash Fiction," 7.6). Even Dean makes occasional comparisons, referencing Mulder and Scully ("The Usual Suspects," 2.7) as well as Sid and Nancy ("Time is On My Side," 3.15). Characters who do not know that the Winchesters are related specifically note the queer erotic potential of their relationship by mistaking them for a couple, seen in "Bugs," "Something Wicked" (1.18), "Playthings" (2.11), and "Bitten" (8.4). This misidentification often comes from hotel managers asking about their sleeping arrangements for the night, tying the brothers' relationship directly to the erotic symbol of the bed. Both boys frequently use the fact that they are brothers as a means of dispelling the notion that their relationship has queer potential; however, this justification is undercut by the fact that, as outlined above, the narrative acknowledges the "queer" nature of the relationship in comparison to hegemonic family bonds. The brothers, and Dean in particular, frequently meet insinuations of the homoerotic with the homosexual panic common in paranoid Gothic texts.

In "Playthings," after the hotel manager mistakes them for an antiquing couple and assumes they will be needing a single bed, Dean wants to know what she meant when she said they "looked the type." In the next scene, as the boys are settling into the room, the misinterpretation still troubles him, as he asks, "Of course, the most troubling question is: why do these people assume we're gay?" In "Something Wicked," when the cheeky teenager checking him in scoffs in skepticism that the brothers will be needing two beds, Dean visibly bristles and confronts him about what he said. Suspicious and visceral reactions to suggestions of secret erotic desire is a common theme of paranoid Queer Gothic texts. This paranoia stems from the fear of recognition, both outward and subsequently inward, of the sexual secret at the center of the Gothic (Rigby 52). Paranoia in the Gothic, and in *Supernatural* as a part of that tradition, derives from the juxtaposition of the open secret and the unspeakable, in this case the potential queer and incestuous desire in the brothers' relationship with one another. Desire creates the anxiety at the center of the Gothic (Haggerty 2), and the Gothic convention that transgressive desire must be repressed (Freud 147) plays out through the trope of the unspeakable.

The Gothic trope of the unspeakable is born out of anxiety surrounding the secret that drives the narrative of Gothic texts. Gothic anxiety builds in part from the tension between the open secret and the unspeakable, defined, like Freud's uncanny, as the secret that should remain suppressed but recognition threatens to reveal (148). The terror evoked by the Gothic therefore builds from a fear of recognition, and the unspeakable as a trope serves as a means of defending against that recognition. The unspeakable is by its very definition automatically associated with queerness, which was historically nameless (Sedgwick 94). As such, excessive male-male desire is frequently subject of the unspeakable, revealing the homophobic thematics of the trope (Sedgwick 53). The anxiety present in paranoid texts therefore creates an explicit connection between homophobic reaction and homoerotic undertones (Sedgwick 92). The unspeakable is in effect itself an acknowledgement of the excessive and homoerotic nature of the male-male dynamic it seeks to repress. In the case of *Supernatural*, the unspeakable manifests through Sam and Dean's inability to name their dynamic or acknowledge the intensity of the bond.

While many other characters comment upon the odd nature of the relationship the brothers share, pointing out both queer potential and an unnatural quality, Sam and Dean themselves are rarely able to fully articulate the relationship between them. When emphasizing their need to distance themselves because of the inherently dangerous nature of their relationship in "The End" (5.4), Dean describes their relationship as "whatever we have between us—love, family, whatever it is" expressing his inability to put their dynamic into definable terms. This moment almost identically echoes other moments of queer recognition through the unspeakable in Gothic novels. Mair Rigby describes the way Gothic novel *Melmoth the Wanderer* (1820) supplies a series of asterisks at the moment of revelation of queer desire by the protagonist. This moment indicates the inability to articulate the unspeakable as indication of characters' homosexual panic in paranoid Gothic texts (Rigby 51). The queer and erotic potential is acknowledged through the absence of language, through the loaded implications of silence. Dean's inability to articulate the nature of the relationship in words not only captures the excess of the brotherhood—it exists somewhere beyond the traditional bounds of love or family—but also indicates the attachment as existing in the realm of the Gothic unspeakable. Ultimately, one of the brothers articulating and therefore acknowledging what exists between them would mean recognizing their relationship's excessive nature, the boundaries it breaks in traditional familial love, and its erotic potential. The unspeakable serves to suppress this self-recognition. However, the series threatens this maintenance of repression through parallels drawn between the boys and the monstrous others they fight, creating paranoia within the narrative that the Winchesters' excessive love for one another will transform them into these monsters. Through the use of monstrous others and doubles, the homoerotic and incestuous nature of the brothers' relationship rears its head.

The series utilizes paranoia about the monstrous other and the double as an articulation of the unspeakable between the Winchesters in a number of different ways. The monstrous other often represents a physical parallel of the desire between the brothers, the terror that their bond may lead them to transform into the monstrous others they hunt, and a willingness to violate the boundaries between human and monstrous for one another. Monstrous figures underscore some of the Winchesters' own inner anxieties, drawing on tropes of the uncanny, the monstrous other, and the Queer Gothic. The Winchesters' anxiety about the intensity of their bond ultimately manifests itself as fear of becoming monstrous. The transformation into something not dissimilar from the monstrous other is often a manifestation or a consequence of a devoted sacrificial act of love between the brothers. Often, the monstrous other is an expression of how excessive the brothers' love for one another truly is, the extents to which they are willing to go for each other, and how potentially unnatural their dynamic is.

Several monstrous figures serve as parallels for the boys, often becoming the object of desire of the other brother. In the fourth season, Sam enters into a sexual and implied romantic relationship with the demon Ruby while Dean is in Hell. Again, this relationship underscores that heterosexual romance only occurs for the boys in the other's absence. In addition, the show draws direct parallels between Dean and the monstrous other Ruby as a means of explaining Sam's connection with and attraction to her. During "I Know What You Did Last Summer," after describing how their relationship transformed in Dean's absence, Sam explains how Ruby saved his life, "What she said to me…. It's what you would've said." Sam directly invokes the parallels that he sees between Ruby and Dean as an explanation for the intimacy that developed between them. This invocation of desire in the figure of the monstrous aligns with the role of the uncanny in Gothic fiction, which acts as "a substitute: the inexact double or surrogate" of the unspeakable (Morris 311). In this case, Ruby acts as a substitute for the true object of Sam's devotion: Dean. The parallel drawn between Dean and Ruby telegraphs the dynamic Sam and Dean share onto the relationship of Sam and Ruby, writing Sam's desire for Dean onto the body of a monstrous other and fully realizing that desire as mirroring sexual desire.

In "Sex and Violence" (4.14), *Supernatural* furthers the monstrous double as an expression of the Winchesters' desire for one another through the erotically coded figure of the siren. The case of the week centers on a hunt for a siren murdering men in the guise of a stripper. Dean becomes unwittingly seduced by the siren as a manifestation of exactly what Dean wants … a brother. The language with which the siren describes his relationship with Dean is heavily coded as romantic and sexual. He tells Dean, "We can be brothers. Forever" and possessively tells Sam, "Dean's all mine." The relationship is explicitly equated with romantic love, when the siren explains his monstrous compulsion is to "fall in love again. And again and again." When describing to Sam how he compelled Dean, he explains, "I gave him what he needed … you. A little brother that looked up to him, that he could trust. And now he loves me. He'd do anything for me." He goes on to describe to Sam the power of the devotion he draws as a siren, a devotion so strong that his victims will kill for him. This excessive devotion, compelled by monstrous power, is not unlike the devotion the brothers display for each other throughout the series, revealing themselves as willing to kill, die, and even defy death for one another. In addition, the siren's role clearly plays on the homoerotic undertones of the brothers' relationship. When faced with a monster who represents desire itself, Dean's desires do not manifest in the form of a heteronormative female romantic partner but as his own brother. The siren thus evokes Gothic terror by confronting the characters with their own repressed desire and the possible nature of their own relationship (Morris 307). By utilizing the siren, who represents the seductive and the erotic, as a stand-in for Sam in his relationship with Dean, the series expresses the Winchesters' own unspeakable desire for one another through the uncanny figure of a monster. Monstrous others serve as doubles for the brothers as an apparition of the unspeakable which cannot be denied, a revelation of the desire that has been unsuccessfully repressed within the open secret.

The series also explores paranoia about repressed desire made manifest in another trope of monstrous doubling: the doppelgänger. In *Supernatural*'s third season, Dean is confronted with a literal double in the form of a demonic doppelgänger of himself. During the season, the narrative arc focuses on the brothers' attempt to free Dean from the deal he struck at the end of the previous season to resurrect Sam in exchange for his soul. Ruby reveals to Dean the origin of demons: each is a former human soul that has been transformed by the torturous horror of Hell. The episode "Dream a Little Dream of Me" (3.10) dramatizes a direct confrontation with Dean's potential fate in the form of Dean's worst nightmare: a vision of himself as a demon. The confrontation between Dean and his double centers chiefly on Dean's primary role and worth as Sam's protector and his own self-loathing. Dean's double taunts that he has, "nothing outside of Sam." His demonic alter ego torments Dean with the teasing demand to know what he wants, what he dreams. The double then deems that Dean is empty, his identity consumed only with his need to protect Sam. Dean's demon self suggests that all there may be to Dean is his bond with Sam. The suggestive nature of the demand to know what Dean wants and dreams, and then the answer that there is nothing but Sam, suggests the all-consuming nature of Dean's devotion to his brother. This connection suggests a revelation of Dean's primary identity, of the only thing he has ever been capable of wanting: to be Sam's brother. When confronted with his demonic self, Dean glibly quips that he is his own worst nightmare, but becomes visibly shaken and then violent in the ensuing confrontation. This shows Dean's true terror, a terror evoked by the role that the double represents: self-knowledge.

In Gothic fiction, the double most frequently represents a portion of the psyche that has been repressed but is ultimately inescapable (Morris 307). In Gothic texts, the terror of the double is a horror at self-revelation (Coates 4). Dean's confrontation with his double centers on the unspeakable and excessive bond between the brothers as Dean's primary desire and suggests that this is the revelation that terrifies him. His unspeakable desire to protect Sam and the possibility that this desire encompasses his entire identity is the self-knowledge his double represents, the part of Dean he wishes to deny but can never eliminate. In addition, this doppelgänger represents Dean's fear of what may come to pass: his own transformation into a monstrous other, a demon, a transformation that is the direct consequence of his sacrifice for Sam.

As monster hunters, the brothers are plagued throughout the series with a fear of the blurring boundaries of their own identity and that of the creatures they hunt. This fear affects Sam in particular, who begins to develop supernatural powers in the beginning of the series and is eventually revealed to have been infected with demon blood as a child ("All Hell Breaks Loose, Part 1," 2.21). On a number of occasions throughout the show, Sam's unnatural or "supernatural" abilities manifest in direct relation to his own excessive devotion to his brother. During the Season One episode "Nightmare" (1.14), after the antagonist of the week traps him in a closet blocked by a large cabinet, Sam has a vision of Dean being killed. His emotional reaction is so intense that he telekinetically moves the cabinet blocking him in, freeing himself so that he can save Dean. This moment suggests Sam's own uncanny nature has its root in his bond with Dean. Sam's own monstrous nature and his love for his brother reside in conjunction with each other deep within his identity, similar to the role monsters play in fiction as representing "radical otherness and … the always already other at the heart of identity" (Shildrick 2). Sam's loyalty to his brother also leads him down the road of monstrous transformation in the series.

During the fourth season, when he is unable to release Dean from Hell, Sam makes it his mission to get vengeance on the demon Lilith who held the contract for his brother's soul. With encouragement from Ruby, Sam embraces his own supernatural abilities as training to defeat Lilith. His excessive devotion to Dean transforms into a rage-filled hunger for vengeance. As his own love transforms his motivations into a darker personal vendetta, so, too, does Sam slowly transform into something less human, monstrous by the show's very definition of monster. The obsessive devotion of the brothers' bond to one another acts as a seed with the potential to embed the uncanny into each brother's identity. Characters' inner selves are often expressed by outward appearances of monstrous others and doubles, creatures who ultimately lurk within (Shildrick 6). In the case of *Supernatural*, monstrous potential literally resides within each brother and manifests from the transgressive compulsions of their loyalty to each other. The monstrous is deeply embedded in each Winchester's primary identity as a brother. The excessive nature of the brothers' bond with one another leads their inner monstrous nature to manifest itself outwardly.

Transformation into these monstrous shadow selves is nearly always the result of one of the Winchesters having violated the natural order for the other, creating a direct connection between anxieties of the monstrous other and the Winchesters' relationship. This breach of the natural and unnatural comes primarily in the brothers' prolonging death for one another. These actions fly directly in the face of one of the central tenets of the hunting culture in the series, the idea that "what's dead should stay dead," which Dean himself verifies in "Children Shouldn't Play with Dead Things" (2.4). Following Dean's deal for Sam's life at the end of the second season, in addition to Dean's own anxiety about transforming into a demon, the series is laced with a paranoia that Sam may have "come back wrong." This anxiety, compelled by the monstrous consequence of violations against death, is a common trope of Gothic fiction, in which the monstrous double can simultaneously stand in as uncanny immortality and the intermediary of death (Freud 142). Immediately following Sam's resurrection, his demeanor seems to become colder, as he kills one of the antagonists of the season finale with a ruthlessness he had rarely displayed up until that point in the series. In "All Hell Breaks Loose, Part 2" (2.22), the demon Azazel taunts Dean, "How certain are you that what you brought back is 100 percent pure Sam?" Sam's ruthless behavior continues into the third season, as does Dean's anxiety and paranoia that his brother may have transformed into something monstrous, something other. He asks Bobby in "Sin City" (3.4) if he thinks something is wrong with Sam. Sam's potentially monstrous transformation as a result of his brother usurping the natural order of death for him suggests the liminal position of the monstrous in fiction, as it exists between the natural and unnatural of the world (Shildrick 2). Sam's developing monstrosity is a reflection of the liminality of the brothers' own excessive relationship with one another; it, too, the series suggests, exists somewhere between the natural and unnatural.

Dean's defiance of death for Sam ultimately has a cyclical effect. When Sam is unable to strike the same deal for Dean's soul to free him from Hell, he ultimately turns to his plan of vengeance, which causes his monstrous nature to intensify. Hence, Sam's slow devolution into the monstrous other is a direct result of the constant cycle of the brothers' attempting to violate nature for one another. The series suggests that Dean's inability to let go of Sam, motivated by his excessive devotion to his brother, potentially awakens the monstrous within Sam. Sam's ultimate demonic transformation, the anxiety that his resurrection may have made him less human, Dean's anxiety about turning into a demon—all stem from the single act of Dean trading his soul for Sam's, an act already erotically coded by being sealed with a kiss. This one act of excessive love has a domino effect throughout the series, awakening the monstrous in both brothers. The monstrous transformation of the Winchesters directly correlates with the boys' excessive bond. This correlation between their bond and the monstrous is one of the most explicit implications that the brothers' connection may be unnatural at its very core, as they literally have the power to corrupt each other into monsters. The transformation into the monstrous other is the Winchesters' paranoid anxiety made manifest, the excessive secret at the center of their relationship revealed.

Through the incestuous undertones in their relationship and the monstrous shadow selves they fear, the Winchesters' relationship draws on the core anxieties of sexual deviancy and monstrous others that create the Queer Gothic and Gothic in general, making it a unique modern addition to the tradition. The paradoxical contrast of the open secret and the unspeakable strikes at the center of the Gothic anxiety that permeates the Winchesters' relationship throughout the series. The brothers' terror of transformation into the other as a consequence of their devotion to each other blurs the boundaries of their identity as hunters with the monsters they hunt. Through the use of these Gothic conventions, *Supernatural* reveals the open secret at the heart of the series: the Winchesters' excessive, incestuous, homoerotic love.

WORKS CITED

"All Hell Breaks Loose, Part 2." *Supernatural: The Complete Second Season*. Writ. Eric Kripke. Dir. Kim Manners. Perf. Jensen Ackles and Jared Padalecki. Warner Bros., 2007. DVD.

Botting, Fred. *Gothic: The New Critical Idiom*. New York: Taylor & Francis, 1996. Web.

"Bugs." *Supernatural: The Complete First Season*. Writ. Rachel Nave and Bill Coakley. Dir. Kim Manners. Perf. Jensen Ackles and Jared Padalecki. Warner Bros., 2006. DVD.

Butler, Judith. *The Psychic Life of Power: Theories in Subjection*. Stanford: Stanford University Press, 1997. Print.

"Children Shouldn't Play with Dead Things." *Supernatural: The Complete Second Season*. Writ. Raelle Tucker. Dir. Kim Manners. Perf. Jensen Ackles and Jared Padalecki. Warner Bros., 2007. DVD.

Coates, Paul. *The Double and the Other: Identity as Ideology in Post-Romantic Fiction*. New York: St. Martin's Press, 1988. Print.

"Dream a Little Dream of Me." *Supernatural: The Complete Third Season*. Writ. Cathryn Humphris. Dir. Steve Boyum. Perf. Jensen Ackles and Jared Padalecki. Warner Bros., 2008. DVD.

Eberle-Sinatra, Michael. "Exploring Gothic Sexuality." *Gothic Studies* 7.2 (2005): 123–126. Web.

"The End." *Supernatural: The Complete Fifth Season*. Writ. Ben Edlund. Dir. Steve Boyum. Perf. Jensen Ackles and Jared Padalecki. Warner Bros., 2010. DVD.

Freud, Sigmund. *The Uncanny*. New York: Penguin, 2003. Print.

Haggerty, George E. *Queer Gothic*. Urbana: University of Illinois Press, 2006. Print.

"I Know What You Did Last Summer." *Supernatural: The Complete Fourth Season*. Writ. Sera Gamble. Dir. Charles Beeson. Perf. Jensen Ackles and Jared Padalecki. Warner Bros., 2009. DVD.

Morris, David B. "Gothic Sublimity." *New Literary History* 16.2 (1985): 299–319. Web.

"Pilot." *Supernatural: The Complete First Season*. Writ. Eric Kripke. Dir. David Nutter. Perf. Jensen Ackles and Jared Padalecki. Warner Bros., 2006. DVD.

"Playthings." *Supernatural: The Complete Second Season*. Writ. Matt Witten. Dir. Charles Beeson. Perf. Jensen Ackles and Jared Padalecki. Warner Bros., 2007. DVD.

"Point of No Return." *Supernatural: The Complete Fifth Season*. Writ. Jeremy Carver. Dir. Phil Sgriccia. Perf. Jensen Ackles and Jared Padalecki. Warner Bros., 2010. DVD.

Rigby, Mair. "Uncanny Recognition: Queer Theory's Debt to the Gothic." *Gothic Studies* 11.1 (2009): 46–57. Web.

Sedgwick, Eve Kosofsky. *Between Men: English Literature and Male Homosocial Desire*. New York: Columbia University Press, 1985. Print.

"Sex and Violence." *Supernatural: The Complete Fourth Season*. Writ. Cathryn Humphris. Dir. Charles Beeson. Perf. Jensen Ackles and Jared Padalecki. Warner Bros., 2009. DVD.

Shildrick, Margrit. "Posthumanism and the Monstrous Body." *Body & Society* 2.1 (1996): 1–15. Print.

Tosenberger, Catherine. "'The Epic Love Story of Sam and Dean': *Supernatural*, Queer Readings, and the Romance of Incestuous Fan Fiction." *Transformative Works and Cultures* 1 (2008). Web.

"You Can't Handle the Truth." *Supernatural: The Complete Sixth Season*. Writ. Eric Charmelo and Nicole Snyder. Dir. Jan Eliasberg. Perf. Jensen Ackles and Jared Padalecki. Warner Bros., 2011. DVD.

We All Have a
Little Monster in Us

*Dean Winchester, the Mark of Cain
and the New Monster Paradigm*

Lisa Schmidt

Once upon a time, monsters were easy to discover. In various narratives—folklore, myth, philosophical discourse and, of course, Gothic fiction—monsters would be found in crypts, castles, and cemeteries. They populated seas, deserts, rivers, forests, and even outer space. Yet, as Stephen T. Asma notes in his *On Monsters: An Unnatural History of Our Worst Fears* (2011), these diverse beings had one thing in common. Going back to the ancients, Asma invokes the once predominant Aristotelian paradigm: Everything in nature has an essence and, with it, a purpose. When this essence is lost, confused, or overthrown, we have a monster; simply put, to be a monster is to be impure.[1] Thus the original and fairly universal understanding of "monster" was as nature transgressed (276). This original monster paradigm seems to have applied equally to "freaks" of nature and supernatural entities.[2] Vampires, ghouls,[3] ghosts, and other revenants of the sort that appear in Gothic literature, were dead bodies that violate their own nature by not remaining inanimate; if the essential purpose of being dead is to lie still and decompose, then vampires and ghosts would unquestionably be "in between," made animate by some profane contamination. Similarly, a creature that is part human and part animal would be subverting the boundaries between philosophical species; and, of course, a demon, witch, or possessed person is transformed by the touch of something unholy and unclean (i.e., Satan). The original meaning of "supernatural" is, for all intents and purposes, *un*-natural.

These old-school, traditional monsters inspired a clear moral imperative. To use the idiom of the television show *Supernatural*, a contemporary Gothic fiction, monsters "gotta be ganked." However, there is something that I would like to call a "new monster" paradigm at work in *Supernatural* (among other texts). To be sure, there are traditional monsters still lurking about, including in *Supernatural*, and contemporary Gothic monsters owe much to the antagonists of classics like *The Castle of Otranto* (1764), *The Monk* (1796), *Frankenstein* (1818), and *Dracula* (1897), or of the horror films of the earlier part of the twentieth century. It goes without saying that cultural notions of monsters always change over time, whether we are talking of monstrosity as applied to individuals or societies, but the old monsters have arrived in 2015 profoundly transformed. The reason, Asma suggests, is this: "We don't *know* the purpose of nature anymore because there are no purposes of nature" (276). That is to say, original cultural understandings of the discursive concept "nature" have been overthrown, initially by the arrival of the Scientific Revolution and the Enlightenment, and then by the real world horrors of the twentieth century. These experiences might be summed up in a well-known apothegm from Friedrich Nietzsche: "He who fights with monsters should be careful lest he thereby also become a monster. And if thou gaze long into an abyss, the abyss also gazes long into thee." By the 1960s, it was quite evident that even "ordinary" human beings could be monsters—fictional or factual, Norman Bates or Charles Manson. But along with these new realizations came increased moral complication. If we are no longer confident of our ability to identify monsters, or to identify them *easily*, can we know when and how to take action? Moreover, if these monsters are so much like "us," if we are somehow responsible for their existence, is it morally correct to just "gank" them and move on, satisfied that we have been righteous?

This loss of moral certainty is not necessarily a step backwards, as critic Robin Wood made abundantly clear in his seminal essay on "modern" horror ("Introduction"). Wood put his analytical finger on the ideological nexus between monster and not-monster, for this place of connection reveals both the best and the worst in us. Using Freudian logic and language, Wood examined the nature of monsters in horror films of the 1960s and 1970s and argued that the transition from classical to modern monsters marked a new, possibly liberatory energy in the horror genre. He discussed some of the contemporary texts (of the time) in terms of being either progressive or reactionary in their attitudes toward monsters. For my purposes here, Wood's critical insight was that there is a fundamental "relationship between the monster and normality" (*Hollywood* 204). In other words, monsters always originate within *us*, and the particulars of our monsters change in tandem with our stance(s) on what it is to be an "ordinary human." Moreover, our capacity to empathize with our monsters (at least in fiction) rather than disowning them is an indicator of a thorny moral landscape, and perhaps also a marker of an increased willingness to engage with knotty problems. For instance, what do we owe to a Charles Manson or Norman Bates if we are responsible, as a society, for his existence? Also, it seems that monstrosity was traditionally (and unjustly) associated with ideas, practices, and desires that were prohibited despite being a part of the ordinary spectrum of human behavior. A world where these problematics are accepted *is* a more difficult one, to be sure. But, as Wood and Asma would agree, the lessons of the twentieth century cannot be unlearned: Complexity is not something that mature moral subjects, acting in good faith, can afford to avoid. Simplicity has the virtue of making decisions easier to arrive at, but it is not necessarily more virtuous.

Supernatural is operating in a genre and television context that understands all of this rather well. The particulars of the dynamic relationship between monster and not-monster will always pose moral questions—questions that are deeply embedded in the storytelling of *Supernatural*. Over the space of ten years, *Supernatural* has delivered a sumptuous buffet of monstrosity. Indeed, the show has long since abandoned the pretense of trying to scare and has become something else, using the trappings of traditional Gothic and horror narratives to make a deep exploration of its own moral world.[4] As early as Season One, the show closed with an emotional epic battle over the right way to deal with a specific monster ("Devil's Trap," 1.22), and it did the same in Season Ten; in Season One, the monster was John Winchester; in Season Ten, it was Dean Winchester ("Brother's Keeper," 10.23). These days, even heroes can be monsters if they make the wrong decisions. In fact, in *Supernatural*, being a monster is not an all-or-nothing proposition but "a choice" ("Ask Jeeves," 10.4). Monsters are not *born* as such; through bad luck, accident, or intended destiny they may find themselves with something in them that predisposes them to violence and chaos, but *Supernatural* insists that free will is both *possible* and *necessary* regardless of *what* you are—creature, demon, angel, or a human with a bad childhood and a cursed mark on your arm. Becoming a monster is an imminent tragedy that can be averted. When the proto-monster abandons choice and surrenders to the idea that nature is destiny, he lets the monsters of the past overtake him and thus becomes a monster of the new paradigm. To subscribe to this old-fashioned and reactionary view of the world is generally presented as immoral within the narrative of *Supernatural*, particularly in seasons eight to ten.[5] Tragedy becomes inevitable. The monster generates horrific damage and suffering and must be destroyed, regardless of what it once might have been.

These monsters who do let themselves be seduced by that older monster paradigm—and there are many—are not only tragic but also melodramatic. As a vibrantly Gothic fiction that also happens to be a heavily serialized television show, *SPN* has seized an opportunity to expound upon the moral status of monsters and, along with them, monster hunters.[6] The text of *Supernatural* often preaches that, while even the most potent monsters may ultimately be dispatched, this can only be accomplished at a cost. While a film can make the same point, the expanded seriality of contemporary television allows shows like *Supernatural* to draw upon years of narrative material to make their case with melodramatic punctuation. In a previous article, "Television: Horror's 'Original' Home," I claimed that horror has always been melodramatic, and that considering the deep connection between horror, the Gothic, and melodrama, and the serialized nature of contemporary television, horror television shows are the perfect expression of horror in its "original" sense.[7] Seriality makes melodrama inevitable by raising the moral stakes of character decisions over narrative time and ensuring intense emotional investment in the outcomes of these dilemmas from the audience. Furthermore, I argued that *Supernatural* perfectly encapsulates the meaning of Peter Brooks's "moral occult," as the narrative struggles to come to terms with different visions of an underlying moral reality via the actions and decisions of Sam and Dean.[8]

We can find all of the abovementioned dynamics percolating in *Supernatural* as recently as the Season Ten finale, in which the Mark of Cain is removed from Dean Winchester's arm by a morally-dubious spell created at the behest of his brother Sam. Prior to this, Sam has been repeatedly warned about the consequences of the spell, and up to the very last moment Dean resists being saved by Sam because they both know that Dean's life and soul cannot possibly be worth more than all the humans they will endanger by their actions—yet, every time they are confronted with this utilitarian calculus, they choose each other like good Kantians, always with horrible consequences. This time, they unleash "The Darkness," a mysterious force that predates and originates all other monsters in the *Supernatural* universe. This was the resolution of the two-season "Mark of Cain" arc, particularly Season Ten, which dwelt luxuriantly on the idea that Dean Winchester, a "righteous man," is doomed to become a monster. Throughout the season, Dean is orbited by characters—i.e., Cole, Charlie, Claire, Crowley—who struggle with monstrosity, not to mention his brother, Sam, who travels his own dark journey in his quest to save Dean from the Mark of Cain. In true Gothic form, almost every one of these characters manifests a dark double, while Dean has his own doppelgänger, the demon version of himself. Intimately tied to Dean's narrative is the tragic arc of Cain, the father of murder and, in some texts, the father of *monsters* (Asma 96). As well, Dean has a brief reunion with his friend Benny (from Season Eight), a vampire and one of many characters in *Supernatural* who exemplify the pitiable trajectory of the new monster. Yet long before Dean receives the Mark of Cain ("First Born," 9.11) there were single episodes and multi-episode arcs that prefigured Dean's Season Ten struggle. In fact, Dean has been on a journey toward monstrosity since the very beginning of the show, and the Mark of Cain only made into a major arc what had been previously a central dynamic of Dean's character.

"It's possible there's a little monster in all of us"

Although the Mark of Cain arc represents the culmination of Dean's journey toward monstrosity, it can easily be said that Dean has always been struggling with the demons of his id. To understand how this is so, it is useful to refer again to Wood, who in his essay makes a crucial distinction between "basic" and "surplus" repression. Basic repression is merely what is necessary for society to function—"universal, necessary and inescapable" ("Introduction" 197)—while surplus repression is excessive and unjust, reaching deeply into our ids and fragmenting the richness of human libidinal expression ("Introduction" 197). Surplus repression is what forces Dean to present a caricature of heterosexual masculinity. Everything about Dean, from his body language, to his way of speaking, to his music preferences, are a part of this restricted ego-performance, as is his categorical inability to express his true feelings other than through acceptable sublimation. So many aspects of Dean's self become forbidden and repressed at an early age—his affectionate heart, his curiosity or desire about anything not connected to his role as protector, his longing for real, long-term connections—that he clings almost maniacally to those things he believes he *can* have: his music, his momentary sexual pleasures, his hamburgers, the trappings of his work (weapons, etc.) and, of course, his car. In Freudian terms, his libidinal energies have been so distorted by the pressures of the reality principle, which includes the unique pressures of Winchester family dynamics and life experiences, that his fierce love can only be expressed as aggression. He has based his self-worth, such as it is, entirely on his ability to protect and save others, especially his brother; the only ego satisfaction he knows is through sacrifice.

As Wood knows, the repressed always returns, but under capitalistic, patriarchal, heteronormative conditions, it will return as a monster. Monsters are literally shaped from the lost parts of ourselves, feared because they have been cruelly repressed, and that which is repressed grows in power until it seems far too powerful and frightening to be confronted; yet far too attractive to resist because it represents parts of our self that we (naturally) want back.[9] These are not vestigial emotions but necessary human desires, yet they appear in a form unbearable (to the superego); one that must be dealt with swiftly and decisively. These would be the monsters of *Supernatural* in "the early years." They were the ghosts, vampires, demons, and other creatures that wanted to hurt, kill, or eat people. It was Sam and Dean's job to destroy them, and there was little debate about it. If it was one of "them," it was wrong and to be destroyed, and "they" obliged by being suitably frightening, dangerous, and grotesque. Just as in Wood's account of modern monsters,[10] the monster is *other*—suppressed and rejected needs transmuted into murderous ghosts, flesh-eating monsters, and savage demons.

In proper melodramatic and Gothic form, Dean and Sam carried their own, personal demons with them on their journey. There was an original "myth-arc" in which we learn, early on, that Sam has some psychic powers of unknown origin. At the beginning of Season Two ("In My Time of Dying," 2.01), Dean is warned by his father that he may have to kill Sam, and by the end of the season Sam has learned the worst: He has been "chosen" to become a monster by the demon Azazel who visited his nursery when he was six months old to feed him some demon blood. At first, it seems that he is meant to lead some kind of uprising of evil, perhaps a demon army ("All Hell Breaks Loose, Part 1," 2.21). But as the Sam-as-evil-prince arc continues, Sam comes to understand that he was chosen to release Lucifer from Hell and trigger the Apocalypse, a war between angels and demons that will more or less incinerate the world ("Lucifer Rising," 4.22). Thus Sam's human nature has been tainted; demon blood is the source of his powers. In a way, this earlier version of Sam is still a part of the old monster paradigm, or perhaps a demonstration that as much as monsters change, they remain the same. Even so, it can be argued that we are within the new monster idiom, where the evil and impurity are not so much projected onto others as introjected, visited back upon the self. The "internalization" of monstrosity observed by Wood is no longer merely geographic and social; the monster is truly, even literally, within.

As this story arc progresses to Season Four, Sam's struggle with his inner monstrosity puts him at risk of becoming a true monster, and this situation becomes a focal point for moral conflict and intense melodrama. On one side, perhaps Sam can use powers derived from evil to do something good, since his power consists mainly of banishing (and later killing) demons; at least he argues as much to Dean. He is assisted (or manipulated) by Ruby, a demon who claims she is helping Sam get vengeance against the much older and more powerful Lilith, the first demon.[11] Sam is led to believe that he can use his powers to avert the Apocalypse by killing Lilith, who is destroying the Seals on Lucifer's Cage. We, along with Sam, are tempted to believe that Ruby does have good intentions, and to consider Sam as having the morally "correct" take on monstrosity. It is certainly a sympathetic one. As Sam rages at Dean in the pivotal episode "Metamorphosis" (4.4): "I've got demon blood in me, Dean...! This disease pumping through my veins and I can't ever rip it out or scrub it clean! I'm a whole new level of freak! And I'm just trying to take this ... this curse ... and make something good out of it ... because I have to." Meanwhile, Dean clings to what could be considered the less evolved, black-and-white morality, the morality of the older paradigm and a much simpler show. Dean believes that any use of demon-derived powers must be dangerous at best and fatal at worst despite the fact that Sam does perform "good deeds" with his power. Even so, Dean is convinced that the Sam who uses these powers is no longer his brother, exhibiting the "us and them" mentality that will come to be a marker of monstrous thinking within *Supernatural*. Dean is still operating within the traditional perspective in which a monster is something whose essential nature is flawed or impure; regardless of what Sam does, his demon powers are grotesque, and in using them he is crossing a line that is absolute. Perhaps the narrative, too, is still clinging to this older paradigm, for Dean is ultimately right.[12] Although Dean has had a role in it, Sam's decisions trigger the Apocalypse, which he and Dean work to avert throughout Season Five. Sam can only atone for his actions by sacrificing his life and joining Lucifer back in his Cage in Hell.

"It doesn't matter what you are.... It only matters what you do"

Even if Dean is right about Sam's demon-legacy, Season Four Sam has reasons to think that his actions are the right ones, not least because, prior to this, the brothers have already encountered so-called traditional monsters whose actions bely their supposedly monstrous nature. In fact, Dean's all-or-nothing stance toward them has been called into question, and will continue to be. Moreover, his rigidity is clearly the product of a dysfunction within him of which he is well aware. Although he seldom admits it, Dean knows that his constrained upbringing as little more than John Winchester's dutiful soldier and Sam's protector has distorted who he might have been, leaving him incomplete and even unstable. In "Salvation" (1.21), an idea is introduced that lurks within the series until fully realized in the Mark of Cain arc: That Dean could become little more than a killing machine, all elements of his personality subsumed into his violence.[13] There are moments scattered throughout the first six seasons where Dean is overtaken by this "demon"; he becomes a dead-eyed, blood-spattered killer. For instance, in "Bloodlust" (2.3), Sam and Dean meet a vampire named Lenore who refuses to kill and drink humans. They also meet a cautionary character named Gordon, a hunter who enjoys killing monsters a bit too much. Gordon is what Dean could become if he closes off any possibility of empathy with monsters.[14] Dean teeters on the brink in "Bloodlust" but is able to accept that Lenore, although a vampire, is not a monster; he confronts Gordon as the true monster. Meanwhile, the fates of Gordon, Lenore, and many other secondary characters in *Supernatural*, are ultimately monster tragedies that play out similarly: Gordon becomes a vampire and is killed by Sam ("Fresh Blood," 3.7), while Lenore, influenced by the presence of Eve (the mother of all monsters) on Earth, feeds on a human and asks to be killed before she loses her humanity ("Mommy Dearest," 6.19). There are others whose stories cannot be told at this point in the interest of brevity. However, I would like to take the time to discuss "Metamorphosis," as I believe it is a pivotal episode, for Dean and Sam's character development as well as the show's perspective on monsters. In context, it is also a warning about the need to battle against the demons of one's nature, in this case directed at Sam, but it applies just as perfectly to Dean's eventual monster arc.

The episode begins with the argument between Sam and Dean that I have summarized above. The argument is left unresolved as they are summoned to help an older hunter named Travis to deal with a Rugaru, a creature that looks normal up to a certain point in its life when it is suddenly consumed by an appetite for "long pig."[15] The man in question, Jack Montgomery, is presented sympathetically; he is an ordinary man with a lovely wife (Michelle), but lately he cannot seem to find satiation no matter how much he eats. Sam and Dean watch him and debate what should be done. Not surprisingly, Dean wants to kill Jack and be done with the matter, even though Jack has not yet hurt anyone. Sam uncovers lore suggesting that if a Rugaru manages not to feed on humans, they will never transform completely; once they take the first bite, however, they are lost. Travis asserts that resistance is impossible, but Sam is invested in the belief that biology is not destiny—he has to be. Dean agrees to confront Jack first; they warn him that if he surrenders to his appetites that they will have to return and burn him alive (the only way to kill a Rugaru). Jack is understandably angry, yet he succeeds in controlling himself, right up to the point that Travis, impatient and no longer trusting Sam and Dean to do what is "right," goes to the couple's house to take care of business. Unfortunately Michelle reveals that she is pregnant, so when Jack arrives he is told (with Travis's condolences) that they will both have to die. At this threat to the woman he loves, Jack uses his Rugaru strength to get free, but he loses control, killing and devouring Travis. When Sam and Dean arrive, Jack gets the jump on them, locking Sam in a closet. As Jack visibly struggles with his desire to make a meal of Dean, Sam pleads with him through the door: "You don't have to be a monster. You have a choice." In a moment of deep pathos, Jack replies, "Have you *seen* me lately?" Sam gets free just in time to save Dean and send Jack up in flames. Meanwhile, Michelle gets away; even transformed into a monster, Jack is still capable of love, having carefully not mentioned Michelle's pregnancy to the brothers. As a final flourish to Jack's tragedy, we are left knowing that all of this will be repeated in thirty years or so.

A similar melodrama shapes the narrative arc of Benny Lafitte, a vampire who becomes Dean's friend and ally after Dean is accidentally sent to Purgatory at the conclusion of Season Seven ("Survival of the Fittest," 7.23). Once again, it is a character's *actions* rather than his *nature* that determines whether or not he is a monster. Benny, like Jack, and Sam earlier on, has something in him that in the original paradigm would make him a de facto monster, that predisposes him to monstrous acts. Yet, like so many vampires in popular fiction lately, he resists a hunger that is supposedly irresistible. He partners with Dean and the two escape Purgatory together, but after escaping, Benny's real struggles with his vampire nature must begin. In Purgatory, it does not matter who he kills because all of the inhabitants are monsters and are technically dead already. Once he is back on Earth, Benny has nowhere to belong, and he must deal with constant temptation, surviving on stolen blood packs. Indeed, the episode "Citizen Fang" (8.6) is almost a complete reboot of "Metamorphosis." Benny has found something like a home, working in a diner in the employ of his human great-granddaughter, Liz. Meanwhile, Sam, who in an interesting reversal, has become the one arguing that vampires are vampires and cannot be trusted, has sent an unstable hunter named Martin to watch Benny. Believing that Benny is responsible for a recent rash of vampire activity, Martin is insistent that Benny be dealt with while Dean refuses (again, a reversal). Despite Dean's best efforts, Martin eventually uses Liz to force the issue, threatening her and demanding that Benny show his true nature. Although Benny at first seems willing to die rather than reveal his worst self, he loses control just as Jack did, attacking and savaging Martin. As a result he loses his home, his connection to Liz, and Dean, who will ultimately decide that he and Benny must part ways.[16]

"Until you become the monster"

In both cases just outlined (Jack and Benny) it is not a lack of willpower that ultimately destroys these characters. It is, in a word, love—but more specifically, a need to act on that love, to protect and save the loved one. Not to put too fine a point on it, Dean has made (repeatedly) the same choice, having turned himself into an increasingly brutal killer over the eight-plus years preceding the Mark of Cain arc. Out of love and a quasi-parental, trauma-based need to "take care of Sammy," Dean repeatedly offers whatever he has, first sacrificing his desires for anything outside the hunter life, then his life and soul and, eventually, his humanity. After his training under his father, he goes on to some special missions in Hell and Purgatory that make him an extremely efficient killer and hunter, while bringing him closer to his demon self. We must bear in mind that, according to *Supernatural* mythology, demons do not come into the universe evil; they become so over time as they are twisted and tormented in Hell. Even worse, it transpires that there was a moment in Hell when Dean chose to pick up a knife and begin torturing other souls in order to escape his own suffering ("Heaven and Hell," 4.10). It seems that demons, just like other monsters in the new paradigm, *choose* to be demons, and unfortunately this choice is inevitable because no one can resist torture forever. Everyone who goes to Hell *will* become a monster, even if they sold themselves for noble reasons.

By Season Eight, Dean has become, in the words of Crowley "quite the killing machine" ("Blade Runners," 9.16). He is ready for an unprecedented act of sacrifice; having given up his life, his soul, and his well-being, all he has left is his bravery and his identity as a hero—which is where the character of Cain enters. Not coincidentally, Dean's story is also Cain's story. Both Dean and Cain are righteous men; both offer to do evil for the brothers they love. Cain tells Dean how he learned that his brother was being tempted by Lucifer; in return for Abel going to Heaven, Cain agreed to take his brother's life and to become a Knight of Hell, a demon, and the father of murder ("First Born," 9.11). With Cain and Dean, the very best in them becomes the core of their monstrosity. Cain decides that Dean is "worthy" to receive his Mark after watching him single-handedly and brutally dispatch a trio of demons; by now he has become the perfect killer he once dreaded being. His willingness to do anything to save his brother regardless of the cost (even his relationship to Sam) is the plot equivalent of Sam's demon blood taint; it is a "power" indeed, but one based in the belief that he himself has no worth, no future, and no right to turn away from violence. He has become a demon of self-loathing, hiding behind an increasingly brittle patina of "okayness," and it is this same demon that drives him to accept the Mark of Cain.

Perhaps it is fitting, then, that as Season Ten unfolds it is sometimes difficult to understand precisely how the Mark is working upon Dean. Even when literally turned into a black-eyed demon at the end of Season Nine and for the first three episodes of Season Ten, Demon Dean is not far removed from his usual self. The Mark's apparently supernatural effects only make sense as an expression of who Dean already is, and the narrative even deploys some popular Freudian analysis to make this point. Indeed, a psychoanalytic explanation of the Mark's effects is suggested in "There's No Place Like Home" (10.11) when Carter/The Wizard (yet another character in Season Ten with a dark double) refers to his darker self as his "id." Dark Charlie underscores this psychoanalytic reading when she says, "You know what's the best part about being dark? You're free." The freedom of which she speaks is freedom from even basic repression; the freedom to give her own anger and murderous impulses full rein. Likewise, the Mark does seem to allow Dean the luxury of anger, but his anger is dangerous and uncontrollable; what might once have been a natural, albeit complex, amoral energy has long since become rage under the tyranny of a murderous superego. Thus while it may be convenient to dismiss Dean's actions while he is under the influence of the Mark as "not-Dean," as Sam does, this is not the case. If anything, he is "more Dean," and when "demonized" he is *most* Dean, only now he can unleash the resentment toward Sam that, on some level, he must have always felt, even if unconsciously. In "Soul Survivor" (10.3), Demon Dean takes the opportunity to lob this truth bomb at his brother: "Your very existence sucked the life outta my life." At the level of supernatural (and plot) mechanism, we know that the Mark, in tandem with the First Blade, supposedly turns its bearer into something he is not, but in terms of Dean's character across ten seasons, it would seem that the Mark manifests Dean just exactly as he is, only amplified. One of the worst things Dean ever does while under its thrall is to speak the brutal truth.

Assuming that this is indeed how the narrative of *Supernatural* understands the influence of the Mark, this allows for a fresh insistence that acts of free will are the cure for monstrosity. After all, if repression can create a monster, repression should be able to subdue a monster. Sam demonstrates this expectation with his speech in "The Hunter Games" (10.10), in which he speculates that since Cain lived with the Mark for years, Dean can also learn to live with the Mark. And Dean is willing to fight but, in a cruel twist, it seems that the common psychic mechanism of sublimation does not work with the Mark and Dean must attempt to control all of his desires, a task that is well beyond most human beings and a particular challenge for Dean who is already a functional alcoholic. He cannot funnel his aggression into food and drink, as much as he tries; indeed, after a short distance on the wagon, Dean hits the bottle harder than ever and is frequently seen in the latter half of the season gorging himself on junk food. Such excess signals that Dean is losing his fight with his demon, that he has given up, and the narrative makes it abundantly clear that giving up, although perhaps understandable, is a prelude to doom. Such is the fate of Cain as played out in "The Executioner's Song" (10.14). After centuries of resistance to the Mark, Cain no longer tries or wishes to try to resist it. He accepts what he considers to be his terrible nature and decides that the only way to "save" those who are tainted with his blood is to eradicate his entire genetic legacy in an act of genocide. He is thus a true monster. He must be saved (killed) by Dean—again, an act of sacrifice for Dean since he has to use the First Blade and has every reason to believe that he will emerge from the fight a monster himself. Even worse, Cain's fate is an obvious predictor of where Dean will end up and he pleads with Cain not to give up, just as he has pleaded with Charlie and Castiel in previous episodes, just as Sam has pleaded with Jack ("Metamorphosis") and the shapeshifter Olivia ("Ask Jeeves") and eventually will with Dean himself. The words are always variations on the theme of agency: "Tell me I don't have to do this." "Tell me you can stop." "You can make a choice." "It isn't what you are that matters; it's what you do." To Dean, Cain's reply is like a death sentence: "I'll never stop." Cain has been lost to Aristotelian inevitability; his essence is all monster, and that leaves no room for choice, neither in him nor in the victims he now sees exclusively as monsters.

Dean must now be the instrument of Cain's tragic destiny; after killing Cain with the First Blade, he somehow manages to retain at least a pretense of free will, yet he seems to be broken. Still, it takes several more episodes for his final plunge to happen. Eventually, when he kills Cyrus Styne without remorse in "The Prisoner" (10.22), we and Sam know that Dean is becoming Cain. In executing all the other Stynes he is still doing his job, i.e., killing monsters. The Stynes are monstrous by any definition, but it is worth observing that they do represent monstrosity from the older, more straightforward paradigm that still makes appearances in *Supernatural* when necessary. They are an ancient, aristocratic family who use the worst kind of magic to increase their privilege and wealth, making them Gothic monsters *par excellence*. This is not to mention the fact that they are originally *Frankensteins*, making them a literal tribute to and interpretation of their Gothic lineage. They also fit easily into the original definition of monstrosity as outlined by Asma. Harvesting organs from other human beings, the Stynes use magic and technology to obtain replacement parts and extend their lives. They are thus walking abominations whose original essence has become contaminated many times over. They are a clear case for ganking. Cyrus is different, though, a young man who could very easily have been Sam once upon a time; he is studious and shy, hates the family business and still has all his original parts. He expresses disgust and horror at what he is forced to do. He is the titular "prisoner," which suggests that under the right circumstances he would turn away from the evil legacy of his family. Having killed all of Cyrus's relatives, Dean could have been a hero to him, setting him free from the nightmare of his family. Instead, Dean commits murder, using Cain's own logic. For Dean in this mindset, Cyrus's blood is sufficient to condemn him. The show makes it clear, by emphasizing Cyrus's perspective, that whether or not Cyrus needed to die, Dean's shooting him through the head with barely a pause is a monstrous act.

Now on the verge of full monster status, Dean attempts, in the season finale "Brother's Keeper" (10.23), one final grab at choice. He asks Death, arguably the most powerful being in the *Supernatural* universe, to put him somewhere he can do no harm. Death agrees, with the proviso that Dean must first murder Sam,[17] for both Dean and Death know that while Sam is alive he will stop at nothing to get his brother back, just as Dean has in the past. The drama in this final confrontation depends upon the knowledge of the committed viewer after ten years of *Supernatural*, the experienced viewer who knows that it would be the ultimate loss of self, the ultimate tragedy, if Dean betrayed his bond with Sam. This would be an act that would put him beyond the reach of redemption. But Dean is able to return from the outermost frontier of monster territory by making another choice, affirming the show's perspective on monsters and, of course, on the power of family.[18] There is also high melodrama in Sam's speech to Dean, which resounds and echoes with many other matters of longstanding debate between the two brothers: "You will never hear me say that you—the real you—is anything other than good." This speech rings with the memory of other, contrary things that Sam has said to Dean;

since the second half of Season Nine, Sam has been angry at Dean and, unlike Dean, has been free with his emotions, telling Dean that he has been selfish and self-serving in his insistence on saving Sam at any cost. He goes so far as to tell Dean that he would not choose to save him under similar circumstances and even that they can no longer be brothers; not long after, Dean flings himself into the Mark of Cain arc. Yet with his speech in "Brother's Keeper," Sam affirms that, having seen everything that Dean is and has done, he still believes in the best of him. Thus reminded, Dean chooses his connection with his brother once again, just as he and Sam have always done. *Supernatural* has remained true to its original defining motif, that family is a redemptive force, or rather, familial *love* will save the world.[19] Even as recently as the finale of Season Ten, Sam and Dean both survive and evade monstrosity because of each other. There is no question that, on their own, they each would have become monsters many times over by now.

Brothers' Keepers

Previously I have argued that *Supernatural* is deploying the tools of seriality and the Gothic to deeply explore the moral status of its characters. The monster is a perfect focus for such an exploration, as it represents the transformation from a morally black-and-white world, in which monsters are relatively easy to identify, to a much more sophisticated one. This is not so much to contradict or overturn the traditional monster as to say that in serialized television our monsters have come home to roost. "Traditional" monsters were defined as evil by nature and, even if somewhat sympathetic, had to be destroyed. In the new paradigm, we still are dealing with familiar creatures— vampires, werewolves, ghosts, ghouls—but we have an increased understanding that these monsters are, in a way, our victims.[20] In the new paradigm, we understand that monsters are not born but made, and that having to destroy them is a tragedy. Such monsters must be destroyed because of the things they *do*, not what they *are*, and they are only unredeemable when they refuse this truth. It may be obvious to say that, in *SPN*, becoming a monster is a process that can always be averted by an act of will—as long as a certain line is not crossed. The line appears to have nothing to do with how many people die, or how many apocalypses are started. It is, rather, the line between old paradigm thinking ("us" versus "them") and new paradigm thinking. This process is manifest in many of the characters of *SPN* but I have chosen here to focus on Dean Winchester, whose character arc best demonstrates the new paradigm. To date, the only thing in *SPN* that seems to separate the "heroes" from true monsters (Those Who Must Be Ganked) is that they are ultimately able to find the will to *choose* not to be monsters.

NOTES

1. In Asma's words: "Monsters are the things that never fulfill their purpose or never make it to their goal, either because the development is accidentally arrested (by internal or external cause) or because matter confused or retarded the realization of form or because some more impurity deformed the creature's true potential. Whatever the particulars, monsters were cases of development that missed their targets" (276).

2. There was always a fairly thin line between supposed "real" monsters and fictional ones, of course. At one time, vampires were denizens of both Gothic literature and official government reports, while creatures that we would now immediately recognize as mythological were sometimes described in the annals of natural philosophy, i.e. science.

3. The popular term for a reanimated corpse that shambles and eats human flesh is, of course, zombie, but I prefer the original term "ghoul" here, since it was only after George Romero's *Night of the Living Dead* (1968) (which, curiously, does not use the word "zombie") that the terminology changed.

4. From the very beginning, the narrative has been dedicated to answering the question: "Can family save the world?," with the relationship between the brothers Sam and Dean being the emotional core of the story and the engine of much of the plot. Throughout its run, the show has expanded and widened its universe, adding various new threats and myth-arcs (while, I would argue, becoming increasingly less "horror" and more "Gothic").

5. Except when it isn't! Even in the complex world they now inhabit, the characters of *Supernatural* do encounter, occasionally, an old-school monster reminiscent of that original, and easier, moral imperative. They are generally nostalgic about that more straightforward world, much as some people mourn a golden past that never really existed.

6. An opportunity previously available only in lengthy, serialized penny dreadfuls such as *Varney the Vampire* (1845–1847) or *The String of Pearls: A Romance* (1846–1847).

7. See Lisa Schmidt, "Television: Horror's 'Original' Home." *Horror Studies* 4.2 (2013): 159–171. http://dx.doi.org/10.1386/host.4.2.159_1.

8. This first "volume" of the show, if I may use that term, culminates at the conclusion of Season Five with the defeat of Lucifer, stopping the (Christian) Apocalypse. The conclusion of this myth-arc coincided with the departure of Eric Kripke, the show's creator, as show-runner. Under show-runner Sera Gamble, Seasons Six and Seven can be seen as a second volume, in which Sam is no longer facing the legacy of his demon blood, but he and Dean wrestle with the fallout of the failed Apocalypse. At the same time, the angel Castiel (who was introduced in Season Four), begins his own quest and is almost responsible for a second Apocalypse. The third volume of the show's text was marked by the installation of Jeremy Carver as showrunner for the eighth season. Each of these three volumes is somewhat distinct from the others in its tone and its plot arcs (not to mention its writing team) but there is nevertheless a continuity to the narrative. Many themes and arcs have been maintained over the ten years, such that it can be viewed as one single, serialized story.

9. Wood was of course deeply indebted to the work of Julia Kristeva on "abjection." In her *Powers of Horror: An Essay on Abjection* (1982), Kristeva demonstrated that the experience of horror is about the violation of boundaries and categories. The abject violates boundaries in ways that arouse disgust, horror, and existential anxiety.

At the levels of bodily integrity, individual and cultural identity, the psychoanalytic mechanism of projection is harnessed to reject elements of our selves that are viewed as undesirable, detaching "I" from "you," "self" from "other," "us" from "them." Anything that threatens the integrity of boundaries also threatens the very concept of boundaries and is therefore appalling. Such mechanisms explain the universal horror of dead bodies, which are the quintessence of abjection even before we consider the possibility of reanimating them. A corpse is still in some sense human/alive and in some sense not, and the visible extrusion of various fluids that accompany the dead body thus abject are signifiers of impurity that arouse intense emotions of disgust. They are literal markers of disintegration. Even while the body is still alive and functional, the fluids produced by the body (blood, piss, pus, shit) are considered grotesque and to be avoided for the survival of the individual and the body politic.

10. Wood's "modern" monsters are linked to the transformation in the horror genre that occurred in the 1960s and 1970s, when important and (in his view) progressive horror texts appeared, such as *Rosemary's Baby* (1968), *Night of the Living Dead* (1968), *The Exorcist* (1973), and *The Texas Chainsaw Massacre* (1974). The transformation from traditional to "modern" horror was triggered by Alfred Hitchcock's *Psycho* (1960), signaling the removal of the monster from geographically and socially external to internal, from foreign or alien to domestic and outwardly familiar. *Psycho* also heralded the beginning of "insecure narratives," in which there is no guarantee of a return to normality (*Hollywood* 209–11).

11. Dean has sold his soul to Hell in order to bring Sam back from death in "All Hell Breaks Loose, Part 2" (2.22) and has only one year to live; that year is Season Three, at the end of which he does indeed die and goes to Hell. It is Lilith who gleefully collects Dean's soul at the end of Season Three in "No Rest for the Wicked" (3.16). Of course, in the very first episode of Season Four ("Lazarus Rising"), he is raised from the dead by the angel Castiel.

12. It turns out that Ruby is in league with Lilith and Lucifer (and Azazel, even though he has been killed by this point), all of them working to manipulate Sam into breaking the final Seal on Lucifer's Cage, which is Lilith herself. We also learn later that Ruby has been keeping Sam in thrall, coaxing him into a sexual relationship while Dean is dead, and also to drink demon blood, mostly hers. The more demon blood Sam drinks, the more powerful he becomes, and eventually he does kill Lilith, mistakenly believing that she is about to break the final Seal. It transpires that he is also meant to be Lucifer's vessel on Earth.

13. Dean himself says in "Devil's Trap" (1.22) that the violence he is capable of in order to protect Sam scares him.

14. Dean has spent most of Season One as a straightforward action man, protector, and hero. In a way, he will continue to be this for six more seasons, always in orbit around Sam's monstrosity, the righteous man whose job is simple: kill the monsters and protect his little brother, often haunted by the possibility that these two duties may be in conflict. He clings to this role even as the world around him becomes increasingly more morally complex, openly lamenting the way that things cannot be as simple as they once were.

15. In other words, human flesh.

16. Later on, much like Lenore, Benny decides that he would rather return to Purgatory (die) than see himself become a monster again.

17. Death has a bone to pick with Sam and Dean, who have evaded their natural death numerous times, thus disturbing the natural order.

18. An important note: The accident of being born into a familial structure is

182 Part 4. Gothic Others: Monstrous Selves

not what is meant by "family." Dean's speech in "Inside Man" (10.17) reinforces the fact that in the world of *Supernatural*, family doesn't have to be connected by blood.

19. Or will it? In "Brother's Keeper," Death makes a fairly strong case that Sam and Dean's insistence on always saving each other at any cost, disregarding the greater good, is a great evil. If Dean is convinced by this logic, we are meant to think, it is because he is under the sway of the Mark. Sam's impassioned speech at Dean's feet gives Dean the strength to stay his hand at the last second. Moments later, the Mark is removed but, just as Death predicted, something terrible happens. Sam and Dean are together and the world is ending—again.

20. Asma discusses this in relation to the tellings and retellings of the Beowulf myth and the treatment of Grendl, who gradually transitions from a pure monster to a "sad, misunderstood" creature: "In the original *Beowulf* the monsters are outcasts *because* they're bad, just as Cain, their progenitor, was an outcast because he killed his brother, but in the new liberal *Beowulf* the monsters are bad *because* they're outcasts" (101).

WORKS CITED

Asma, Stephen T. *On Monsters: An Unnatural History of Our Worst Fears.* Oxford: Oxford University Press, 2009. Print.

"Blade Runners." *Supernatural: The Complete Ninth Season.* Writ. Brad Bucker and Eugenie Ross-Leming. Dir. Serge Ladouceur. Perf. Jensen Ackles and Jared Padalecki. Warner Bros., 2014. DVD.

Brooks, Peter. *The Melodramatic Imagination: Balzac, Henry James, Melodrama and the Mode of Excess.* New Haven: Yale University Press, 1976. Print.

"Brother's Keeper." *Supernatural.* Writ. Jeremy Carver. Dir. Phil Sgriccia. Perf. Jensen Ackles and Jared Padalecki. CW Network, 20 May 2015. Television.

"The Executioner's Song." *Supernatural.* Writ. Robert Berens. Dir. Phil Sgriccia. Perf. Jensen Ackles and Jared Padalecki. CW Network, 17 February 2015. Television.

Kristeva, Julia. *Powers of Horror: An Essay on Abjection.* Trans. Leon S. Roudiez. New York: Columbia University Press, 1982. Print.

"Metamorphosis." *Supernatural: The Complete Fourth Season.* Writ. Cathryn Humphries. Dir. Kim Manners. Perf. Jensen Ackles and Jared Padalecki. Warner Bros., 2009. DVD.

Nietzsche, Friedrich. *Beyond Good and Evil.* Trans. Helen Zimmern. Project Gutenberg. 2009. http://www.gutenberg.org/files/4363/4363-h/4363-h.htm.

"Soul Survivor." *Supernatural.* Writ. Brad Buckner and Eugenie Ross-Leming. Dir. Jensen Ackles. Perf. Jensen Ackles and Jared Padalecki. CW Network, 21 October 2014. Television.

"There's No Place Like Home." *Supernatural.* Writ. Robbie Thompson. Dir. Phil Sgriccia. Perf. Jensen Ackles and Jared Padalecki. CW Network, 27 January 2015. Television.

Wood, Robin. "An Introduction to the American Horror Film" Ed. Bill Nichols. *Movies and Methods*, Vol. II. Berkeley: University of California Press, 1985. 195–220. Print.

_____. *Hollywood from Vietnam to Reagan ... and Beyond*, exp. and rev. New York: Columbia University Press, 2003. Print.

About the Contributors

Daniel P. **Compora** is an associate professor at the University of Toledo, where he teaches literature. His recent publications include "Ghostly Attractions: The Ghost-lore of Television, College Campuses and Tourism" in *New Series* 9 (2006) and "Undead America: The Emergence of the Modern Zombie in American Culture" in 1.1 of *Supernatural Studies* (2013).

Melissa **Edmundson** specializes in nineteenth and early twentieth-century British women writers, with particular interests in women's ghost stories, the Gothic, and Anglo-Indian popular fiction. She is the editor of a critical edition of Alice Perrin's 1901 collection of short stories, *East of Suez* (2011), and author of *Women's Ghost Literature in Nineteenth-Century Britain* (2013).

Dana **Fore** is interested in Victorian British literature (1798–1900), disability theory, film studies, and the literature of fantasy and horror. His previous analyses of the fantasy/horror genre have discussed disability issues in the early *Saw* films, James Cameron's *Avatar*, and Robert Louis Stevenson's *Dr. Jekyll and Mr. Hyde.*

Megan **Fowler** is a Ph.D candidate at the University of Florida. Her research interests include television and new media studies, fandom studies, feminist and queer theory, postcolonial and critical race theory, science fiction, and the Gothic. Her primary research is in intersectional representations of race, gender, and queerness in contemporary television.

Michael **Fuchs** teaches American literature and media studies at the University of Graz (Austria). He has co-edited three books and written more than a dozen journal articles and book chapters on adult and horror cinema, American television, and video games.

Thomas **Knowles** teaches on a range of subjects at Birmingham City University, including Romanticism and the Gothic. He co-edited *Insanity and the Lunatic Asylum in the Nineteenth Century* (2014), contributed two pieces on ecocriticism to the Higher Education Academy–funded project "The Virtual Theorist," and contributed to a forthcoming book on J. G. Ballard (2016).

Leow Hui Min Annabeth is a master's student in modern thought and literature at Stanford University. Her research focuses on the narrative construction and representation of race and nationalism in fiction. She is also interested in portrayals of race and gender in popular culture, and her essays have appeared in *Transformative Works and Cultures, Bitch, The WisCon Chronicles,* and *Speculative Fiction.*

Alexandra **Lykissas** is a Ph.D. candidate in literature and criticism in the Department of English at Indiana University of Pennsylvania where she is also a part-time faculty member. Her research interests include traditional fairy tales and Gothic fiction and their modern adaptations in movies, television, and graphic novels.

Jamil **Mustafa** is a professor at Lewis University, where he chairs the English Department and teaches courses in Victorian literature, Gothic fiction, and the horror film. His publications include "'A good horror has its place in art': Hardy's Gothic Strategy in *Tess of the d'Urbervilles*," "'The Lady of the House of Love': Angela Carter's Vampiric Sleeping Beauty," and the Bethlehem Blog.

E. J. **Nielsen** is a Ph.D. candidate at the University of Massachusetts–Amherst in the Department of Communication with a focus on media studies and popular culture. Her research interests include monsters and the monstrous, gender studies, and fan studies. She was the guest editor for "Virtual and Physical Fan Spaces" of the *Journal of Fandom Studies* 4.3.

Lisa **Schmidt** is an independent scholar. She writes about genre film and television, particularly horror and science fiction. Her publications include "Monstrous Melodrama: Expanding the Scope of Melodramatic Identification to Interpret Negative Fan Responses to *Supernatural*" in *Transformative Works and Cultures* 4 (2010) and "Television: Horror's 'Original' Home" in *Horror Studies* 4.2 (2013).

Jessica **Seymour**, a researcher at Southern Cross University, is co-editor of *Fan Studies: Researching Popular Audiences* (2014). Her work includes "Holmes's Girls: Genderbending and Feminizing the Canon in *Elementary*" and "Lizzie Bennet: Storytelling, Fan-Creator Interactions, and New Online Models." Her interests include children's and young adult literature, pop culture, and transmedia storytelling.

Samantha J. **Vertosick** is a Ph.D. candidate in literature and criticism at the Indiana University of Pennsylvania. Her specialty area is modern and contemporary British literature with a focus on the Gothic, children's literature, fantasy literature, and the occult.

Ashley **Walton** writes pop-culture criticism on the website *Geek Appetite* and edits the horror webcomic *False Positive.* She has published in *Channeling Wonder: Fairy Tales on Television* (2014) and in various online publications, including *USA Today's* Pop Candy.

Index

Abaddon (character) 106, 107, 109, 110, 111, 140, 147
"Abandon All Hope" (episode) 140
Abbott, Stacey 3, 5, 64, 65
abhuman traits 104, 105, 107, 110, 111
abjection 180–181*n*9
Ackles, Jensen 2, 4, 67
Adam (character) 30, 36*n*8, 112*n*3, 145, 149, 152*n*4, 158
After the Fall: American Literature Since 9/11 22
Aladdin 98
Alan J. Corbett (character) 59–60
Alice in Wonderland 55
Alien 116
Alistair (character) 106
"All Hell Breaks Loose, Part 1" (episode) 163
"All Hell Breaks Loose, Part 2" (episode) 164, 181*n*11
Allen, Robert 63–64
allusions 51, 64, 66–68, 158; *see also* intertextuality
Ambrosio (the Monk) 9, 39–43
Amelia Richardson (character) 22
America 31
American Gothic 34
The Amityville Horror 66
Amy Pond (character) 43
And Their Dogs Came with Them 99
Andrews, Virginia 27, 36*n*6
angel condoms 104, 107
"angel in the house" concept 17
Angel Tablet 56, 139
Angela (character) 81
angels 17, 42; fragmentation of 132–138; vessels for 105–106
"Angels, Demons, and Damsels in Distress: The Representation of Women in *Supernatural*" 104
Anna Milton (character) 19, 43, 133, 145
anxieties 1–2, 3, 34; death 78; gender-related 116, 130; homosexuality/incest 28, 52 (*see also* repression); of identity and authentic-

ity 34; influence on monster creation 5; of the monstrous other 160–165; transforming into suspense 7; and the unspeakable 157, 159–160
Apocalypse 9, 30, 42, 64, 100, 111, 139, 146, 172, 173, 179, 180*n*8
Apocalypse, Four Horsemen of 30, 150
"Appointment in Samarra" (episode) 149, 158
archangels 9, 30, 136, 144
"Are Monsters Members of the Moral Community?" 152
"Are You There, God? It's Me, Dean Winchester" (episode) 109, 111, 133
Armitt, Lucie 85
Art of Darkness: A Poetics of Gothic 24*n*3
"Ask Jeeves" (episode) 169, 177
Asma, Stephen T. 167, 169, 180*n*1, 181*n*20
assbutt 30
"Asylum" (episode) 66, 70
audience-narrative relationship 10, 63–74
authenticity 36*n*7
Azazel (character) 103, 106, 151, 164, 172, 181*n*12

backstory, tragic 143, 144
"Bad Day at Black Rock" (episode) 3
Ballard, J.G. 35*n*2
Balthazar (character) 129, 135–138, 141
Barnes (character) 54, 60
Barthes, Roland 31, 33, 63
Bartholomew (character) 106
Baudrillard, Jean 31
Baughman folklore motif system 76, 80
Beal, Timothy K. 151
Becky Rosen (character) 56, 57, 58
"Bedtime Stories" (episode) 3, 85–86
Beeler, Stan 26–27
Bela Talbot (character) 103, 114
belief systems, distortion of 44
Beloved 95
"The Benders" (episode) 4
Benny Lafitte (character) 9, 83, 84, 170, 174–175, 181*n*16

185